LUTHER AND THE REFORMATION

LUTHER AND THE REFORMATION

BY

JAMES MACKINNON, Ph.D., D.D.

Regius Professor of Ecclesiastical History, University of Edinburgh

VOL. I.

EARLY LIFE AND RELIGIOUS DEVELOPMENT TO 1517

NEW YORK

RUSSELL & RUSSELL · INC

1962

3/1962
Genl.

FIRST PUBLISHED IN 1925
PUBLISHED, 1962, BY RUSSELL & RUSSELL, INC.
L. C. CATALOG CARD NO: 62—10691

PRINTED IN THE UNITED STATES OF AMERICA

PREFACE

THE evangelical Reformation of the sixteenth century is unthinkable without Luther. As a religious movement it owed its origin directly to him and it bears the stamp of his personality and religious experience.

At the same time, it was a complex movement. Its factors were not exclusively religious and moral. A variety of forces—political, economic, social, and intellectual as well as religious and moral—went to the making of it. Without the co-operation of these forces, Luther would hardly have succeeded in bringing about the evangelical Reformation, of which he became the main instrument. Even as a religious reformer, he had precursors who had striven to effect a thorough amelioration of the Church during the previous two centuries. Wiclif, Hus, Savonarola, for instance. In the early years of the sixteenth century attempts to bring about a practical Reformation were also being made by reforming churchmen like Ximenes and Colet, and reforming humanists like Erasmus and More. The Reformation of the Church was, in fact, a general aspiration of the age in which Luther appeared, and this aspiration had periodically found expression on the part of individuals, councils, and fraternities within it, before, and up to, his advent.

Apart from these direct attempts, the trend of history in the late mediæval age was making towards the religious climax of the early sixteenth century. During the fourteenth and fifteenth there were forces at work tending to transform mediæval society and civilisation. This period witnessed, for instance, the rise of the national state in Western Europe, and the national state brought into play the force of nationality as a factor to be reckoned with not merely in the political, but in the ecclesiastical sphere. This factor was bound ultimately to react on the claim of the mediæval Papacy to a universal ecclesiastical supremacy over the

State as well as the Church. It might, and in fact eventually did, lead to the establishment of the national Church, independent of the Papacy, on national as well as religious grounds, in Germany, Scandinavia, Holland, England, and Scotland. It might also, and eventually did, result in aggravating the national antagonism, on economic grounds, to the fiscal system by which the Papacy drained so large a portion of the national wealth in the form of a variety of taxes and other contributions, which were increasingly resented as an intolerable source of oppression and grievance. Again, the reaction against the feudal social system, with which the Church as well as the State was so closely identified, was, and had long been, finding expression in the striving of the people to secure emancipation from serfage and the amelioration of their social condition. Here, too, was a force which might make itself powerfully felt in abetting the work of the religious reformer. A new social order was not possible without a far-reaching reform of the Church in its feudalised form, and the masses might well see in such a reformation the means of bringing about a new and better social order.

Moreover, in the rise of the new culture, the humanist movement, a force was likewise at work preparing the way for the Reformation. It was not without reason that the age of the Reformation was also the age of the Renaissance —the rebirth of culture in the wide sense of energising the faculties of mind and soul and transforming the whole sphere of human activity in art, literature, science, theology, philosophy, education, invention, and discovery. In virtue of this factor alone, the world could not go on in the old mediæval routine. More especially, it brought into play the power of individuality, which sought and found expression through this movement, as it had not done for centuries. Through it, too, the critical spirit was becoming alive and being applied to the independent study of history, ideas, and institutions. The system of authority which dominated the mediæval Church and the mediæval schools could not indefinitely subsist unscathed by the critical, inquiring spirit, which claimed and asserted the right of the individual conscience and judgment.

It was in the age in which these transforming forces were already in powerful operation that Luther was born and grew to manhood. They unquestionably contributed indirectly to prepare the way for the great religious transformation which he was instrumental in effecting. In this sense the Reformation was a co-operative and complex movement. Some historians have seen in it, in fact, largely, if not solely, the play of these forces, and have been inclined to emphasise them to the extent of ignoring or belittling the religious and moral side of the movement. In so doing they have not adequately apprehended or correctly judged it. The Reformation was not simply a matter of politics, or economics, or social reform, or humanist culture. It was not even all these put together. Neither singly nor collectively would they have achieved the great religious transformation which Luther brought about. Without the religious conviction, the religious genius, the personal faith, the dynamic of a potent personality, there would have been no far-reaching Reformation of the Church. The attempt to explain the Reformation without this cardinal element is like the attempt to explain the action of an electric machine without the dynamo. As a religious movement the Reformation without Luther is unthinkable.

All previous individual or corporate attempts to reform the Church on the part of reforming churchmen, humanists, statesmen, or reforming councils and fraternities had proved unavailing or were only temporarily, and in quite a limited degree, effective. Luther alone succeeded in this hitherto hopeless enterprise by initiating and directing a reform movement, which made an end of the scandal of an unreformed Papacy and the system of absolute and oppressive ecclesiastical government which the Papacy represented. He alone contributed the impelling force which effected such far-reaching religious results in Germany and spread the movement to other lands. This impelling force consisted in the new conception of the relation of the individual soul to God, which found expression in his distinctive doctrine of justification by faith. He thus imparted to the Reformation the religious dynamic which was hitherto lacking, or only imperfectly operative in previous attempts, and with which other factors might co-operate, but could not adequately replace.

Hence the cardinal importance of the problem how he attained to this new religious conception. The answer to this problem is to be sought in his early religious experience as a monk, with which Luther research in Germany has been particularly occupied in recent years. A great impulse was given to this research by the discovery of his notes on the works of Augustine, Petrus Lombardus, Anselm, and Tauler, which go back to 1509 and the immediately succeeding years. These notes were written on the margin of copies of these works, of which he made use as a student of theology and as a theological lecturer, and the copies themselves were discovered by Buchwald in the Municipal Library of Zwickau in 1889-90. Some years earlier the notes of his early lectures on the Epistle to the Galatians (1516), which had been made by a student, and a few of his early sermons came to light. In 1885 his first course on the Psalms (1513-15), which had been discovered in the Royal Library at Dresden, was published in complete form, along with the manuscript of the same course in the library at Wolfenbüttel, by Kawerau in the Weimar edition of his works (vols. iii. and iv.). In 1899 Vopel found in the Vatican Library a manuscript copy of the lectures on the Epistle to the Romans (1515-16) and a student's notebook of those on the Epistle to the Hebrews (1517). Shortly afterwards Luther's original manuscript of the lectures on Romans was found in the Royal Library at Berlin and published by Ficker in 1908.

These successive discoveries threw a flood of light on his religious development to 1517, and furnished the materials for a more thorough study of his early life and religious experience. The result has been largely to antiquate the older biographies and monographs on Luther, as far as they deal with the period up to 1517. On the other hand, these discoveries have during the last decade and a half added to the enormous Luther literature a considerable number of important works by both German Protestant and Roman Catholic writers. In this field of historic research the Germans are, of course, supreme. Roman Catholics like the Dominicans Denifle and A. M. Weiss and the Jesuit

Grisar have devoted no inconsiderable learning and research to the elucidation of this period of the life of the man who is perforce to them the arch-heretic of modern times. Unfortunately they have not always brought to bear on this task the objective and judicial spirit which is a first requisite in the study of history, and which it is so difficult to exemplify in the sphere of ecclesiastical history in particular. Denifle's " Luther und Lutherthum " is a bad example of the application of the dogmatic spirit to the interpretation of ecclesiastical history. Grisar's biography of Luther, though professedly more objective, is vitiated by the same tendency, inasmuch as he writes not only under the influence of his Roman Catholic prepossessions, but of Denifle's grossly prejudiced interpretation of Luther's religious development, which more reasonable Roman Catholic writers like Kiefl have rejected.[1]

On the other hand, research on this subject has been materially advanced by the recent works of German Protestant writers like Scheel, Holl, Köhler, Boehmer, A. V. Müller, Ficker, Preuss, von Below, and others mentioned in the footnotes, and, in the more limited field of the history of dogma, of Harnack, Loofs, Seeberg, O. Ritschl, Tschackert, etc. They may be unconsciously coloured to a certain extent by the antagonisms aroused by the contributions of Denifle and other extreme Roman Catholic writers. They are more or less pleas for the defence on the evangelical side. But their authors are evidently all trained in the application of scientific historic method, and from this point of view are generally actuated by the striving to elucidate the truth in accordance with this method. The

---

[1] Another excellent example of Roman Catholic fairness towards Luther is Merkle's " Reformations-Geschichtliche Streitfragen " (1904). This is a crushing exposure of the misrepresentations contained in Baron von Berlichingen's popular lectures on " Luther and the Reformation " (1902-03), by a Roman Catholic expert in the history of the Reformation, who at the time was professor of Church History in the Roman Catholic Faculty of Würzburg University. This interesting production appeared in the year in which the first volume of Denifle's work was published, and contains no reference to this work. In it the true historic spirit finds admirable expression and it is happily not exceptional. It is, in fact, characteristic of liberal-minded Catholicism.

same merit characterises the recent work of the French
Protestant scholar, M. Strohl, of Strassburg.   Moreover,
in a case of this kind sympathy is a surer guide to the actual
truth than hatred, which, in the case of writers like Denifle,
inevitably tends to distort it.

At the same time, in virtue of his special knowledge of
the scholastic theology, Denifle was fitted to expose the
weakness of previous Protestant theologians and biographers
of Luther in this field of research.   He deserves at least the
merit of having compelled subsequent German Protestant
writers to improve upon their predecessors in this respect,
and to bring to the study of Luther's early religious
development a more adequate knowledge of the theological
system in which, as a monk, he was trained.   At the same
time, it is only just to point out that some of these
writers, like Seeberg and A. V. Müller, show a mastery
of the scholastic theology equal, if not superior, to
that of Roman Catholic experts.   A. V. Müller is, in
fact, an ex-monk and possesses a remarkable knowledge
of this subject.

Luther came to his distinctive conception of religion by
the scholastic approach.   It was the scholastic theology,
particularly in its later Nominalist form, which he studied
in the Augustinian monastery and the university at Erfurt,
that formed the staple of his thought during this formative
period.   Together with the monastic conception of the
religious life, it was largely responsible for the spiritual
conflict that clouded his early religious experience before
he learned to seek in the Bible itself, backed by the writings
of Augustine and the mystics, the key to the solution of the
problem of his personal salvation.   It was with this theology
that he had to reckon in his striving to clarify and develop
his new conception of religion during the momentous years
between 1512 and 1517, when his creative mind was
working out the main lineaments of his own theology.   In
the opinion of Holl, one of the most capable of present-day
experts in Luther research, these years form the most
creative period in the whole of Luther's life.   There is no
little force in this contention, and the fact emphasises the
importance of the period before 1517 both for the religious

origins of the Reformation in general and the history of
Luther's life in particular. The student cannot, therefore,
attain to an adequate understanding of either without
taking the trouble to grasp the distinctive content of the
scholastic theology in which Luther's mind was so profoundly absorbed during this period, and which exercised
a truly moulding influence on his development both by way
of attraction and repulsion.

So far as the writer is aware there is not in English any
work specially and adequately dealing with Luther's early
life and development down to 1517. Few, if any, of the
recent German monographs on this subject have appeared
in English. Denifle's ponderous volumes have been translated into Italian by Mercati and into French by Paquier.
But no English translation has, to my knowledge, so far
appeared. This is not surprising in view of the heavy
style and ill-conceived arrangement of the book, which
make it very laborious to read and digest. Grisar has been
more fortunate and his biography of Luther has appeared
in English in six volumes, though its arrangement is also
faulty. It has thus contributed to diffuse a one-sided view
of Luther among English-speaking readers, and it would
appear that it has had some influence in accentuating the
anti-Luther spirit in certain circles. German Protestant
research, on the other hand—much of it accomplished during
and subsequent to the war, which has tended to discredit
German scientific research even in circles which ought to
know better—has been less fortunate. Neither the works
of Scheel nor those of Holl, for instance, have as yet found
an English translator, and apart from a few specialists,
this laborious and fruitful research is little known in Britain
and, I suppose, also in America. There was thus ample
reason for undertaking the present work on the formative
period in the great Reformer's life from his early years to
1517.

The work is the fruit of an intensive study of the original
sources as well as the results of the more recent research
referred to.   It is meant as a contribution to the early
history of an epoch-making movement. All—the foes as
well as the friends of Luther—are agreed on the fact that

the Reformation, both in itself and in its effects on modern history, was such a movement. Those who disbelieve in and dislike it cannot ignore it, and the fact of the continued interest in it, manifested by Roman Catholic writers, is a striking testimony to the religious genius of the man who initiated and brought it to fruition, as far as Germany was concerned, and also contributed, directly or indirectly, to its diffusion and its triumph in other lands. To those who believe in it the heritage of the Reformation is of immeasurable value, even if they are conscious that, like all human movements, it is not above criticism, and that in some respects its spirit and its aspirations, even more than its actual achievement, are the supremely important things in it. The writer has, at all events, striven to treat the particular aspect of it with which this work deals in the spirit of the historian, whilst striving to bring to bear on it a knowledge acquired by a long-continued and special study of theological thought. Sympathy for the man in his soul-searching quest for a gracious God and in his struggle to emancipate himself from the bonds of traditional mediæval beliefs, he frankly admits that he feels. In view of what Luther accomplished in this formative period and of the long drawn-out searching for and reasoning out a faith on which to live and for which, if need be, to die, he was unquestionably a man of genius and a great heroic soul. At the same time, he was called on to exemplify this genius and exhibit this heroism in an age whose mental and religious horizon was narrow compared with ours, and whose outlook conditioned and inevitably hampered his thought. The writer could hardly help feeling at times not quite at home in the labyrinth of scholastic and monastic ideas, from which Luther was seeking deliverance and could only escape by threading his way through the intricate intellectual and religious concepts of his time. Frankly speaking, he would have been glad if the Reformer had succeeded in effecting this deliverance with less of scholastic disputation with his opponents and in a style more appropriate to the Gospel. From the religious point of view, much of this disputation is not to us the supremely important thing it was to the age of Luther. Part of it at least has become merely antiquarian. The writer has, at all events, tried to confine his exposition to the things that really mattered for Luther in his toilsome and trying progress towards that conception of religion which ultimately dealt the fatal stroke to the mediæval papal and ecclesiastical system.

The edition of Luther's works mainly used by the writer is the Weimar edition, begun in 1883 and still in course of publication. It has superseded the Erlangen edition, though the earlier volumes have not been adequately edited in some respects. Six volumes of his "Table Talk" have also appeared in this edition and form a great improvement on the older edition of Bindseil and Förstemann. The more recent edition of his letters by Enders (from 1884 onwards) has been used in preference to that of De Wette. Ficker's edition of the lectures on the Epistle to the Romans (1908) forms the first volume of the "Anfänge Reformatorischer Bibelauslegung."

The study of his works, as far as they bear on his early life and religious development, affords ample scope for the exercise of the critical faculty. His utterances on this subject must be discriminatingly viewed in the light of his tendency to judge the past from his later evangelical standpoint. His letters, sermons, commentaries, and controversial writings contain a great deal of matter relative to his personal religious experience, and whilst this biographical element is valuable for the light it throws on the early period of his life, its value varies in exactitude. His memory did not always truly reflect the events or facts of the past, and his standard of judgment was inevitably influenced by the great transformation of his religious life and by the antagonisms and controversies to which it gave rise. Moreover, like most great men who write and talk much, he was not above contradicting himself at times. The exercise of critical alertness is still more applicable to the reports of his sayings and doings recorded in the vast repository of his "Tischreden" or "Table Talk" and to the versions of his works which others edited, and which had not the benefit of his personal revision.

TABLE OF CONTENTS

CHAPTER I

xiii

Contents

CHAPTER IV

CHAPTER V

Contents

Contents

LUTHER
AND THE REFORMATION

CHAPTER I

EARLY LIFE AND EDUCATION (1483-1505)

I. Home and Early Religious Atmosphere

LUTHER, whose name is the modern equivalent of the old German Lothair,[1] sprang from peasant stock. His ancestors belonged to the small farmer class—freemen who owned their holdings at Möhra in Thuringia,[2] and transmitted them through the youngest, not the eldest, son, from generation to generation. In later life he took pride in his free peasant origin and, in spite of his university education, he remained in manner, temperament, and drastic mode of expression a true son of the Thuringian soil. From Möhra his father, Hans Luther, one of several brothers, migrated with his young wife, Margaret Ziegler, to Eisleben in the county of Mansfeld, in search of a living. Here his eldest son was born on the 10th November 1483,[3] and was baptized Martin on the morrow, St Martin's Day, in honour of the saint. Within six months his parents, who

---

[1] Köstlin, " Martin Luther," i. 21, 3rd edition, 1883.

[2] Enders, " Luther's Briefwechsel," ii. 293, where Luther speaks of his relatives in this district.

[3] Melanchthon (sketch of Luther's life in " Opera Corpus Reformatorum," vi. 156) says that his mother, whom he questioned on the subject, remembered the day, but not the year of his birth. Up to Luther's death Melanchthon believed that the year was 1484, but changed his belief on being informed by Luther's brother Jacob that the correct date was 1483. Oergel decides for the 7th December 1482, and argues with considerable force in favour of the earlier date. " Vom Jungen Luther," 1 f., 1899. He has hardly succeeded, however, in discrediting the family tradition in favour of 1483.

1

evidently failed to find subsistence at Eisleben, removed to Mansfeld, the centre of the iron mining and smelting industry. Prosperity ere long rewarded this second venture in search of a livelihood. After several years of hard toil his father became the lessee of several pits and furnaces, and as early as 1491 he appears as a notable member of the community, which in this year chose him as one of the four burgesses annually elected from the four quarters of the town to maintain their interests in the Town Council.[4] In later life Luther speaks of the poverty of his early years. He tells us that his father was " a poor miner," and that his mother carried home on her back the firewood from the forest for the household use. He says that he himself sang in the streets of Mansfeld.[5] From these later utterances his modern biographers have concluded that his childhood was one of abject poverty. He was the eldest of seven children— four boys and three girls—and there was doubtless at first a stiff struggle to keep the wolf from the door. But the description of the straitened circumstances of the household applies at most only to the first half-dozen years after the settlement at Mansfeld.[6] By the year 1491 the father was no longer " a poor miner," but, by dint of his energy and economy, had raised himself and his growing family above the poverty line. The carrying of firewood from the forest was usual in peasant families, and street singing for philanthropic or religious purposes was customary among the children of even affluent burgesses. It was a pious exercise in connection with the Church festivals, and Luther's reference [7] to it shows that he took part in it for this purpose.

Both parents seem to have been of choleric temperament and deeply imbued with the current notion of unquestioning obedience to parental authority and the

---

[4] Melanchthon says that he was a member of the Town Council (*magistratus gessit*), " Vita," 156. But he was rather what we should term one of the four assessors elected by the burgesses to assist the Council in the administration. Scheel, " Martin Luther," i. 265.

[5] " Tischreden," i. 60 ; iii. 51 (Weimar edition).

[6] Luther speaks of his father's poverty only " as a young man " (*in adolescentia*). " Tischreden," iii. 51.

[7] " Tischreden," i. 60 ; and see Scheel, i. 6-9, 265-267.

efficacy of an unsparing use of the rod in securing it. In accordance with the practice of the time they were harsh disciplinarians, and Luther never forgot his sufferings under the harsh discipline of the home. " My father once flogged me so severely that I fled from him and was bitterly estranged from him until he again accustomed me to himself." [8] " My mother once flogged me on account of a nut, till the blood flowed." [9] He deplores the lack of insight and self-restraint on the part of parents in the treatment of their children, and cites his own case as an example of the evil effects on the child mind of this inconsiderate harshness. " My parents treated me so harshly that I became prone to timidity." [10] He even says that this excessive harshness begat a frame of mind that ultimately drove him into the monastery.[11] This is evidently an exaggeration, due to a defective memory which frequently led him in later life to confuse the motives or causes of the events of an earlier time. But he deliberately says that his parents were lacking in sympathetic discernment in the management of their children,[12] and Scheel, in his striving to tone down the harshness of the home discipline,[13] seems to overlook too much this aspect of the evidence. On the other hand, Luther admits that they meant well by him.[14] In later life he cherished a deep affection and gratitude towards them, and some of his modern biographers have gone too far in representing his home life as a continuous martyrdom.[15] Luther also tells us that his father had his joyous hours, and could let himself go in jest and song over a glass of beer with his friends, sometimes taking more than his thirst required.[16] Nor was his mother always scolding and thrashing her young brood, and Luther mentions

[8] " Colloquia," ii. 76 (Förstemann and Bindseil, 1848).

[9] *Ibid.*, ii. 129.   [10] *Ibid.*, ii. 129.   [11] *Ibid.*, ii. 129.

[12] Sed non poterant discernere ingenia, secundum quæ essent temperandæ correctiones. *Ibid.*, ii. 130.

[13] " Luther," i. 11.

[14] " Colloquia," ii. 129, sie meineten es herzlich gut.

[15] For example, Hausrath, " Luther's Leben," i. 2 (1904) ; Berger, " Luther," i. 6 (1895) ; Preserved Smith, *American Journal of Psychology* (1913), 362.

[16] Reliqui ebrii sunt læti et suaves, ut pater meus, cantant, jocantur. Homines læti possunt interdum uti vino largiori. " Tischreden," iv. 636.

a little song which she used to sing to him [17] and which tends to show that, if she was not too well liked among her neighbours, she too had her jocose moments. Melanchthon, who later knew her intimately, speaks admiringly of her matronly virtues and her piety, and says that she was held in high esteem by other respectable women as an example of a virtuous life.[18]

The atmosphere of the home was a pious one. The children were taught by precept and example the fear of God and the observance of the religious usages of the time. There seems to be no real ground for assuming that the piety of the Luther household differed in any respect from the conventional type, or that the germs of Luther's subsequent revolt against the Church may be traced to his father's sympathy with the anti-ecclesiastical spirit prevalent in certain sections of the German people at the close of the Middle Ages. Hans Luther is supposed to have disliked the monks and to have adopted a rather critical attitude towards the Church and the priesthood. But there is very slender ground for this supposition. Luther's enemies later circulated the tale that the father was a Hussite and that the son was born in Bohemia. The tale gave Luther an opportunity for poking fun at his detractors in one of his sermons.[19] That he was not an indiscriminating admirer of the monks might be inferred from his chagrin at his son's sudden resolve to enter a monastery. This chagrin was, however, caused, not by any dislike to the monastic life in itself, but by the fact that this impulsive act was a direct defiance of the paternal will and completely upset the career which he had planned for him. It was on these grounds alone that he bitterly reproached his son for his unfilial and visionary conduct. The passage in the " Table Talk," [20] in which he is said to have always hated monkery, seems to be a reflection backwards, probably on the part of the reporter, of the view which, under his son's influence, he later came to entertain. Equally unfounded is the assumption that the father, in contrast to the mother, was not in sympathy with the conventional piety as embodied

[17] " Werke," xxxviii. 338 (Weimar edition).
[18] " Vita," 156.   [19] " Werke," vi. 81.   [20] I. 440.

in the teaching and usages of the Church. Assertions of this kind are disproved by the municipal records of Mansfeld which reveal Hans Luther as a good churchman, who associates with the priest and other burgesses in observing and maintaining the ecclesiastical usages of the time.[21]

From this pious atmosphere Luther's early religious experience drew its nurture. He learned in the home the Lord's Prayer, the Creed, and the Ten Commandments. He might have learned to read the Bible in the vernacular, to judge from the numerous German versions that appeared in the second half of the fifteenth century and the early sixteenth. None of these seems, however, to have been available in his home, since, on his own testimony, it was only later that he became acquainted with the Bible as a whole, and so far only knew the portions of it prescribed in the Church services.[22] When a boy (*puer aliquando*), he tells us in a passage of his " Table Talk," he chanced on a Bible (perhaps at Magdeburg or Eisenach), and on reading the story of Hannah, he was greatly delighted and thought to himself how fortunate he would be if ever he could possess such a book. Afterwards he bought a postil, or collection of passages of Scripture, and found in it more of the Gospel than they were wont to be taught in a whole year.[23] In the Church services he was introduced to the mediæval conception of religion as embodied in the liturgy and expounded from the pulpit. He learned to sing the popular hymns which were also a feature of the religious life of the age long before his own religious muse burst into evangelical song. In the church he would join in the devotion which found expression in the Confiteor, the Magnificat, the Benedictus, the Gloria, the Psalms, and other liturgical compositions. He took part in the Church Festivals, in processions and pilgrimages, and shared in the invocation of the saints, especially of the Virgin and her mother St Anna, the patron saint of the miners. In the years of his boyhood and early manhood there was a popular religious revival which took the form of a craze for visiting religious

[21] See Scheel, i. 14-15.
[22] Scheel, " Documente zu Luther's Entwicklung," 29 (1911).
[23] " Tischreden," i. 44.

shrines. He later mentions this craze in connection with various shrines in the neighbourhood of Mansfeld, such as Wimmelberg, which were believed to work miraculous cures, or add to the stock of the sinner's merits, or insure indulgence from the pains of purgatory. There can be no doubt that at this early period he devoutly believed in the efficacy of this shrine worship, which he was one day to denounce on both moral and religious grounds. Doubtless, too, the elaborate cultus of the Church was fitted in its way to be the nurse of deep religious emotion and upright living, if it also tended to nurture crude and mercenary views of religion. In this respect the young Luther appears as the product of his age. Even his later breach with the conventional religion was very gradual. It is a mistake to search in the early period for evidence of any essential antagonism to the teaching or cultus of the mediæval Church. The evidence, on the contrary, goes to show that he was a devout believer in its institutions, doctrines, and usages. When he later looks back from his evangelical standpoint, what strikes him in the retrospect is his zeal for the traditional faith and usages, which he had learned in the interval to criticise and denounce. He tells us again and again that he was a thorough-going papalist. Not only would he have looked on the burning of heretics, who denied the authority of the Pope and the teaching of the Church, with approval ; he himself would have helped to burn them.[24] In his early lectures as a teacher, he is careful to show his hatred of heretical views and to emphasise the orthodox beliefs in which he had grown to manhood.[25] Even when he began to develop his characteristic doctrine of salvation, he is still explicit in his condemnation of heretics and is long unconscious of being one himself. It was long before he discovered that he was out of harmony in essential respects with the received ecclesiastical teaching, and it would be vain to seek for any trace of this disharmony in the early period of his life.

True, he tells us that he was at times far from finding complete peace of mind or conscience in the old religious

[24] " Documente," 11-12, 34.
[25] See " Werke," ix. 30, for instance.

system. The thought of Christ as judge filled him with terror even in his boyhood. For while the Church taught the forgiveness of sins in virtue of the death of Christ, it also taught and emphasised in the sacrament of penance the necessity of satisfaction for sin on the part of the sinner against the day of reckoning, when Christ would hold the great assize of the merits and demerits of the individual. Christ, the stern judge, seated on the rainbow, as depicted in the church at Mansfeld—the Christ, too, as He was too often depicted in the sermons which he later described as "judgment sermons" (*gerichtspredigt*)—made such an impression on the heart of the young Martin that, as he later says again and again, he trembled every time he heard the mention of His name. For who could be certain that the satisfactions rendered by penitential good works would suffice in the presence of this awful judge.[26] He had, too, in common with his age, a very realistic belief in the devil, purgatory, and hell, of which the Church made ample use as an adjunct of the religious life. It sought thereby to dominate human nature and enforce its sway. This realistic belief in the devil and hell was a dread reality to imaginative souls, and it clung to Luther and caused him many an hour of torment to the end of his life. The superstition of the age filled the world with a host of maleficent spirits, through whom the devil worked his wiles on human beings. It believed in witches and warlocks, who were the devil's minions; in apparitions, charms, and spells. His mother, he tells us, had much to suffer from a neighbour whom she believed to be a witch, who frightened the children that they cried themselves almost to death, and to whom she ascribed the death of one of his brothers.[27] Luther grew up in a world of occult forces, which worked harm to both body and soul — a world of fancy and fear, which undoubtedly threw its shadow over his early years and seems to have aggravated a temperamental tendency to sombre introspection. This popular superstition was entwined with

[26] "Werke," xlv. 86; "Documente," 24, 25, 27, 31, 35-36, and many other passages in his works.

[27] "Tischreden," iii. 131; *cf.* "Werke," xl., Pt. I., 315 f., where he mentions this incident and enlarges on the machinations of the devil.

the religious experience of the time and tended to intensify the more sombre side of religious belief, which concerned itself with death and judgment to come and to which the Church gave a prominent place in its ritual and teaching. On the one hand, Christ the stern judge to whom the sinner has to give an account and render satisfaction for his sin. On the other, the powers of evil lurking around him, seeking to do harm to body and soul in this life and to get possession of him in the next. Well might the sinner tremble at the thought of both God and devil.

But the Church had its remedy for those terrors, and though Luther trembled at the name of Christ and feared the powers of evil, his young life was not, therefore, necessarily a continual nightmare, as some of his utterances may seem to imply. For he also reminds us that the Christ of judgment was not the only conception that he learned to know. Christ as the Saviour was also discernible in the liturgy and symbolism of the Church,[28] and if the Christian was taught that he still required to make satisfaction for sin against the day of reckoning, he was also taught that he could rely on the effective intercession of the virgin, the apostles, and the saints in his behalf. Luther was destined to discover the insufficiency of this expedient in the dark days of his search for a gracious God in the monastery. But these days were still distant, and he does not say that in those of his youthful fears and doubts he was unable to find comfort in the doctrine of the intercession of the saints. He implies, in fact, that he implicitly accepted the Church's teaching on this head, and he continued long after the discovery of his characteristic doctrine of justification by faith to cherish the belief in its efficacy.[29] Even as " a frenzied papalist " he had experienced the virtue of saving faith, though the term implied something very different from what it ultimately came to mean to him. In some of his later utterances, indeed, he seems to see nothing in his early religious experience but a haunting fear and servitude, from which he would fain have broken loose. But these sombre reflections are, to a certain extent at least, coloured by his later

[28] " Werke," xlii. 134.
[29] See, for instance, a sermon of 1519 in " Werke," ii. 696-697.

religious experience. His young mind was too undeveloped to be more than the receptacle of current beliefs and impressions, and it would absorb the light as well as the shade reflected by these beliefs and impressions. Looking back on his boyhood across the stormy period of his spiritual conflict in the monastery and its agitated sequel, the shade rather than the light was apt to seem the predominant feature, and it certainly would be premature to assume that his youthful religious experience was a sort of anticipation of the dark days of spiritual trial in the monastery.[30]

Even the popular superstition which believed so realistically and crudely in the devil and his baneful agents does not necessarily betoken a pessimistic view of life. Here, too, the Church, whilst sharing in this superstition, provided the remedy. Not only were there charms and spells and talismans of proved efficacy in warding off the malign influence of the spirit world. The devil and his minions were helpless against the cross and the sacraments, and in this case also the protection of the saints was available. Luther, on his own confession, made ample use of this assurance against the powers of darkness, and we must beware of assuming that because he tells us that he believed so realistically in these occult powers as well as in a retributive God, his early life was all cloud and no sunshine. Like other children he would not always be shuddering at the thought of a maleficent devil, against whose machinations the sign of the cross or the protection of the saints was an effective remedy.

[30] Strohl dissents from this view which has been forcibly handled by Scheel. He thinks that some of the later utterances of Luther warrant the conclusion that his youth was habitually clouded by the fear of a retributive God, and that already as a boy he was the victim of religious unrest. " Il semble donc bien que la jeunesse de Luther ait été assombrie par une religion dont, par une disposition speciale, il sentait plus profondément que d'autres l'insuffisance. La préparation de sa mission a commencé dès son enfance." " L'Évolution Religieuse de Luther jusq'en 1515," 53 (1922).

II. School and University Career

Luther's treatment in the Mansfeld Latin school, to which he was sent in his seventh year, is usually represented as the counterpart of the harsh discipline of the home.[31]   To the barbarity of his teachers, Hausrath ascribes the nervous disorder which manifested itself in the periodic fits of terror to which he was subject from his childhood onwards.[32] It is, however, questionable whether those terroristic attacks, to which he was undoubtedly liable in later years, and which took the form of intense religious trepidation, are traceable to his school days.   The fact seems to be that he inherited a strong constitution from his parents and that he was too sturdy a child to be thrashed into a chronic neurotic.[33] Melanchthon says that these terrors first began, at all events in acute form, at a later period, at earliest apparently during his student course, and he notices the fact in connection with his entrance into the Erfurt monastery and ascribes to them a purely religious cause.[34]   Scheel questions the usual version of the unbridled brutality of his teachers at Mansfeld, in view of the general testimony of the regulations applicable to the schools of the period of Luther's youth. Whilst these show the firm belief, on the part of the municipal authorities, in the efficacy of the rod in the maintenance of discipline, they forbid arbitrary and excessive punishments.[35]   It is, however, a fair question whether these regulations were scrupulously observed, and Luther's experience certainly shows that brutal and excessive punishment was not unknown in the Mansfeld school.   He tells us that he was thrashed fifteen times in a single forenoon, evidently without justification.   He seems to have in mind his own experience at Mansfeld when he speaks in the same passage of his " Table Talk " of the blustering, storming, and violent methods of schoolmasters, who showed neither insight nor skill in their treatment of their pupils,

[31] See, for instance, Hausrath, i. 4, and Berger, i. 18-20.
[32] I. 264.
[33] " Erat autem natura, quod sæpe miratus sum," says Melanchthon, " in corpore nec parvo nec imbecilli."   " Vita," 158.
[34] *Ibid.*, 158.   [35] " Luther," i. 34-36.

and adopted the attitude of the hangman or the gaoler towards them. Whilst discipline is essential, severity ought to be tempered by love and discernment.[36] Under this brutal régime school life was a martyrdom.[37] In another passage, which also refers to his experience in the Mansfeld school, he says that he and his fellow-pupils were the victims of the perpetual threats and cruelty of their teachers who kept their nerves on the rack.[38]

There seems also to be a reminiscence of his own sufferings under this régime in the manifesto to the German municipal authorities, written in 1524, in behalf of scholastic reform on humanist and evangelical lines. He denounces the pre-Reformation schools as nothing else than " hell and purgatory," in which the children were terrorised by brutal, ignorant schoolmasters, and learned nothing worth knowing, neither Latin nor German properly, in spite of the endless mechanical drill in cases and tenses.[39] In this drastic philippic against the old educational system he is undoubtedly thinking of his own sufferings at the hands of incapable and irascible pedagogues. At the same time, it is evident that he also writes from the standpoint of the aggressive evangelical reformer, to whom this system appears as unmitigated error and bondage. Whilst there was much to be said for the new education on the humanist, evangelical model, which he would fain substitute for the old in all the municipal schools, the spirit of the indictment is too bitter and biased to be an objective statement of facts. Even

[36] " Colloquia," ii. 130. Quodlibet regimen debet observare discrimen ingeniorum.

[37] *Ibid.*, ii. 542.

[38] " Werke," xliv. 548. Nisi forte animi assiduis minis et crudelitate magistrorum, qua tum in scholasticos sævire solebant, perculsi, facilius repentino terrore concuterentur. *Cf.* " Tischreden," i. 60, where he refers to the same incident without, however, mentioning the brutality of his teachers. The first version was published without his revision. But there seems to be no reason for inferring that the editor added the words referring to the teachers in the Mansfeld school.

[39] " Werke," xv. 46 ; *cf.* **31, 51.** Und isst nicht mehr die helle und das fegfewr unser schulen, da wir innen gemartert sind über den Casualibus und Temporalibus, da wir doch nichts denn eyttel nichts gelernt haben durch so viel steupen, zittern, angst und jamer.

so, the old system was certainly far from being an ideal one. It was not only unduly harsh and lacking in discernment. It was largely a system of cram, fitted to exercise the memory rather than develop the understanding and form the character of the pupil. In the Latin school, the instruction, of which Latin was the exclusive medium, consisted in memorising certain school books, graded according to the age of the pupils. The use of the vernacular was strictly prohibited and delinquents who contravened these regulations were systematically punished. " Better bad Latin than good German," was a current scholastic saying, and the bad Latin from the alphabet upwards was drummed into the young mind with the aid of the *asinus* and the *lupus* which, along with the rod, were the ubiquitous adjuncts of discipline.

In the first years of the Latin school course the pupil was taught the Latin primer, or elementary reading book, known as the " Fibula." In the next stage he acquired a knowledge of elementary Latin grammar, with Donatus as text-book, and this was followed by more advanced instruction in grammar and syntax, as contained in the "Doctrinale," as the higher text-book, composed by Alexander de Ville Dieu about the beginning of the thirteenth century, was termed. The reading books used in connection with Donatus and Alexander consisted of extracts from Æsop, Cato, and other ancient moralists, and towards the end of the fifteenth century from Plautus and Terrence.[40] Whilst the curriculum in the Latin schools of the larger towns included Rhetoric (composition) and Logic, which, with Grammar formed the Trivium, in those of the smaller towns, like Mansfeld, the more advanced instruction received little or no attention. Religious knowledge and music were taught in all schools, large and small, and this part of the instruction was intended to fit the pupils to take a part in the Church services, Church and school being closely associated.

So much of this curriculum as could be mastered from his seventh to his fourteenth year, Luther had passed through

[40] Paulsen, " Geschichte des Gelehrten Unterrichts," i. 20-22 (1896), and " Das Deutsche Bildungswesen," 18 (1909) ; Scheel, " Luther," i. 44 f.

before he left the Mansfeld school for Magdeburg. He had learned to speak the colloquial Latin of his time and had been drilled in Latin grammar, in the elements of the faith, and the moral tales and maxims which formed the subject matter of the reading books. In spite of his later contempt for the method and content of this mediæval instruction, those early years in the Mansfeld school were not altogether wasted. According to Mathesius he was a diligent and apt pupil.[41] In a passage of the " Table Talk " Luther himself materially qualifies the statement in the manifesto to the municipalities that the pupils learned nothing worth knowing in these schools. He expresses his appreciation of Donatus [42] and ascribes to the reading of "Æsop's Fables" and Cato's moral maxims a high educational value. He ranks them second only to the Bible and rejoices that they have been retained in the schools.[43]

In his fourteenth year (probably Easter, 1497) he was sent to Magdeburg to continue his education [44] in accordance with the practice of moving from school to school in search of instruction. The wandering student or scholar, like the wandering apprentice or artisan, was a feature of the social life of the period. This wandering life began even during the school age, when the pupil went forth, under the name of " Schütz " or " Bachant," to finish his education at a distance from home, or, in not a few cases, seek adventure and waste his time. Luther's father made choice of Magdeburg for this purpose, and the son is supposed to have attended a school of the Brethren of the Common Life. He himself says that " he went to school with the Nollbrüder," a popular name for the members of this late mediæval fraternity.[45] From this statement it

[41] " Fein fleissig und schleunig gelernet," Scheel, i. 54.

[42] Donatus est optimus grammaticus.

[43] "Tischreden," iii. 353. Post biblia Catonis et Æsopi scripta, me judice, sunt optima.

[44] Enders, " Briefwechsel," ii. 294 ; cf. " Werke," xxxviii. 105.

[45] Noll is probably the German for Lollard. See Luther's letter to the burgomaster of Magdeburg, Sturm, with whom as a youth he was acquainted during his residence at Magdeburg. The letter is dated 15th June 1522. "Werke," Erlangen edition, liii. 137 ; cf. Enders, " Briefwechsel," iii. 402.

has been inferred that he attended a Latin school of the Brethren in the town. But, as Scheel has shown, there is no evidence for the existence of such a school at Magdeburg, and what evidence there is goes to show the contrary. Luther, he thinks, attended the Cathedral school, which at this period was the chief educational institution of the town and the only one that could have provided instruction superior to that of Mansfeld.[46] In this school he was, it would seem, taught by members of the Brethren of the Common Life, who apparently served on the school staff, and it is only in this sense that we should interpret his assertion that he went to school with the Nollbrüder at Magdeburg.[47] In accordance with the custom of the time, he earned his bread by singing in the streets.[48]

It is also supposed that the Brethren exercised an influence on his subsequent religious development. The aim of their instruction was specifically religious, and they doubtless strove to nurture the piety of their pupil. They were religious reformers in the sense of seeking to improve the religious usages of the time and laying stress on inwardness in religion against the prevailing formalism. To this end they fostered the reading of the Bible in the vernacular and a devout life in keeping with its teaching and spirit. It may have been due to their influence that Luther first became acquainted with the vernacular Bible, if the incident related in the " Table Talk," [49] to which we have already referred, took place during his Magdeburg sojourn. But this Bible reading did not imply any essential divergence on the part of the Magdeburg Brethren or their pupil from the teaching or usages of the Church. They were certainly not reformers in the later doctrinal sense, but orthodox churchmen who, whilst striving to deepen the traditional piety and reform ecclesiastical abuses, conformed to conventional belief and

[46] The municipal school was not yet established.

[47] Scheel, " Luther," i. 67 f.

[48] The term " Partekenhengst " was applied to the school children who sang for bread, and Luther himself implies that he maintained himself by this method at Magdeburg, in referring to his use of it at Eisenach. " Werke," xxx., Pt. II., 576.

[49] " Tischreden," i. 44.

practice. Their influence on Luther, such as it was, would only tend to confirm him in the piety in which he had been nurtured, and there appears to be no real ground for inferring that it sowed in him the seeds of his future revolt against the teaching and institutions of the Church.[50] The environment in which he spent this Magdeburg year was certainly not fitted to estrange him from either. Magdeburg was the seat of an archbishopric. The ecclesiastical interest dominated the city, with its numerous clergy, churches, and monasteries. The young Luther would be impressed, not estranged, by the ecclesiastical pomp, the stately ceremonies which its streets and its Church services witnessed, and this impression would strengthen the religious spirit which the Brethren nurtured by their teaching. An incident, later mentioned by him, points unmistakably to this conclusion. He was struck by the realistic presentation of monastic self-denial and devotion given by the guardian of the Franciscan monastery, Prince William of Anhalt-Zerbst, whom he saw walking in the streets barefooted, begging alms and carrying a heavy sack filled with the offerings of the faithful on his bent back, accompanied by a fellow-monk, who carried no load, in order that he might show in his own person his readiness to serve Christ in the lowliest fashion. " He had so fasted," Luther tells us, " watched, and mortified his body, that he looked like a dead man, sheer skin and bone, so that he died soon after. Whoever looked on him was deeply stirred by his devotion and felt ashamed of himself." [51] The incident evidently made a deep impression on his imagination and may possibly have recurred to him in serious moments as an example for him to follow.

[50] Scheel, i. 82 f., makes out a strong case against the supposed far-reaching influence of the Brethren on Luther in opposition to Barnikol, " Luther in Magdeburg und die dortige Brüderschule " (1917), and Börner, the editor of Dieburg's " Annalen und Acten der Brüder des Gemeinsamen Lebens zu Hildesheim " (1905). Ullmann, " Reformers before the Reformation," ii., also recognises that the religious views and reforming activity of the Brethren did not really go beyond the Catholic standpoint.

[51] " Werke," xxxviii. 105.

After the close of the school year at Magdeburg his father sent him to Eisenach, where he had many relatives— a fact which decided the choice of a new school.[52] It did not, however, assure him free lodging and maintenance. At Eisenach, as at Magdeburg, he sang in the streets for his bread.[53] There was nothing unusual in this, for though his father was probably in a position to provide for his education, as he certainly was three years later, when he became a student at Erfurt, it was not unusual for boys thus to fend for themselves whilst attending school away from home. Happily, Martin was erelong relieved from the necessity of relying on this haphazard means of subsistence by the kindness of the wife of an opulent burgher, named Kuntz Cotta. The ordinary version of his good fortune is of late origin and seems to have been gradually expanded into the circumstantial tale of later writers, who draw a touching picture of the forlorn lad singing in vain from door to door and ready to despair, when the motherly Frau Cotta took pity on him and opened her home to him. That he sang for his bread in the streets is indubitable. But the earlier accounts of how he came to find a home under Frau Cotta's roof know nothing of the picturesque details of the later popular tale. Ratzeberger simply says that he had lodging and maintenance from Kuntz Cotta, and Mathesius adds that a devout matron (whose name he does not give) was touched by Luther's singing in church and conceived such an affection for him that she took him into her home. Luther also mentions that he was received as a guest by one whom he calls Henricianus (Heinrich Schalbe), and it seems that while he found a lodging with the Cotta's, he was in the habit of partaking also of the hospitality of this additional benefactor.[54]

It appears from his later correspondence that he also enjoyed the friendship of Johann Braun, vicar of St Mary's Church, whom he invited to his ordination as priest in 1507, and that he had grateful memories of his intercourse with the members of the Minorite monastery at the foot of the

[52] Melanchthon, " Vita," 157.
[53] " Werke," xxx., Pt. II., 576.
[54] For a critical discussion of the evidence, see Scheel, i. 104 f.

Wartburg.[55] The genial vicar, who combined piety with a taste for poetry and music, attracted a number of young people of similar tastes, and of this circle Martin was a member. In it he would appear to have come into contact with a wider culture than in the circle of the Brethren at Magdeburg, or in his simple home at Mansfeld. This wider culture was, however, conjoined with a sincere piety of the conventional type, which reverently believed in the papal indulgence vouchsafed to those who once a year visited the grave of a holy man, Heinrich Raspe, in the church of St Catherine's monastery, and in the wonderful image of the Virgin and Child which turned away from, or graciously received the sick suppliant, according as he approached it with or without gifts for the monastery. Luther later tells how the movement was the result of a hidden mechanism worked by the monks.[56] At the time of his residence at Eisenach, he apparently shared in the superstition which seems not to have suspected the real explanation of this pious fraud. He appears also to have heard much about the saintly Princess Elizabeth of Thuringia, so closely associated with the Wartburg, who in the thirteenth century had devoted herself with rare self-denial to works of mercy, the tradition of which was cherished by the inhabitants. Among those to whom he later expressed his indebtedness was the Rector of the Latin School, Trebonius, who, according to Melanchthon, " taught grammar more thoroughly and aptly than elsewhere." [57] That he was an ardent humanist is an assumption of later biographers.[58] It finds no support in the details given by Melanchthon, who would hardly have omitted to mention the fact. What he does say is that it was at Erfurt that he turned his attention to the Latin classics as a welcome diversion from the scholastic philosophy.[59] What Trebonius

[55] Enders, " Briefwechsel," i. 1-3 ; *cf.* Debering, " Aus Luther's Frühzeit, Briefe aus dem Eisenacher und Erfurter Lutherkreis, 1497-1510," *Zentralblatt für Bibliothekswesen*, Jahrgang 33, Hefte 4 and 5 (1916).
[56] " Werke," Erlangen edition, lx. 288 f.　　　　[57] " Vita," 157.
[58] Hausrath, i. 7 ; M'Giffert, " Martin Luther," 11 (1911), for instance.　　　　[59] " Vita," 157.

taught him more efficiently than elsewhere was the more
advanced course of grammar, rhetoric, and poetry, as
contained in the mediæval text-books. Under his instruction Luther made marked progress in the higher Latin
grammar, in composition, versification, and discourse, and
easily outdistanced his fellow-pupils.[60] The worthy rector
also distinguished himself from the ordinary pedagogue
by the respect which he showed towards the older pupils.
On entering the schoolroom, he would doff his magister's
cap before taking his seat at his desk, and he required
his assistants to follow his example, reminding them
that sitting on the benches were burgomasters, chancellors,
learned doctors, and masters of the future. Luther
evidently had no little reason to cherish the memory of
the kindly rector, who strove to make the most of the
mediæval system of instruction for the benefit of his
pupils. Besides the rector, he held one of his assistants,
Wigand, in high esteem.[61] By this careful training,
extending over three years, he was fitted to enter on
a course of academic study at Erfurt in the spring
of 1501.

Erfurt, which owned the feudal superiority of the Archbishop of Maintz and the Elector of Saxony, was the seat
of a suffragan bishop. At the beginning of the sixteenth
century it counted over 100 buildings—churches, monasteries, hospitals, etc.—devoted to religion in a city of about
20,000 inhabitants. It was known locally as " little Rome "
and evidently merited the designation. Its numerous
monastic orders included the Augustinian Eremites, of whom
he was ultimately to become a member, and a Scottish
monastery, whose members repelled him by their over-
bearing manners, and of whom he gives a very
unfavourable, but evidently prejudiced description.[62] Once
more he found himself in a pre-eminently ecclesiastical
environment. Its position on the highway between north
and south Germany, its privileges as a staple, the fertility
of the surrounding district made it also the centre of a

[60] Melanchthon, " Vita," 157.
[61] Enders, " Briefwechsel," i. 48.
[62] " Tischreden," iv. 270.

considerable trade and industry. Luther celebrates its eminence in this respect among the German cities, though he exaggerates the number of the population, which at this period probably did not much exceed 20,000.[63] Its fame was increased by its university, which, though instituted by a Bull of Clement VII., granting the city the privilege of a *Studium Generale* on the conventional mediæval model, in 1379, was not actually opened till 1392, when 523 students were entered on the matriculation roll. In Luther's day its fame far exceeded that of any other German university, and years afterwards the Reformer looked back with pride on the stately " promotion " ceremonies of his time.[64] Some of his reminiscences were by no means favourable, and he expressed himself very drastically on the prevailing laxity of the student life of his time.[65] As usual his later generalities must not be taken too literally, and allowance must always be made for the effect of the change in his religious standpoint, which inevitably coloured his judgment. The students were as a rule required to live in colleges (*collegia*), or hostels (*bursæ*), which were strictly supervised, and serious breach of the regulations rendered them liable to expulsion and jeopardised their chance of taking a degree. As Luther distinguished himself by his industry and ability as a student and took his degree with distinction, it is evident that he was not adversely influenced by the moral laxity which he attributed to the students generally and seems to have exaggerated.

The curriculum of study for the Bachelor's degree in Arts included courses, extending over eighteen months, in grammar, logic, rhetoric, physics, and philosophy, in accordance with the system of Aristotle, who dominated the instruction of the Faculty. The method of this instruction was what we should call the tutorial and consisted of the comments of the lecturer on the text-books, which were noted by the students, and of disputations and exercises on the themes treated in the books, or suggested by the lecturer.

[63] " Tischreden," ii. 486 ; iii. 372.

[64] *Ibid.*, ii. 660.

[65] *Ibid.*, ii. 613-614; *cf.* 669. Erphurdt ist nichts besseres gewest dann ein hurhaus und bierhaus.

As the result of his work, Luther took the degree of Bachelor of Arts in the autumn of 1502 and thereby came under the obligation to teach the more elementary knowledge, in which he had thus given proof of his proficiency, to the younger students. Two years' further study were required for the Master's degree, the courses including, besides higher instruction on the subjects previously studied, mathematics,[66] metaphysics, and ethics. At the age of twenty-two his ability and industry secured him second place in a list of seventeen candidates who passed the Master's examination in the winter of 1505.

Luther held his teachers, especially Trutvetter and Usingen, in high esteem, and seems to have implicitly accepted their philosophic teaching. In his later years, even after he began to take a line of his own in theology, and to criticise the scholastic method and doctrines in which they had trained him, he continued to express this esteem. Trutvetter he calls " the prince of the dialecticians of our age," [67] and he confesses his obligations to him and his reverence for his authority.[68] He expresses an equal veneration for Usingen,[69] who subsequently joined the Augustinian Order, of which Luther himself was erelong to become a member. Erfurt was an exclusively " modern," i.e., Occamist, university, and all the Masters of Arts professed the Nominalist philosophy as expounded by William Occam, the great Franciscan doctor of the fourteenth century. Under their teaching Luther became an enthusiastic " modern," or Occamist, against " the sects " of the Thomists and Scotists, as the followers of Thomas Aquinas and Duns Scotus were called. He regarded Occam as " the most skilled and the most learned of all schoolmen," [70] " the greatest dialectician of the middle age," though he did not esteem him a good writer.[71] He calls him " my master "

---

[66] Embracing music, arithmetic, geometry, and astronomy—the Quadrivium in contrast to the Trivium of the schools—grammar, logic, and rhetoric.

[67] Enders, " Briefwechsel," i. 160.

[68] *Ibid.*, i. 188, 190.   [69] *Ibid.*, i. 31.   [70] " Tischreden," i. 137.

[71] Summus fuit dialecticus, sed gratiam non habuit loquendi. *Ibid.*, ii. 516.

(*magister meus*) and speaks of the Occamist school of philosophy as " my sect." [72] " Occam," he says, " was the prince of the Moderns, and conquered all the others by his genius, if he was but an indifferent theologian and understood nothing of Christ." [73] He retained his predilection for his philosophic teaching even after he had come to differ from him in theology. In the endless controversy, for instance, over the reality, outside the mind, of universal or abstract ideas, apart from the mind conceiving them, he was, as a student, the votary of the Nominalism of Occam, who believed that they were mere generalisations of the mind, against the various forms of Realism represented by Thomas Aquinas and Duns Scotus.[74] In after years he retained his preference for the Nominalism of Occam, though, as a passage in his " Table Talk " shows, he had lost taste for these wordy disputations.[75]

As in all the mediæval universities, Aristotle was the dominant authority in dialectics and philosophy for the various " sects," including that of Occam. It was on the Aristotelian logic, natural philosophy, ethics, and metaphysics that Luther's mind was nurtured at Erfurt, and in its general features this culture remained the dominant influence in his intellectual life, despite the estrangement from it in essential respects in consequence of his later religious experience. Even as the militant reformer he could boast of his knowledge of Aristotle, and in his " Address to the German Nobility," written fifteen years after his Erfurt student days, claimed to have a clearer understanding of his philosophy than Aquinas or Scotus.[76] He retained

---

[72] "Werke," vi. 195. Meæ sectæ, scilicet Occanicæ seu Modernorum.

[73] "Tischreden," iv. 679-680.

[74] The question whether our general conceptions have something corresponding to them in external objects, apart from the conceiving mind (Universalia), or are merely general terms by which the mind expresses the features common to these objects, had long been the subject of keen dispute between Realist and Nominalist. It was a question as old as the days of Plato, who regarded the visible universe as the expression of the divine ideas antecedent to or underlying all things, and Luther learned from his Erfurt teachers to take the side of Occam in this and other questions against both the Thomist and the Scotist schools or sects.

[75] "Tischreden," iv. 679.   [76] "Werke," vi. 458.

a high opinion of the educational value of his logic, rhetoric, and poetics in the training of youth, if divested of the mere quibbling of the schools.[77] He continued to make use of the dialectic method as a means of solving difficult problems even in theology [78] and he favoured and encouraged in the University of Wittenberg the method of dialectic disputation, in which he had taken part with such zeal in that of Erfurt, where he was known among his fellow-students as " the philosopher." [79] There is no real ground for inferring from Melanchthon's disparaging reference to " the thorny dialectic " [80] in which he was trained at Erfurt, that he had no relish at this time for these dialectic studies, even if he later ridiculed the tendency to split logic over trifles and would greatly simplify its terminology.[81] His early notes on Augustine's works show his familiarity with the Aristotelian philosophy, which he accepts as authoritative in speculative questions,[82] and both these early lecture notes and his later controversial works show the skill with which he could turn it against his opponents. He expresses contradictory opinions on the value of the Physics. In one passage in his " Table Talk " he says that Aristotle as a natural philosopher is of no value [83] and he includes the Physics in his condemnation of his works in the " Address to the German Nobility." [84] In another he praises the Physics as the best of books on the subject,[85] and whilst learning from Trutvetter to mistrust astrology and distrusting all the persuasions of Melanchthon to believe in it, he accepted the Aristotelian astronomy.[86] He expresses equally contradictory opinions on the Ethics, for while in the Address he condemns it on Christian grounds and places the ethical

[77] " Werke," vi. 458 ; cf. " Tischreden," ii. 186.
[78] " Tischreden," ii. 555-558.
[79] Enders, " Briefwechsel," ii. 391 ; cf. Drews, " Disputationen Luther's " (1895-96), and Stange, " Die ältesten Ethischen Disputationen Luther's " (1904).

[80] " Vita," 157.
[81] " Tischreden," iii. 230.
[82] " Werke," ix. 9.
[83] " Tischreden," i. 178.
[84] " Werke," vi. 457.
[85] " Tischreden," i. 57.
[86] " Tischreden," ii. 457, 619 ; iii. 12-13, 448-449.

teaching of Cicero on a higher level,[87] he rates it highly in the " Table Talk." [88] The same inconsistency appears in his judgment of the Metaphysics. These judgments seem to have been swayed by the mood of the moment, and Luther, like some other great men, who talk much and are prone to impulsive generalisations, was not above being inconsistent at times. The true explanation seems, however, to be that his judgment of the Aristotelian philosophy varied according as he thought of it from the purely philosophical, or from the purely Christian standpoint. From the former, it is evident that he cherished a deep sense of its value and owed much to it as an intellectual discipline. " Formerly," i.e., at Erfurt, he says, " I read diligently the works of Aristotle, and because he observes the right method, he is to be highly esteemed." He describes the Metaphysics and the De Anima as well as the Physics as the best of books and adds that he understands them perfectly.[89] In reference to his conception of God as the eternal principle of energy in the universe, he admits that, if understood and better applied than Aristotle himself was able to do, his ideas might be made to render useful service to theology as well as philosophy.[90] From the Christian standpoint, on the other hand, he subjects him to severe criticism and makes ample use of his gift of strong language in denouncing him. " Aristotle," he says, " knows nothing of the soul, of God, and of immortality, and Cicero far excels him in these subjects." [91]

Even in the lecture rooms at Erfurt, Aristotle was no infallible authority, for Occam and his school, in opposition to the older scholastics, insisted on the antagonism of reason and faith and on the futility of attempting to demonstrate the truth of Christian doctrine by dialectics. Rational knowledge, they held, is limited to what is demonstrable by reason, whereas the knowledge of faith is based on revelation and ecclesiastical authority, and is not capable of rational

[87] " Tischreden," iii. 451.
[88] Ibid., i. 178, Aristoteles est optimus in morali philosophia.
[89] Ibid., i..57.   [90] " Werke," i. 28.   [91] " Tischreden," iii. 451.

proof, though, being based on revelation, it is the most certain. Even in philosophy Luther's teachers did not blindly accept his authority, and already in his early lecture notes on Augustine their pupil is found denouncing those who say that Aristotle's philosophy is not in disharmony with the Christian faith, as " shameless chatterers." [92] In this he was only repeating what he had learned in the Erfurt class-rooms, and even in his later onslaught on the great " heathen " as a misleading guide in theology, he was only expressing in more vehement language what Occam and his school had said less offensively before him.[93] At the same time it is evident that he owed not a little to his Erfurt training in the Aristotelian dialectics and philosophy, and he remained to a considerable extent his disciple even in speculative theology, though, like his teachers, he could only read him in a Latin translation.

There is no real ground for the inference that Luther came under the influence of a free, anti-ecclesiastical spirit [94] at Erfurt. Occam, indeed, was a daring rebel against the papal authority in the conflict between the emperor and the pope, in which he bore an active part as the champion of the Emperor Ludwig. But it does not appear that at this period of his career Luther concerned himself with this side of the great Franciscan's teaching. He is also supposed to have been influenced by the teaching of John of Wesel, who had lectured at Erfurt for a number of years from about the middle of the fifteenth century, and was esteemed one of its most famous doctors. Luther says that in his time Wesel ruled the university through his books and that he studied his works for his Master's degree.[95] These works seem to have been of a philosophical, not a theological

[92] " Werke," ix. 27.

[93] See his letter to Trutvetter, 9th May 1518, in which he says that he had learned from him to give credence to the Scriptures alone in theology and that, in writing against the scholastics, he was only doing what had been permitted to Trutvetter and all others hitherto. Enders, " Briefwechsel," i. 190.

[94] Ullmann, " Reformers before the Reformation," i. 223 f., English translation (1855).

[95] " Werke," xxv. 325 (Erlangen edition).

character, and it was only after he had left Erfurt to become cathedral preacher at Worms that he was condemned for heresy. It does not appear that he had laid himself open to this charge as professor. It has also been supposed that, as a student, Luther had doubts about the condemnation of Hus, and he does note in one of his later writings that one of his Erfurt teachers, Johann von Grefenstein, remarked to him that John Hus had been condemned by the Council of Constance without sufficient evidence.[96] This casual remark does not, however, seem to have predisposed him at the time in favour of the Bohemian reformer, and he repeatedly gives expression to his detestation of heresy (including that of Hus) in his earliest writings. He also remembered long after how, as a student, an old man had said to him that a great change must come about, since things could not remain as they were.[97] The remark seems to have made little impression on him at the time and certainly did not transform him into a rebel against the existing ecclesiastical authority. Again, he tells us that, as a young master, he took to reading the Bible in the Erfurt Library and thereby discovered many errors in the Papacy. His doubts were, however, only evanescent and the thought of the authority of the Pope and the Church speedily silenced them. " Should you alone be so wise ? " he asked himself. " Nay, you may be sure that you are wrong." With these words he stifled the passing doubts induced by his Bible reading.[98]

Nor is there much ground for assuming that, as a student and young master, he devoted himself specially to humanist studies and was already conscious of a jar with the old culture. The fact seems to be that in his case, as in that of his fellow-masters, the degree betokened, not the humanist expert, but the proficient exponent of the scholastic philosophy. The only teachers at Erfurt at this period who could be said to represent the humanist spirit were Nicolas Marschalk, Maternus, and Emser. Marschalk, who taught Greek and Latin, left Erfurt the year after

---

[96] "Werke," vi. 591.   [97] "Tischreden," ii. 74.   [98] *Ibid.*, iii. 439.

Luther became a student for the newly-founded University of Wittenberg. Maternus lectured occasionally on the classics besides the scholastic philosophy, and Luther may have attended these lectures, though they were not obligatory for the degree. He certainly attended those of Emser in the summer of 1504 on Reuchlin's Latin comedy, *Sergius*. But Emser, who later mentioned the fact in a philippic against the Reformer, spent only a short time at Erfurt, and it was not till fully a decade after Luther had taken his degree that humanism took an appreciable hold on the university. He certainly read a number of the Latin classics, and, according to Melanchthon, found in them a welcome change from the schoolmen. Erfurt was not professedly hostile to such study. The course in poetry included the reading of some of these writers, and Luther's predilection for Cicero, Virgil, Livy, and other classic authors does not necessarily signify a leaning towards the humanist *versus* the scholastic ideal in education. Scholasticism, not humanism, was the characteristic feature of the university curriculum, and his intellectual training was of the conventional mediæval type, even if he learned besides to interest himself, chiefly on account of their practical value,[99] in Cicero, Virgil, Livy, and Plautus. His scholastic studies, he later tells, left him little time to devote to the classics. We hear, indeed, of a circle of ardent young humanists at Erfurt, whose recognised leader was Mutianus Rufus, Canon of Gotha. But it does not seem to have been formed before Luther entered the Augustinian monastery. His former fellow-student Crotus Rubianus, who later became a distinguished humanist, reminds him in a letter of October 1519 of the fellowship (*consortium*) to which both belonged in their student days. But he does not say that it was a humanist circle, and Crotus was at this period still a votary of the scholastic philosophy. It seems, in fact, to have been a student society which met to discuss philosophy (*bonæ artes*), and in whose discussions and pastimes Luther took an active part before he distressed

[99] Melanchthon, " Vita," 157.

its members by suddenly becoming a monk.[100] In a subsequent letter (April 1520) Crotus refers to this society (this time under the name of *contubernium*) in which Luther excelled as "the musician and erudite philosopher" of the company.[101] Whilst interest in the classics was not necessarily excluded from these social gatherings, it is evident that they were mainly devoted to discussions of the conventional scholastic type.

[100] Enders, "Briefwechsel," ii. 204-208.
[101] *Ibid.*, ii. 391.

CHAPTER II

BEGINNINGS OF LUTHER'S MONASTIC CAREER
(1505-1507)

I. Entrance into the Erfurt Monastery

As Master of Arts, Luther came under an obligation to
teach in the faculty for two years.[1] The obligation did
not, however, preclude him from pursuing a course of study
in another faculty. His father was proud of his promotion
as magister and showed his sense of his new dignity by
addressing him as " You " (Jhr) instead of the familiar
" Thou " (Du).[2] As in the case of the father of Calvin,
his ambition contemplated for him a larger career than
that available to the ordinary magister. He had planned
for him a rich and honourable marriage.[3] A juristic career
opened the most feasible avenue to the realisation of his
ambition to see his talented son rise in the world. At his
desire he became a student in the Faculty of Law at the
beginning of the summer session, 1505. As in the case of
Calvin, he seems to have yielded to the paternal wish rather
than to any personal inclination for the study of law, and
was perhaps not too happy in the possession of the *corpus
juris* with which his father presented him. From a letter
to Trebonius two years later (April 1507), it is evident that
he was not so keen as his father on mere material advancement. As he reminds his old preceptor, he had in the
Eisenach days been " careless of the things of the world

---

[1] Scheel, " Luther," i. 237.

[2] " Documente zu Luther's Entwicklung," 19.

[3] " Werke," viii. 573. Destinabas vero me vincire honesto et opulento
conjugio, as Luther reminded him in the dedication of his work on
" Monastic Vows " (1521).

and little concerned about riches." [4] In his " Table Talk "
he was wont to speak disparagingly of the study of juris-
prudence. He calls it a sordid profession concerned only
with the getting of money.[5] Such utterances may not
necessarily be an echo of his impressions as a law student.
They at least lend some confirmation to the inference that
even then he was not particularly enthusiastic for the profession of law. It is rather significant in this connection
that he speaks of the depression to which he was liable as
a young magister at Erfurt, *i.e.*, during the months that
elapsed between his promotion as Master of Arts and his
entrance into the monastery.[6] In any case, in view of the
spiritual crisis that intervened within a few weeks after he
became a student of law and changed the whole course of
his life, he can hardly have been wholeheartedly devoted to
the course that his father had marked out for him. His
mind, it would appear, was not absorbed in the pursuit of an
ambitious career to the exclusion of other-worldly thoughts.
He began the study of law in May 1505. On 17th July he
renounced the world and entered the monastery of the
Augustinian Eremites at Erfurt. To his fellow-students
he had hitherto appeared as " a lively and cheery
companion," as Mathesius calls him.

What had happened ? Was this startling transition
from the law class-room to the monastery the result of a
sudden conversion from one conception or ideal of life to
another ? Or was it the climax of a religious experience
that was gradually and surely tending this way ? The
result of a protracted inner conflict over the question of
his relation to God and the salvation of his soul ? The
biographers are by no means agreed on the answer. One
set holds that Luther's temperament and previous religious
experience were gradually and surely leading him to a spiritual
crisis, and that the climax must have come sooner or later.

[4] In memoria habes quam fuerim prodigus in sæculo et minus amans
lucra. " Briefwechsel," xvii. 84.
[5] Juris studium est plane sordidum et nisi pecunia esset, nemo illi
studio vacaret. " Tischreden," iii. 4 ; *cf.* ii. 626. Omnes lucri et quæstus
causa student.
[6] " Tischreden," iii. 439.

They see in it the ultimate effect of his harsh upbringing in home and school which disordered his nerves and fostered a morbid imagination. They stress the terroristic conception of God and Christ which made him liable to periodic fits of anguish and despair. They assume that he was from an early period haunted by the thought of judgment and damnation and obsessed by the question, How shall I find a gracious God? They emphasise every religious influence that might have tended to direct his mind to the monastic life as the only sure way of winning the divine favour and as in itself the ideal of the perfect life. They thus tend to read what is known of his early life in the light of this *a priori* conception of it—to make the crisis of 1505 throw its shadow back over his school and student days.[7]

There is something to be said for the tendency to trace the making of such a crisis in previous experience. Sudden conversions like that of Luther to the monastic life have often their presuppositions in previous experience. But not necessarily in every instance, and in any case there must be reasonable evidence on which to found them. In the case of Luther, in particular, what evidence there is, is rather scanty and most of it consists either of his own later utterances, or those of his friends and biographers, and is not to be accepted without critical discrimination.

Hence the reaction against this tendency which has found expression in the recent works of Köhler,[8] Scheel,[9] and A. V. Müller,[10] who maintain that Luther's decision to become a monk was unpremeditated. Scheel, for instance, criticises the usual conception of his early religious life and

---

[7] This is especially the standpoint of Hausrath, Chap. i. of the first volume of his more recent biography, particularly the conclusion of it, pp. 20-21. It is more or less shared by the older biographers. See, for instance, Kolde, " Luther," i. 42 f. (1884) ; Köstlin, i. 57 ; Berger, i. 47 f. See also Jundt, " Le Développement de la Pensée Religieuse de Luther," 38 f. (1906) ; Lindsay, " History of the Reformation," i. 198-199 (2nd edition, 1909) ; Preserved Smith, " Life and Letters of Martin Luther," 8-9 (1911).

[8] " Luther und die Deutsche Reformation," 16 (1917).

[9] " Martin Luther," i. 241 f. (3rd edition, 1921).

[10] " Luther's Werdegang Bis zum Thurmerlebnis," 2 f. (1920).

development, and modifies the older theory of his conversion to monasticism accordingly. He thinks that his piety was of the normal type, and sees little or nothing in his early life to justify the usual version of his abnormal religious experience, or to foreshadow the crisis of 1505. Luther may have had his seasons of serious religious reflection, but this reflection was not out of harmony with the ordinary piety of the time, and does not seem to have differed from that of serious-minded youths brought up in a pious atmosphere.

On the other hand, Holl, who is also one of the experts in recent Luther research, is disposed to conclude from some of Luther's later utterances that he had thoughts of the monastic life before (he does not say how long) he took the actual resolution to become a monk, and that this resolution was " probably the fulfilment of a secret wish " which he had for some time been cherishing.[11] The passages which he quotes seem to me too indefinite to warrant this conclusion, especially in view of other explicit utterances, which seem to leave no room for doubt that the actual decision to enter the monastery was both sudden and unpremeditated. The chief and also the earliest passage in which he refers to the subject occurs in the dedication to his father of his work on " Monastic Vows "[12] in 1521. Here Luther explicitly says that his vow to become a monk was a sudden and involuntary act, wrested from him in a moment of extreme terror. " I was called to this vocation by the terrors of heaven, for neither willingly nor by my own desire did I become a monk, but, surrounded by the terror and agony of a sudden death, I vowed a forced and unavoidable vow."[13] In a letter to Melanchthon in

[11] " Gesammelte Aufsätze zur Kirchengeschichte," i. 13-14 (1921). See also Kattenbusch, " Lutherana," ii. 363, and Hirsch, *ibid.*, 307 f. (1920) ; Schubert, " Luther's Frühentwickelung," 12 f. (1916) ; Strohl, " L'Évolution Religieuse de Luther," 37 f.

[12] De Votis Monasticis, " Werke," viii.

[13] " Werke," viii. 573-574. Memini enim nimis præsente memoria, cum jam placatus mecum loquereris, et ego de cœlo terroribus me vocatum assererem, neque enim libens et cupiens fiebam monachus, multo minus vero ventris gratia, sed terrore et agone mortis subitæ circumvallatus, vovi coactum et necessarium votum.

the same year he is equally explicit : " I was forced, more than drawn into making this vow, for God so willed it." [14]

The incident to which he refers took place, according to a later passage in the " Table Talk," on the 2nd of July when he was returning to Erfurt from a visit to Mansfeld.[15] Near the village of Stotternheim and not far from Erfurt, he was overtaken by a terrific thunderstorm. A flash of lightning prostrated him to the ground and in his terror of sudden death he called on St Anna for help and vowed to become a monk.[16]

The testimony of the Dedication agrees with several later passages in the " Table Talk " in which he asserts that it was only by force that he became a monk.[17] It is also in accord with that of his fellow-student, Crotus Rubianus, which is earlier by a couple of years than his own, and in which he says that " like a second Paul " [18] he was thrown to the ground by a flash of lightning and compelled to enter the Erfurt monastery. The incident near Stotternheim was for his friends as well as for himself what the incident on the road to Damascus was for Paul— a sudden breach with the past. The suddenness of his resolution is further shown by the fact that he repented of his vow.[19] One does not repent of a resolution which one has long premeditated, and it evidently cost him no little effort to carry it out. The surprise of his friends, to whom he communicated it and who strove to dissuade him from his purpose, points in the same direction. Once made, however, he felt bound on moral and religious grounds to implement it,[20] and on the 16th of July—St Alexius' Day— he invited his friends to a valedictory meal. To their

[14] Enders, " Briefwechsel," iii. 225. Magis fui raptus quam tractus, Deus ita voluit.

[15] Justus Jonas incorrectly says from Gotha (" Documente zu Luther's Entwicklung," 30) ; Crotus Rubianus, correctly, from a visit to his parents. Enders, ii. 208.

[16] " Tischreden," iv. 440.

[17] *Ibid.*, i. 294 ; ii. 407 ; iv. 303.

[18] Veluti alterum Paulum. Enders, " Briefwechsel," ii. 208.

[19] " Tischreden," iv. 440.

[20] Ego vero perseveravi.

remonstrances he firmly replied, " To-day you see me, and henceforth nevermore." On the morrow, the 17th, they accompanied him to the door of the Augustinian monastery and bade him a tearful farewell.[21]

Strangely enough, Melanchthon mentions the resolution to become a monk not in connection with the thunderstorm, of which he knows nothing, but with the sudden death of a friend which took place apparently not long before. Mathesius and Oldecop also mention this incident as well as the thunderstorm, and though both do so with evident inaccuracy of detail, it seems to be historic.[22] In the university list of the graduates in Arts, which contains Luther's name, one of them, Hieronymus Buntz, is notified as having suddenly died from an attack of pleurisy before the graduation day, and Oergel concludes that this was the friend to whom Melanchthon refers, and with whose death he connects Luther's entrance into the monastery. This may be so, though it is no more than an inference and is not in accordance with Melanchthon's belief that his death was due to violence.[23] Luther himself, however, never mentions the loss of this friend, and certainly never ascribes to such a cause his entrance into the monastery. In any case, Melanchthon distinctly says that his resolution to become a monk was the result of a sudden impulse, which completely surprised his parents and his friends.[24] This does not indeed exclude the possibility that Luther, unknown to them, had been grappling with the problem of his salvation and contemplating such a step as the ultimate solution of this problem. If so, it is strange that an accident which befell him as he was walking with a friend near Erfurt, and threatened him with death from loss of blood during

---

[21] " Tischreden," iv. 440 ; see also the account of Justus Jonas (" Documente zu Luther's Entwicklung," 30), which differs in detail.

[22] Later tradition invented for this friend the name of Alexius or Alexis, which was the name of the saint on whose day Luther entered the monastery—a fact which shows the untrustworthiness of the later additions to the story.

[23] " Vita," 158. Nescio quo casu interfectum.

[24] *Ibid.*, 158. Subito præter parentum et propinquorum opinionem venit ad solloquium monachorum Augustinianorum Erphordiæ, seque recipi petit.

his student career, did not precipitate the crisis. On this occasion he called, indeed, on the Virgin for help. But he did not vow himself to the monastic life in the presence of imminent death, and happily for him a surgeon succeeded in stanching in time the flow of blood.[25] Another student incident—an illness which is said to have brought him to the point of death—is also supposed to have turned his thoughts to the monastic life. In Luther's own version of it, it appears as merely a passing indisposition [26] and no religious significance is ascribed to it.

In one utterance in a sermon on baptism he does, indeed, seem to imply that his resolution to become a monk was preceded by a long inner conflict in his quest for a gracious God.[27] In the German version of the sermon he is made by his editor to say that he was driven to monkery by the oft-recurring question, When wilt thou at last become pious and do enough to make God gracious to thee? But the passage in the German version is an attempt by the editor to make sense of the original Latin notes of the sermon made by Rörer,[28] which, as they stand, are unintelligible. Whilst the language of the original is obscure enough, it is clear that Luther is referring, not to the motives that drove him into the monastery, but to his trying experience in the quest for a gracious God after he had entered it.[29]

The evidence bearing on his resolution to become a monk thus appears to afford no ground for the assumption that it was the climax of a protracted period of religious anxiety, dating in fact from his childhood. So far as we can judge, this resolution was unpremeditated and involuntary. Was it, then, solely the result of physical fright? There can be no doubt of his terror-stricken condition when he made it. The lightning prostrated him to the ground. The fear of death gripped him. He was brought face to face with eternity without the sacramental preparation and consolation which the Church assured to those about to depart into the unseen world. Luther later suffered from fits of terror, which perhaps are traceable

[25] " Tischreden," i. 46.   [26] *Ibid.*, i. 95.   [27] " Werke," xxxvii. 661.
[28] *Ibid.*, xxxvi. 274.   [29] See Scheel, i. 243-448, 319-320.

to the impression produced on mind and imagination by this terrible ordeal. These fits later bore a spiritual rather than a physical character, and he was later to show the highest courage when occasion called for it. On this occasion there was undoubtedly physical fear of a very acute kind and the vow appears as a desperate device to save his life. But it had a religious as well as a physical significance. For him as for the prophets of old the thunderstorm was the voice of God, calling him to do His will. It was a call from heaven, as he told his father, who doubted whether his rash act was not the fruit of a mere illusion.[30] He made the vow, " not for the sake of the belly, but for the sake of his salvation." [31] It came to mean for him the offering of himself in a great act of obedience to God.[32] Hence the determination with which he kept it against the will of his father and the remonstrances of his friends. To his father he did not announce his resolution till the door of the monastery had closed behind him, and he maintained it against his anger and his reproaches.[33] True, he repented it, but even his own regret did not succeed in making him swerve from what he believed to be the divine will.[34]

Moreover, having vowed, he felt that he could not con- scientiously evade the obligation. Whether he was free to change his mind and resile from such a personal under- taking is a debatable point. Grisar is of opinion that, if he found, after conscientious self-examination, that he had no real vocation for the monastic life, it was not binding from the ecclesiastical point of view and that, before formally taking the monastic vow at the completion of his preliminary period of training in the monastery, he was free to return

[30] Et ego de cœlo terroribus me vocatum assererem. " Werke," viii. 573. It is not necessary to assume with Scheel (i. 249-250) that these words imply a heavenly vision. They imply no more than that Luther interpreted the lightning flash as a call to him from God to devote himself to His service as a monk.

[31] Ego enim non ventris, sed salutis meæ causa vovebam. " Tischreden," iv. 303.

[32] Persuasum habebam me eo genere vitæ et laboribus illis tetricis magnun obsequium Deo præstare. " Werke," xliv. 782.

[33] Ibid., viii. 573.

[34] Nunquam cogitavi egredi monasterium. "Tischreden," iv. 440.

to the world.[35] A self-imposed vow is not necessarily obligatory before such formal profession. Apparently Luther might have obtained dispensation from entering the monastery at all. A. V. Müller, on the other hand, contends, in opposition to Scheel, that his vow, even in the extraordinary circumstances in which he made it, was obligatory, and that the terms in which he refers to it, in the dedication to his father, show that he so regarded it.[36] Whilst the passage certainly shows that he felt bound to implement it, it does not necessarily decide the question whether it was absolutely binding on him from the ecclesiastical point of view. The difference of opinion between these two experts, both of whom can claim experience of the monastic life, makes it difficult to arrive at a definite conclusion.[37] The important point is, however, that Luther evidently held himself bound in conscience to carry it out.

At first and for some time his father was implacable.[38] He was maddened by the impulsive act which had suddenly dashed his plans for his son's advancement. He feared, moreover, that he was the victim of an illusion and he had misgivings about his fitness for such a life.[39] Apart from the wreck of all his hopes, what if his son should discover, when too late to undo it, the rashness of his impulsive act? No wonder that he was furious. "When I became a monk my father almost went mad. He was bitterly chagrined and would on no account give his consent."[40] His letter to him on the subject only called forth an angry refusal, and he would have persisted in this refusal but for an outbreak of the plague which carried off two of his younger sons. The news reached Mansfeld that Luther himself had succumbed. The report happily proved to be unfounded, and it was only in response to the entreaties of his friends who took the opportunity of this sore bereave-

[35] " Luther," i. 8-9.
[36] " Werdegang," 1 f.
[37] Scheel, in the third edition of his work, has subjected Müller's objections to forcible criticism, i. 325.
[38] Indignatio tua in me aliquamdiu implacabilis. " Werke," viii. 573.
[39] Metuabas tu paterno affectu imbecillitati meæ. *Ibid.*
[40] " Documente," 19.

ment to plead with him to make this sacrifice to the honour of God, that he at last reluctantly consented. " So be it and God grant that it may turn out well." " But," adds Luther, " he gave his consent not willingly, with a free and happy heart. His approbation was lacking." [41]

II. His Novitiate

The Erfurt monastery belonged to the Reformed or Observantine section of the Augustinian Order. Founded in Italy about the middle of the thirteenth century, it had developed into a powerful organisation in Germany, where at the beginning of the sixteenth it numbered over a hundred establishments. As in the case of the other Orders, its prosperity led to laxity and worldliness, and in the second half of the fifteenth century Andreas Proles started a reform movement in Saxony in opposition to the Vicar-General of the Saxon province, which resulted in the formation of a separate Union or Congregation of about thirty monasteries within and beyond the province. This Union, of which Proles became the Vicar-General and which stood for a stricter observance of the Rule, was known as the Observantines, in contrast to the Conventuals, or laxer section. Its Vicar-General at the time of Luther's entrance was John von Staupitz, who had succeeded Proles in 1503 and in the following year revised its constitution.[42] It was to this constitution, which differed from the old one in the greater stringency of its discipline,[43] that Luther,

[41] " Documente," 19-20 ; cf. " Werke," viii. 573. The withholding of his consent evidently lasted a considerable time, frustra suadentibus amicis ut, si quid offerre deo velles, clarissimium et optimum tuum offerres.

[42] Kolde, " Die Deutsche Augustiner-Congregation und Johann von Staupitz " (1879), and " Martin Luther," i. 46 f. ; Benrath, " Luther im Kloster," 32 (1905) ; Oergel, " Vom Jungen Luther," 42 f. ; Müller, " Luther's Werdegang," 21 f.

[43] The old constitution whilst, for instance, enlarging the periods of fasting throughout the year, had amplified the power of dispensation. The revised constitution, on the other hand, whilst reducing these periods of fasting, limited the power of dispensation so as to secure the stricter observance of them. Müller, " Werdegang," 25-26.

first as a novice and then as a professed monk, became subject. The reputation of the Erfurt monastery, which combined with a strict observance of the monastic life a flourishing theological school, probably decided his choice of the Augustinian, in preference to any of the other monasteries in the city.

The constitution prescribed the careful examination of the motives or " spirit " of the applicant before his formal reception, and this preliminary seems to have necessitated an interval of observation. It has been supposed that this interval was protracted by Luther's desire to secure the consent of his father to his formal reception.[44] Certain it is that, after his entry into the monastery, he earnestly strove to gain the paternal approval and that some time elapsed before he succeeded. Whether he actually delayed his reception on this ground does not appear from his own account of the relations with his father after his entry, and A. V. Müller rejects the supposition as baseless. He thinks that only a short time elapsed before the reception and insists, against Scheel, that at most a couple of weeks, instead of a couple of months, would suffice for the preliminaries. This short delay was due, he maintains, not to Luther's desire to secure the approval of his father, but to the fact that the prior was under obligation to obtain the consent of the Vicar-General of the Order to his reception.[45] He forgets, however, that this provision of the constitution applied only to those under the age of eighteen, whereas Luther was twenty-two when he entered the monastery, and it is likely enough that he was anxious to receive his father's approbation before his formal admission as a novice.[45]

The elaborate ceremonial prescribed by the constitution included an explanation by the prior, Winand von Diedenhofen, of the self-denying obligations of the monastic life as " the warfare of Christ " (*militia Christi*), the investiture of the novice with the habit of the Order, and the

[44] Scheel, i. 259 ; Oergel, 72-73.

[45] Müller, " Werdegang," 14-17. Müller writes in a very insistent strain, and Scheel has certainly caught him napping here. " Luther," i. 329.

tonsure. He thereby became a member of the clerical section of the community, as distinct from the lay brethren or uneducated section, who were unfitted for the higher service of God and performed the more menial duties of the establishment. This distinction did not, however, necessarily exempt Luther from taking his part in these duties. He had to learn the fundamental lesson of humility, and there is no reason to doubt the later accounts of the lowly and even demeaning services which he was required to render, though it is not necessary to ascribe, with these later biographers, unworthy motives to his fellow-monks in so doing.[46] Even a distinguished Master of Arts like Luther could not expect or receive exemption from this training in humility during his novitiate, and he does not seem to have felt any grievance on this ground.[47] He would thus submissively take his turn in begging for alms in the streets of Erfurt, scrubbing his own cell and those of others, and performing even more menial service as an essential of the discipline of the soldier of Christ.[48]

This hard discipline was, however, subordinate to the preparatory training in the minutiæ of conduct and the principles of the monastic life under the preceptor or master of the novices. He was as carefully drilled as any raw army recruit in the intricate formal observances which regulated all external acts. He was, for instance, taught how to sit and how to get up at table, how to eat and drink, to observe the appropriate postures, to walk with downcast eyes, to keep silence and understand the signs of the preceptor. He was initiated into the complicated ritual of the religious services which began at dawn, followed each other at stated intervals till vespers, and interrupted the slumbers of the monks at midnight.[49] He was instructed in the duty of unquestioning obedience to his

[46] Scheel subjects the traditional accounts to a detailed criticism and succeeds in disproving such later charges; ii. 9. See also Oergel, 80 f.

[47] Sic cum ego ingrederer monasterium dicebunt ad me, sicut mihi factum est, ita fiat tibi quoque. " Werke," xlii. 641.

[48] See Müller, " Werdegang," 32-33, who writes from personal experience of the menial duties of the novice.

[49] See the detailed account in Müller, " Werdegang," 27-30.

superiors and the observance of the Rule of the Order, of daily confession, of fasting and watching, of self-mortification and solitary self-scrutiny, of reading the Scripture and the breviary. Under this complicated regulation [50] of the outward and inner life of the novice there was no room for individuality, for free self-development. It was, indeed, based on the principle of absolute self-surrender in all things. Neglect or mistake in the exact performance of its minute prescriptions was a transgression which had to be made good, and which it required the utmost vigilance to avoid. It was thus fitted to keep the sensitive conscience in a state of incessant anxiety till routine had made the novice familiar with its multifarious details, and even then there was liability enough to incur guilt and induce self-torment.

Luther seems to have been an apt and zealous pupil, and there is no ground for the charges of wilful insubordination and neglect of duty which his later opponents [51] attribute to him even during his novitiate. Such charges are evidently due to the assumption that he must have been a bad monk because he later became a heretic, and that the devil must have been at work within him even from the outset. The discipline to which he was subjected precluded anything in the novice but the most complete submission, and the fact that at the end of his year of probation he was found worthy to take the vows and was admitted to the full status of a brother is sufficient to show the baselessness of the malicious gossip of his later enemies. He is said, for instance, to have been careless in the repetition of his breviary. Later, indeed, when he was overwhelmed with work and was consequently at times in arrear with the prescribed prayers, he adopted the method of repeating them *en bloc* at the end of the week. But this, he tells us, was in contrast to his earlier practice

[50] See the details in Oergel, " Vom Jungen Luther," 77 f.

[51] Cochlaeus, Oldecop, Emser, and Dungersheim. Grisar does not accept these charges as applying to the period of his novitiate, though he thinks that they hold good of his conduct as a professed monk. " It appears that during his novitiate he was attentive to the rules." " Luther," i. 9 ; *cf.* 24.

when he scrupulously observed the canonical regulations.[52]
On the other hand, later Protestant tradition knows of
incidents reflecting on his harsh treatment by members
of the Order which seem equally unfounded. It tells how
he found a Bible in the monastery library, how the monks
disliked his Bible reading and took the book from him,
giving him instead their " sophistic books " to read, how he
would steal in a spare moment to the library to continue
his study of it, how they envied the distinguished magister
and assigned him the most menial tasks, how they dis-
couraged his studies by sending him out to beg, telling him
that study was a waste of time and that it was more profit-
able to go from door to door with a sack on his back and
gather gear for the monastery.[53] This tradition begins
with Mathesius, one of Luther's disciples and table com-
panions, and with Ratzeberger, his physician, and it grows
in bulk with later writers. The embargo laid on the reading
of the Bible is at variance with the express regulation of the
constitution that the novice shall eagerly read the holy
Scripture, reverently hear and zealously learn it.[54] Luther
himself tells that on his entrance into the monastery the
monks gave him a Bible bound in red leather and that he
acquired such a familiarity with it that he knew the contents
of every page and where to find any particular text.[55] In
another passage, professing to record one of his conversa-
tions,[56] the story of his being deprived of it seems not to
reflect correctly what he had said, and is not in keeping with
the above statement. He speaks, indeed, in several other
passages [57] of the ignorance prevailing in the monasteries of
his time, the mechanical reading of the Bible without interest
or intelligence, the contempt for study and learning, on the
assumption that a studious brother would be inclined to play

[52] "Tischreden," ii. 220; cf. ii. 11. Cum essem monachus nihil
volebam obmittere de precibus.
[53] Mathesius, " Historien," " Documente," 2-3.
[54] Chap. 17; Benrath, " Luther im Kloster," 35; Oergel, "Vom
Jungen Luther," 64-65.
[55] "Tischreden," i. 44.
[56] " Archiv für Reformations Geschichte," 5te Yahrgang, 345;
Scheel, ii. 9-10.
[57] "Tischreden," iii. 429, 579-580.

the master over his fellow-monks, and that the way to cure
him of this zeal was to hang the sack on his neck.[58] This
rather exaggerated generalisation is not, however, connected
with his personal experience as a novice in the Erfurt
monastery. Nor is there anything in his own authentic
utterances to support the later tradition that it was for this
reason that the monks sent him a-begging and that it
was only through the intervention of the university in
behalf of its distinguished member that he was freed from
this obligation.[59] His own version of his early life in the
monastery in his conversation with his father, on the occasion
of his first Mass, lends no support to these later stories. He
expresses his complete satisfaction with the lot to which God
had called him and speaks of it as " a peaceful and God-like
life." [60] Instead of repining under the monastic yoke, it
could hardly be made heavy enough for the zealous novice,
who imposed on himself more than the Rule prescribed in
the matter of ascetic exercises.[61] Certain it is that he later
distinguished himself as District Vicar of his Order by his
energetic maintenance of discipline.[62] He speaks in terms
of deep appreciation of his preceptor, who treated him with
consideration and insight and gave him one of Athanasius'
works to read during his novitiate, and whom he described
as " a truly excellent man (*vir sane optimus*) and assuredly
a good Christian under the cursed cowl." [63]

At the conclusion of his probationary instruction he
was deemed worthy, after a strict investigation by the
prior into his character and conduct as a novice, to enter
into the full membership of the Order. At the commencement of the ritual prescribed by the constitution for this
ceremony, he was asked whether he was prepared to renounce
the world and dedicate himself to God and the monastic
life. The young novice answered in the affirmative and
in the course of the elaborate ritual that followed made

[58] Ergo sackum per nackum.
[59] Mathesius, " Documente," 3. Ratzeberger adds that it was
Staupitz who used his influence with the prior. The tradition is thus
not uniform.
[60] " Documente," 20.   [62] Enders, " Briefwechsel," i. 99.
[61] *Ibid.*, 34 ; *cf.* 36.   [63] " Documente," 38.

solemn profession and took upon himself the vows of obedience, poverty, and chastity. At its conclusion he received the kiss of peace from the prior and the brethren and their gratulations on his " monk's baptism." For the profession of the monastic vows was esteemed a second baptism which carried with it remission of the guilt and punishment of sin. Luther has been severely handled by Denifle for asserting [64] that his fellow-monks held and expressed such a view, though it was not the official teaching of the Church.[65] He characterises his statement as a lying distortion. It nevertheless appears to have widely prevailed in monastic circles and to have been held by Paltz, the most notable theologian of the Erfurt monastery, and there is no ground for thus crassly questioning Luther's veracity.[66]

III. Ordination as Priest

After his " profession " (probably September 1506),[67] Luther, as a distinguished magister, was directed by the Vicar-General to enter on a course of theological study with a view to his ordination as priest, and ultimately the vocation of a theological teacher in the interest of his Order.[68] In preparation for his ordination he studied Biel's book on the " Canon of the Mass," which at this

[64] " Werke," viii. 596 ; cf. " Documente," 36.
[65] " Luther und Lutherthum," i. 220 f.
[66] See Benrath, " Luther im Kloster," 36 f. ; Scheel, ii. 26-28.
[67] See Scheel, ii. 23. Müller, on what seem insufficient grounds, thinks that he was admitted to make his profession as early as December 1505. " Werdegang," 36-39.
[68] Müller, 42 f. Scheel, on the other hand, is of opinion that the prior was empowered to decide his future course without any reference to the Vicar-General. The constitution, however, as Müller shows, required the consent of the Vicar-General and conferred on him and the Chapter of the Order the final decision in the question of theological study in the case of the members of the Order. Scheel is further of opinion that he did not commence the systematic study of theology till after his ordination as priest. Müller controverts this opinion and thinks that he commenced this study immediately after his profession. " Werdegang," 53-54. This is also the view of Hausrath, " Luther," i. 26, and Kolde, i. 55.

time was esteemed the best on the subject.[69] " The authority of the Bible," he says, " was as nothing compared to that of Biel." This famous schoolman had been the teacher at Tübingen of both Staupitz, the Vicar-General of the Order, and Nathin, Luther's theological preceptor, and this personal connection is sufficient to explain the vogue of this treatise in the Erfurt monastery. Luther studied it with heart-searching zeal. It initiated him into the doctrine underlying the supreme mystery of the Mass, which he then held to be the fundamental of all religion. He adored the Mass with all his heart, he tells us, and if anyone would have deprived him of this sublime treasure, he would have opposed him with all his might.[70] Biel's book expounded to him the high vocation of the priest, who " makes the body of Christ " and brings to God's remembrance Christ's offering on the Cross and thereby propitiates His justice in favour of the sinner. It emphasised the tremendous responsibility of the priestly function and the need for the scrupulous observance of all the details of the rite, which is essential to its efficacy, and the disregard of which, through mistake or oversight in its performance, is a more or less grave offence. It taught him further the priestly conception of the Church as the medium of the divine grace and exalted its authority and that of the Pope, its supreme head, as the embodiment of the divine law and purpose and the superior of every other authority on earth. The reading of this and other books appeared to him, looking back long afterwards, as " a martyrdom." [71] At the same time it is evident from his own words that at this period he valued them very highly and read them with edification, if the thought of the Mass and what it signified filled him with awe and misgiving under the sense of his own unworthiness. " When I read therein my heart bled." [72] They were to him, notwithstanding, the best of books, and as the result of his study of them he learned to adore the rite which he was erelong to perform as priest. He learned,

---

[69] " Tischreden," iii. 564. Qui liber meo judicio tum optimus fuerat.
[70] Ibid., iii. 566-567. Nam ego toto pectore illam adorabam.
[71] Ibid., iii. 564.
[72] Wenn ich darin las da blutte mein hertz. Ibid., iii. 564.

too, the profound reverence for the authority of the Church and the devotion to the Pope which the Augustinian Order in particular exemplified, and of which he himself in his earlier career as monk was the fervid champion. In this respect Biel differed from the anti-papal Occam, to whose school he belonged, and Luther did not derive his later anti-papal teaching from him. His exposition of the Mass would, in fact, tend to nurture in him the fervent "papalism" which found expression in some of his early works. In one of his early sermons, for instance, he insists on the divine institution of the Papacy as an essential of the Church and on its supreme power, against which no other power of earth or hell can prevail.[73] Long afterwards in the preface to his collected works (1545) he reminds his readers that at this early period he was so fanatic a papalist that he would have burned anyone who would have detracted by a single syllable from his obedience to the Pope.[74]

In the course of this instruction he was ordained stage by stage subdeacon, deacon, and priest. Some weeks after his ordination as priest he celebrated his first Mass (2nd May 1507).[75] It was a joyous as well as a solemn occasion for the young celebrant and his fellow-monks. It brought the monastery special gifts from relatives and friends and was concluded with a festive meal in the refectory.[76] In accordance with custom Luther invited his parents from Mansfeld and his friends from Eisenach.[77] His father seems still to have grudged the sacrifice of his ambition. But he accepted the invitation and appeared with befitting *éclat*. He rode into the courtyard of the monastery at the head of twenty horsemen and presented the monks with twenty gulden to pay for the entertainment.[78] For Luther the meeting must have been a trying one, though he seems to have been gratified by this exhibition of his father's

[73] "Werke," i. 69. [74] "Documente," 11-12.

[75] Hausrath ("Luther," i. 26-28) and others incorrectly state that he performed his first Mass on the occasion of his ordination, which had in fact taken place some weeks earlier. Enders, "Briefwechsel," i. 3 ; Oergel, 90 ; Scheel, ii. 32-34.

[76] "Tischreden," iv. 180.

[77] Enders, i. 1-3 ; xvii. 84. [78] "Tischreden," ii. 133.

generosity. Still more trying was the rite which he was to perform for the first time. In his letter of invitation to his Eisenach friend, Braun, he expresses his sense of the high vocation to which God had called him, " an unworthy sinner," and his gratitude for the greatness of the divine goodness in thus exalting him to this sublime ministry, which he feels bound to accept.[79] There is nothing in the letter to indicate trepidation at the prospect of undertaking the priestly office. Awe is mingled with gratitude that God has found him worthy to be entrusted with it. But as the day of his first celebration drew near the tremendous responsibility, which the belief in transubstantiation associated with it, seems to have filled him with a nervous dread which was aggravated by the reflection that the slightest mistake in the ritual was regarded as a transgression, and might make the performance of no effect. He remarks in one passage of the " Table Talk " that he had known priests who were habitually overcome with such terror in consecrating the wine and the bread that they stammered through the words of consecration,[80] and the reminiscence seems to have included his own experience. He refers to the subject in several passages of his " Table Talk " and his Commentary on Genesis,[81] and though they contain some discrepancies and evident inaccuracies, they agree in stating that he was struck with terror when standing at the altar, in the presence of God, as the minister of what was to the mediæval Church the supreme mystery. During the ritual he was, we are told, on the point of rushing from the altar and would actually have fled had not the prior (in one passage his preceptor) intervened with the admonition to go on. The reports do not, however, agree as to the part of the ritual at which this feeling of terror overcame him. One says that it was when he began the opening prayer of the Canon of the Mass with the words

[79] Enders, i. 1-2.
[80] " Tischreden," iv. 607.
[81] *Ibid.*, ii. 133 ; iii. 410-411 ; iv. 180 ; v. 86 ; " Werke," xliii. 382 ; Preger, " Tischreden Luther's," 89 ; " Archiv für Reformations Geschichte," v. 354 (1908) ; Ericeus, " Sylvula Sententiarum," " Documente," 42.

" Thee O most element Father." [82]   Another says that
the fit of terror occurred at the prayer, " We offer to Thee,
the Eternal, Living, and True God," which it quotes
wrongly and which in the Missal preceded the other.   The
later reporters thus seem to have confused what Luther
said, or he must have forgotten the order of the prayers,
which is not likely in view of his long familiarity with the
ritual of the Mass.   In his Commentary on Genesis
he himself, indeed, seems to confuse the order.   But the
part of the Commentary in which the passage occurs was
edited and printed after his death and had not the advantage
of his personal revision.   It is, therefore, more probable that
the editor has not given the passage correctly.   In this and
other respects the reports thus bear trace of confusion and
inaccuracy and cannot be accepted as exact representations
of what took place.   Moreover, the intervention of the prior
or the preceptor (another trace of confusion on the part of
the reporters) [83] seems most unlikely, if not impossible, in
view of the fact that Luther, attended by a deacon and a
subdeacon, must have faced the altar with his back to those
present and was not, therefore, in a position to address
either.   The additional assertion that he already had a
foreboding of the blasphemy of the Mass [84] is out of the
question at this stage of his religious development.   The
dramatic element thus imparted to the incident looks like
a later colouring by details which betray a confused
knowledge of the ritual of the Mass and tend to exaggerate
the experience of the moment.   In the Commentary on
Genesis Luther says that what he felt was dread at the
thought of the unspeakable divine majesty.[85]   He says
nothing in this passage of the impulse to rush away from the
altar or the intervention of the prior.   At the same time the
words used in describing his emotions are very vivid,[86] and
even if they have been intensified by the editors in accordance

[82] " Tischreden," iii. 410.
[83] One version of the tradition says it was the prior, another the
preceptor that intervened.
[84] Preger, " Tischreden," 89.
[85] " Werke," xliii. 382.
[86] Totus stupebam et cohorrescebam ad illas voces.

with the prevailing tradition of the incident, it appears that at the opening prayer of the Canon of the Mass his mental condition was one of great trepidation. Scheel thinks that what he experienced was no more than a deep sense of the significance of the rite.[87] At all events the experience was a trying one.

There is less dubiety about the other incident connected with his first Mass, though here also the later reports are to some extent misleading. The incident occurred during the repast in the refectory after Mass.[88] Luther was anxious to obtain at last an explicit avowal of his father's approval of his self-dedication to the monastic life. The father had reconciled himself to the inevitable and had accepted his son's invitation. But he was still far from being convinced of the wisdom or the propriety of his conduct. It was the first time they had met since the fateful 17th July 1505, and at table Luther took advantage of the occasion to vindicate himself. He adduced the divine call which had come to him on the road near Stotternheim. His father, he found, was still sceptical. "Would that it may not have been a mere illusion and deception," was the blunt reply.[89] Such a possibility had evidently never entered Luther's mind. For the moment he was startled by this matter-of-fact outburst. But it did not succeed in shaking his confidence in what he believed to be the divine will,[90] and he met it by adducing his subsequent experience of the monastic life as proof to the contrary. Still sceptical, his father reminded him of the obligation of the divine command of obedience to parents, which rested on the indubitable authority of Scripture, and this even in the presence of the doctors, masters, and other ecclesiastics at table. " Have you not read in Scripture that one shall honour one's father

[87] II. 51-52. He has subjected the received accounts to trenchant criticism.

[88] "Tischreden," ii. 294, 439 ; iii. 410.

[89] *Ibid.*, ii. 439. Hans Luther is represented as making this reply by letter in answer to Luther's telling him of his entry into the monastery. This is inaccurate.

[90] Id verbi, quasi deus per os tuum sonaret, penetravit et insedit in intimis meis, sed obfirmabam ego cor, quantum potui, adversus te et verbum tuum. "Werke," viii. 574.

and mother ? " This appeal to Scripture against his appeal
to ecclesiastical institution made a still deeper impression [91]
and reduced Luther to silence. He never forgot it and in
later life it seemed to him that through it " God had spoken
to him from afar," though as yet he felt " secure in his own
righteousness," and maintained his confidence in the
superiority of the monastic life as the most acceptable to
God and the assured way of salvation. [92]

[91] In tota vita mea ex homine vix audierem verbum quod potentius in
me sonuerit et heserit. " Werke," viii. 574.

[92] The earliest account is that given in the Dedication to his father of
his work on " Monastic Vows," November 1521 ; cf. his letter to Melanchthon, September 1521 (Enders, iii. 225). Next in importance are the
passages in the " Tischreden " already referred to and that in a sermon of
1544, " Documente," 19-20. The account in the Commentary on
Genesis, " Werke," xliv. 711-712, is less accurate.

CHAPTER III

LUTHER AND THE SCHOLASTIC THEOLOGY
(1507-1512)

I. STUDENT OF THEOLOGY

THE Augustinian Order distinguished itself by its interest in education of the scholastic type and encouraged study as an adjunct of the monastic life.[1] The Erfurt monastery was pre-eminent within the Order as an educational as well as a religious establishment. It provided courses in both arts and theology for its inmates and conferred appropriate degrees in both branches of study. After a preliminary course in grammar and logic (*studia particularia*) extending over several years,[2] the student was promoted to the degree of *Cursor*. He then entered on the study of theology (*studia generalia*) and after two or three years attained the degree of *Lector*, which entitled him to lecture on the Bible and the Sentences of Lombardus, the official theological text-book of the mediæval universities and the monastic schools. The Erfurt monastery thus possessed the status of a *Studium generale* in theology and its reputation attracted a considerable number of students from the other Augustinian monasteries in which this higher instruction was not attainable.[3] These monastic degrees were not,

[1] Chap. 40 of the " Constitution." Attente provideant quomodo studia in quibus fundamentum ordinis consistit per universum ordinem sollicite continuentur. Müller, " Werdegang," 44; Oergel, " Vom Jungen Luther," 97-98 ; Scheel, ii. 59 f.

[2] Müller thinks that the course for the Cursor degree included philosophy and theology as well as grammar and logic, and lasted not less than five years (52). Oergel (99) and Scheel (ii. 60) hold that the course lasted four years and was concerned exclusively with grammar and logic.

[3] Oergel, 54 f.

indeed, of equal value or validity with those of the university, and monastic students of theology who desired to obtain the latter were obliged in addition to attend the courses of the university Faculty, which were both longer and more advanced. For the university degree of *Baccalaureus Biblicus*, for instance, the candidate must not only be a Master of Arts, but have attended the courses of the Theological Faculty for five years. The professors of theology in the monastery school at Erfurt were, however, as a rule, also members of the university Faculty, and in the case of monastic students the Faculty relaxed the regulations, and not only waived the preliminary qualification of the Master's degree, but materially reduced the ordinary period of study for the degree of Bachelor and the higher degrees of Master of the Sentences, Licentiate, and Doctor.[4]

As a magister Luther would be exempted from the Arts course in the monastery school and probably began the study of theology after his " profession " in 1506. He appears to have attended the theological courses in the university as well as those in the monastery, his teachers being members of the Faculty as well as lecturers in the monastery. He thus, as a student in the Faculty of Theology, renewed his connection with the university which he had left so abruptly, though, as a monk, he was entitled to acquire the various theological degrees within a shorter period than was permissible in the case of non-monastic students.[5]

The professors of the monastic seminary when he became a monk were Johann Paltz and Johann Nathin. Paltz, who was a theologian of widespread repute, left Erfurt in 1507 to become prior of a monastery near Coblentz, as the result of a dispute with his fellow-monks.[6] Luther thus enjoyed for only a short time the advantage of his guidance in his early study of the scholastic theology, and it was mainly to Nathin that he owed this service. Like his pupil,

[4] Scheel, ii. 59-64.

[5] The monastic students were, however, required to make up for the shorter period of study by more intensive work.

[6] Enders, " Briefwechsel," i. 17 ; Oergel, 56-57, 103-104.

he had graduated as Master of Arts in the University of Erfurt in 1472 and had then entered the Augustinian monastery. He continued the study of theology, which he had begun in its theological school, under Biel at Tübingen, where he lectured on the Sentences. In 1493 he took his Doctor's degree at Erfurt and became Professor of Theology ᵢn the monastery seminary in the same year.[7] The humanist Mutianus describes him as a barbarous and morose pedant, and his scholastic Latin would certainly give offence to humanist taste, whilst his scholastic method and austere life would not otherwise commend him to the easy-going, cultured Canon of Gotha. Narrow and opinionated, he seems to have been more learned than inspiring as a teacher, and Luther's inquiring mind would not find much edification in his prelections. Some years later, as we learn from Luther's letter to the prior and brethren of the Erfurt monastery, he was estranged from his old pupil over what he considered as his unconstitutional and inconsiderate conduct in graduating as Doctor at Wittenberg instead of at Erfurt. Luther spiritedly defended himself against an aspersion which he shows to have been unfounded.[8] But the estrangement was only temporary, though his old teacher later became his uncompromising opponent as a Reformer, and there is no reason to assume that the relation between professor and pupil in the monastery was other than that of mutual esteem. Nathin seems to have regarded his pupil, in view of what he deemed his miraculous conversion to the monastic life, as " a second Paul,"[9] and the fact that Luther was in 1510 entrusted, along with him, with a petition in behalf of the monastery to the Archbishop of Magdeburg,[10] tends to disprove the assumption of most of his later biographers of their unharmonious relations. This assumption rests on the authority of Mathesius and others who, as we have noted,

[7] Kolde, " Augustiner Kongregation," 137 ; Oergel, 104 ; Scheel, ii. 65-66.

[8] Enders, i. 17-19.

[9] See the quotation from Dungersheim's work against Luther (1530) in Boehmer, " Luther's Romfahrt," 57 (1914).

[10] Ibid., 57.

tell of the opposition of his fellow-monks to the study of the Bible, which is supposed to have been due mainly to his teacher Nathin, who, they say, directed him to restrict his attention solely to the study of the scholastic theology, and to have been frustrated by the intervention of Staupitz. It is not, as we have also seen, applicable to the year of his novitiate, and it seems to be equally inapplicable to those which he devoted to the systematic study of theology. True, a passage in the " Table Talk " informs us that his " Preceptor " told him that the Bible was the source of all rebellion, and advised him to read the ancient doctors who had imbibed the truth contained in it.[11] But it names Usingen, not Nathin, as the preceptor in question, and Usingen, who only entered the monastery at the earliest in 1512,[12] was never his theological teacher. Moreover, the passage does not prohibit the reading of the Bible and has nothing to do with any official deliverance to this effect on the part of Luther's superiors. On the contrary, the study of the Bible, along with the Sentences of Peter Lombard, was an essential part of the course for the lowest theological degree, that of *Baccalaureus Biblicus*, whose office it was to expound the Scriptures, and Melanchthon explicitly tells us that Luther diligently prosecuted the study of both. Even Mathesius says that he was free to read the Bible in the monastery library when his time was not taken up with the scholastic books.[13] Luther himself knows nothing of any such prohibition. He continued to make use of the copy in red leather which he had received at his entrance into the monastery and only relinquished when he was finally transferred from Erfurt to Wittenberg. As a student of theology, he was furnished, in addition, with a " Glossa Ordinaria " to guide him in his interpretation in accordance with the teaching of the Church.[14] He later made use of the Commentary of Nicolas of Lyra which he at first disliked, but ultimately learned to value for the light it threw on the historic meaning of the text.[15]

[11] " Tischreden," ii. 5-6.
[12] Oergel, 104-105. Luther evidently refers in this passage to the time when Usingen was his preceptor in the Faculty of Arts at Erfurt.
[13] " Documente," 3.   [14] " Tischreden," i. 44.   [15] *Ibid.*, i. 44.

Besides the Bible and the Sentences, he read, according to Melanchthon,[16] the works of Gabriel Biel and Pierre D'Ailly, both of them disciples of Occam, and those of Occam himself whom he preferred to Aquinas and Scotus. "Biel and D'Ailly he knew almost by heart. Long and much he read the writings of Occam." Melanchthon further says that he began and continued these studies at Erfurt, *i.e.*, in the years between 1506 and 1512 which, with the exception of his sojourn at Wittenberg from the autumn of 1508 to that of 1509 and his visit to Rome in the winter of 1510-11, he spent in the Erfurt monastery. What we learn from Luther himself tends generally to confirm these statements. There is no reason to suppose with Oergel [17] that at this period he had a dislike for the scholastic theology, and only took up the study of it with reluctance. His own testimony in an early letter to his friend Braun [18] shows, on the contrary, that he much preferred it to the study of philosophy. He speaks of himself, in reference to his early studies, as an Occamist and a Gabrielist.[19] His early lecture notes on the Sentences (1510-11) show a knowledge of Scotus as well as Occam, Biel, D'Ailly, and others.[20] Scotus he esteemed the best commentator on the third book of the Sentences. "We monks read him instead of Augustine." [21] Though he speaks in the first person plural, he himself must have been an exception, for his notes on some of Augustine's works show that he was already, as early as 1509, keenly interested in the great African Father.[22] Next to Augustine he appreciated

[16] "Vita," 159.

[17] "Vom Jungen Luther," 105-106. Oergel qualifies this statement on p. 109, where he says that he zealously studied the scholastic theology after he had received, under the supposed influence of Staupitz, the right to study also the Bible !

[18] Enders, "Briefwechsel," i. 6 (1509).

[19] *Ibid.*, i. 55 ; "Werke," vi. 195.

[20] "Werke," ix. 29 f.

[21] Scotus optime scripsit 3 librum Sententiarum. "Documente," 30; *cf.* "Tischreden," i. 117; "Werke," ii. 403; and "Documente," 23-24.

[22] "Werke," ix. 3 f. In a letter of 1516 he says that at the time of his "profession" (1506), he had no interest in him.

Gerson most highly,[23] and we learn from Melanchthon that he became familiar with the writings of Bernard.[24] With Aquinas he was also to some extent familiar. Though he pronounces Scotus on the Sentences to be his superior, Thomas is nevertheless most praiseworthy   He had evidently dipped into the " Summa Theologiæ," [25] and there is no ground for Denifle's contemptuous allegation that he was a complete ignoramus in the Thomist theology,[26] even if his knowledge of him was not very deep and he later underrated his powers as a theologian.   But as a Realist the great mediæval theologian was not in much favour with the Occamists, and his " Summa " was, he says, little studied in the schools, though he found it fairly acceptable.[27]   On this account he was less attracted to him and his school [28] than to " the Moderns," as the Occamists designated themselves, and for the same reason he regarded Scotus as inferior to Occam.   He disliked the Thomist maxim, " Thus saith   Aristotle,"   as   applied   to   the   interpretation   of Scripture, and learned from the Occamists to distrust the application of the Aristotelian logic to prove the truth of Christian doctrine.[29]   He found his work against the heathen ridiculous.[30]

II. Augustine's Doctrine of Salvation and its Influence on the Scholastic Theology

The scholastic theology which Luther studied was based on that of Augustine, which gave to western Christianity its specific character.   His doctrine of salvation and his

[23] " Documente," 20, 40 ; cf. Melanchthon, " Vita," 159.   Diligenter et Gersonem legerat.

[24] " Vita," 159.

[25] "Tischreden," i. 117-118 ; and see Scheel, ii. 74.

[26] " Luther und Lutherthum," i. 522-523.

[27] "Tischreden," i. 118.   Man lase es selten en scholis.

[28] Thomas est loquacissimus, quia metaphysica est seductus. " Documente," 30.

[29] Aristoteles autem sic dicit, et secundum Aristotelem interpretatur scripturam. " Tischreden," i. 118.

[30] Interim legebantur ridiculi libri contra gentiles.   *Ibid.*, i. 118.

conception of the Church largely conditioned those of the scholastic theology, which sought by the aid of the Aristotelian logic and philosophy to set forth a rational system of Christian truth as embodied in Scripture, tradition, and ecclesiastical belief and practice. His teaching was derived from various sources which he did not succeed in fashioning into a consistent unity. Whilst he took a great deal from Paul, he assimilated not a little from Neo-Platonism, and something even from Manichæism,[31] in which, before his conversion, he sought the truth in philosophy and religion. It bears in addition the stamp of his own religious experience which he strove to accommodate to the teaching and practice of the Church. The result is an incongruous body of religious thought, in which the contradictions and inconsistencies are not really unified.

His doctrine of salvation is based on the fact of sin and the impotence of the sinful will to realise the good, to attain to God, who is the highest good, the perfection of being. In this respect he is a Paulinist, though, as a Neo-Platonist, he at first believed in the freedom of the will to turn to the good. It was in the course of the controversy with Pelagius, who denied original sin and maintained the capacity of the will to attain the good, that he developed his characteristic doctrine of salvation. Like Paul, too, he proceeds on the scriptural theory of an original sinless man and a fall from the state of sinless felicity. Man was created good with the power freely to will the good, though, even in the state of goodness, he required the assistance of divine grace in the exercise of his freedom, and without this grace he could not remain in this state. So assisted, he possessed the power not to sin, not to die, not to forsake God, and to cleave to God, which is his true being.[32] From this state of goodness he fell through sin, which is, metaphysically considered, a defect in being, morally considered, a defect in goodness.[33] It subjected the soul as well as the body to

[31] Harnack asserts ("History of Dogma," v. 211-212, 219, English translation, 1898), and Seeberg ("Lehrbuch der Dogmen-Geschichte," i. 272 (1895)) controverts the influence of Manichæism.

[32] Posse non peccare, non mori, non deserere Deum, adhærere Deo.

[33] Harnack, "History of Dogma," v. 210.

death. It involved the deprivation of the good,[34] substituted the love of self (*amor sui*) for the love of God, self-will for the divine will, and induced the sinful tendency—pride and evil desire in the sense especially of sexual lust (*superbia* and *concupiscentia*). Augustine, it must be remembered, had been the slave of sexual desire before he became a believing Christian, and judges of human nature by his own experience. In this state of sin man lost the power to will the good and the assistance of the divine grace in the exercise of the will, and came under the domination of the devil and the necessity of sinning.[35] Formal freedom in the sense of freedom of choice might remain, but it was practically of no avail in virtue of the necessity to sin. He, and humanity along with him, became in fact "a mass of perdition." [36] For this original sin affects his posterity. In Adam all sinned and died ethically as well as physically. The generative power became subject to carnal con- cupiscence and conveyed sin and the disposition of the will to evil to his posterity.[37] Mankind passed into that state of impotence, corruption, and guilt which justly merits damnation and which, if God's grace should not intervene, involves eternal death—the lot even of those dying in infancy and without actual sin. This he assumes, by a mistranslation of Romans v. 12,[38] to be the Pauline theory of original sin and its effects, though he expresses it in more philosophical language.

This intervention of God's grace took place through the Logos, who became incarnate in Christ, and who suffered death in order to ransom man from the power of the devil, whose captive he has become through sin, and also, by his vicarious suffering and his offering of himself as a sacrifice for sin, to satisfy God's justice and free man

---

[34] Privatio boni.

[35] Misera necessitas non posse non peccandi.

[36] Massa perditionis, or peccati.

[37] Seeberg, " Lehrbuch der Dogmen-Geschichte," i. 271-272.

[38] He incorrectly translates the original Greek by *in quo*, " in whom all have sinned," instead of by " since all have sinned," and thus makes Paul teach that in Adam all his posterity actually sinned, whereas Paul is referring to actual sin in all men.

from its guilt and power. Thus through Christ, and
through Him alone, God's grace becomes operative in the
salvation of those whom He has decreed or predestined to
be saved and elected for this purpose. For not all, even
of those who are called (*vocati*), are saved, but only those
whom God has elected, whose number is fixed and can
neither be increased nor diminished. Salvation depends in
the last resort on the divine decree, and this decree is not
based on God's foreknowledge of man's action, but on His
own purpose. The realisation of this purpose is, further,
a matter entirely of grace. Salvation is the gift of God,
of grace freely given (*gratia gratis data*), for man, whose
will is enslaved by sin, is impotent without grace to turn
to God. It is grace alone that begets the will to believe,
to be saved, and only after grace [39] has thus influenced the
will, does the will actively co-operate with it in the work of
salvation.[40] In reality the distinction between prevenient
and co-operating grace is a distinction without a difference,
since without God's grace man can neither will to be saved,
nor, after willing, can he effect it without grace. Moreover,
salvation, it must be remembered, depends ultimately on
God's sovereign decree, and only those whom He has in
His sovereign purpose elected will be saved. This is in
keeping with the teaching of Paul, though Paul does not
reason out the subject philosophically, and is practically a
universalist.

God's gift of grace becomes operative in the recipient
of it by faith in Christ. Faith is, in the first place, the
unquestioning acceptance of the truth—assent that what
God has proclaimed is true. It is so far an act of
the intellect rather than of the heart. But it is also the
medium by which grace becomes effective in the renewal
of the will and the inspiration of the love of God in the
heart, and thus changes the will to evil into the will to the
good, evil desire into good desire.[41] This conception of
the renewing power of grace in the heart, of which faith

[39] Gratia præveniens, predisposing grace.
[40] Gratia co-operans.
[41] Mala concupiscentia into bona concupiscentia.

is the medium or condition, imparts its special character to Augustine's doctrine of justification. Justification by faith consists not in the remission of sin through faith in Christ. Remission is attained in baptism, by which original sin and past actual sins are washed away and which, on this account, is termed "the bath of regeneration." This is, indeed, an element of justification. But justification is not specially brought into connection with the remission of sin in baptism. Nor is it so much a definite act as a lifelong process, by which man's nature is gradually renewed or healed (*reparata, sanata*) from sin, and he becomes righteous, participates in the divine goodness or righteousness which he has lost through sin. It is thus really equivalent to sanctification, operated by God's spirit or God's grace infused into the heart [42] and begetting the love of the highest good, which is God. His formula is " justification by faith working through love." [43]

This is not exactly the Pauline doctrine. With Paul the stress is laid on faith, and justification is associated with the remission of sin through faith in Christ.[44] With Augustine the stress is laid on love operated by God's grace in the believing heart. With Paul it means the definite appropriation of Christ's righteousness by faith which makes the sinner righteous in the sight of God, brings him the assurance of salvation, and emancipates him from the power as well as the guilt of sin. With Augustine this definite experience is lacking and with it the conviction of salvation as an actual, present reality. Apart from the divine decree, which in any case renders it a matter of God's inscrutable will, and regarded from the human standpoint, it is a contingency rather than a certainty, a process rather than a definite experience. He makes use, indeed, of the Pauline phraseology. But there is not the Pauline conviction of having passed by faith from death to life, here and now and for evermore. His conception is governed by his philosophic view of God as the highest

---

[42] The gratia infusa, or infusio gratiæ.
[43] Fides quæ per dilectionem operatur.
[44] Romans iv. 24 f. ; v. 1 f.

good and man's gradual restoration to this highest good, rather than by the Pauline antithesis of law and grace, works and faith, and of the definite transformation from death to life wrought by faith, trust in God's saving mercy in Christ.[45]

God's grace which works in us justification is not, however, given in return for any merits apart from it. It is gratuitously given on account of Christ (*gratia gratis data*). Salvation is due to God's grace in Christ, imparting the will to believe and co-operating with the renewed will in nurturing love. Moreover, it is only effectively given to the elect, to those whom God has decreed and purposed to save. For the grace that begets the will to believe and co-operates with the renewed will, is, as it were, probationary. Only the grace of perseverance to the end, irresistible grace, which God gives to some and refuses to others, can finally ensure justification, salvation. Perseverance, not regeneration, is the final test and guarantee of salvation, election. Who shall finally be saved is known to God only. Why many are called and few chosen must be left to God's inscrutable judgment. Apart from the method and the means of it, salvation is really a matter of God's sovereignty, and from this point of view it is independent of all other conditions or considerations.

Such is Augustine's doctrine of salvation. It is coloured by his philosophical (Neo-Platonist) conception of God as the highest good, the perfection of being, and the attainment of goodness by man (the *adhærere Deo*).[46] It is also powerfully influenced by the teaching of Paul, though he fails in essential respects to understand this teaching.

The Pauline, evangelical-mystic element in it is unmistakable. It has, however, also a sacerdotal and ecclesiastical side. For Augustine does not solely envisage the problem of salvation from the subjective or the transcendental point

[45] On Augustine's doctrine of justification, see Loofs, " Leitfaden zum Studium der Dogmen-Geschichte," 386 f. (4th edition, 1906) ; Harnack, " History of Dogma," v. 207-208 ; Seeberg, " Lehrbuch," i. 276-278.

[46] On the Neo-Platonist influence on Augustine's teaching, see Loofs, " Leitfaden," 348 f., 393 f.

of view. He brings it into relation to the teaching and practice of the Church, as these had developed in his time. The Church, especially as the result of the Donatist controversy, assumes for him a superlative importance and significance as a factor in man's salvation. He magnifies its authority as the guardian and guarantee of divine truth, and whilst emphasising the authority of Scripture as the highest revelation, he also emphasises that of the Church as the authoritative witness of the truth of revelation. He goes, in fact, so far as to say that without its authoritative testimony he would not have believed the Gospel. He had been a sceptic before he became a believer, and he needed the help of an external authority to confirm his faith. Moreover, by its sacraments it is the medium and the sphere of divine grace, and outside of it there is no salvation. St Paul had also magnified the Church as the mystical body of Christ, the community of the saints, bound together under Christ its spiritual head by a common faith and living the life of faith in mystic union with Him. But for Augustine the Church is the historic institution as it had developed during the previous four centuries, with its moralist conception of the Gospel, its organised hierarchy, its sacerdotalism, its ascetic view of the Christian life. It is this conception of the Church that he elaborated in the controversy with the Donatists and bequeathed to the Middle Ages.

In its apprehension of the Gospel the historic Church had diverged from the Pauline view of faith and works, law and Gospel. The Gospel is not really for it, as for Paul, the emancipation of the sinner from the guilt and power of sin by the faith that, in virtue of Christ's death, definitely reconciles the sinner to God, translates him from death to life, and becomes the dynamic of the new creature in Christ Jesus. The Church might retain the Pauline phraseology, but it had long ceased to understand the Pauline Gospel. The Gospel is rather a new law which the baptized Christian is to realise under the direction of the Church and with the aid of sacramental grace, which the Church dispenses. Faith in Christ, indeed, secures the remission of sin—of original sin and past actual sins—in baptism. But the remission of sin in baptism by faith in Christ does not extend to subsequent sins, to which, in virtue of the sinful tendency (concupiscence), man is still liable and which, at least in the case of sins wilfully committed, *i.e.*, with the consent of the will, still involve guilt.[47] For such sins the sinner must make satisfaction (*placere, satisfacere Deo*) by penance.[48] Moreover, the idea of meriting eternal life by means of good works, especially by the ascetic form of the Christian life, which the monastic movement had intensified—the idea of attaining superior merit and even a supererogation of merit by ascetic self-denial[49]—was really incompatible with the Pauline view of the gospel of faith *versus* works. By making satisfaction for sin through penance, by striving to augment his stock of merit the sinner can prepare himself to stand the great trial at the judgment seat of God, when Christ will make the great reckoning of merits as against demerits, and finally decide his eternal destiny.

It was with this conventional type of piety that Augustine combined his doctrine of salvation by grace. He thus related it to the teaching and practice of the developing Church—to its sacerdotalism, its moralism, its penitential ordinances, its doctrine of merits. The Christian receives, through the Church, the grace of faith and love which works justification. He attains thereby the goodness which merits salvation, though in virtue of the operation of grace these merits are only God's gifts.[50] But the idea of merit is recognised and God finally crowns these divinely inspired merits in man's salvation. This combination of the evangelical-mystic element with the sacerdotal-ecclesiastical element is an artificial one and really conflicts with the conception of salvation in virtue of God's sovereign decree and God's sovereign grace. This conception really nullifies

[47] Fisher, " History of Christian Doctrine," 218.

[48] Loofs, " Leitfaden," 399.

[49] The evangelical counsels, in contrast to the mere " precepts of the Gospel."

[50] The saying that God finally crowns only His own gifts cannot be traced to Augustine. But it substantially expresses the idea of merit as a feature of salvation.

any scheme of salvation that does not rest on absolute dependence on trust in a merciful God and Father, as Jesus Himself revealed Him and Paul apprehended through faith. It was to this faith that Luther ultimately came in his search for a gracious God, and it is obvious that, while his study of Augustine, as far as he had absorbed the Pauline teaching, might take him some distance on the way to it, it could not take him all the way. The Pauline Epistles, experimentally understood, alone could do this.

There were, indeed, difficulties in the Pauline as in the Augustinian doctrine of salvation—difficulties springing from the Biblical representation of the origin of man and sin in man, and from St Paul's rabbinic interpretation of Scripture in support of his individualist religious experience. Its foundation does not rest on a scientific knowledge of human origins, and the demonstration of it is vitiated by an unhistoric interpretation of Old Testament passages. But these were not difficulties that exercised the mind of Luther, as they do the mind of the modern student. The difficulty with him was purely religious and ethical. It lay in the problem how to find the righteousness that would avail in the presence of a perfectly righteous God ; how to surmount such a pessimistic view of human nature ; how to reconcile the divine decree with the divine goodness and mercy ; how to find the sure way to an assured salvation ? In this quest the study of Augustine could both help and hinder.

III. THE SCHOLASTIC THEOLOGY—DOCTRINE OF SALVATION

From Augustine to the scholastic theologians of the twelfth to the fifteenth centuries, in whose teaching Luther was trained, is a long leap, and the transition takes us into a widely different world of culture and life. But his influence on western theological thought prevailed throughout the intervening centuries and impressed itself on the scholastic theology, which took its rise with Anselm, Abelard, and Lombardus in the twelfth century. This is true in respect of both the evangelical-mystic and the

sacerdotal element in his doctrine of salvation. His fundamental conceptions of original goodness and original sin,
grace and free will, predestination and election condition
those of the great schoolmen. They follow him, too, in his
tendency to accommodate this doctrine to the current
beliefs and usages of the Church, to keep it in harmony
with ecclesiastical teaching and practice as these had
developed in the intervening seven centuries.

At the same time, there is a tendency to diverge from his
teaching in certain important respects, to modify his doctrine
in accordance with later theological and ecclesiastical
development. This divergence is already discernible
throughout the intervening seven centuries—from the fifth
to the twelfth. From the outset, in fact, there is a certain
reaction against his teaching on predestination, free will,
and grace in the direction of practically identifying God's
decree with his foreknowledge of man's future action,
making grace available for all, and recognising to a certain
extent at least the freedom of the will. This divergence
was natural and even inevitable. For Augustine's teaching
on these subjects was too extreme to secure a whole-hearted
and uniform assent. He was too prone, under the influence
of controversy, to express extreme views, in magisterial
fashion, on questions like predestination and the freedom
of the will, to sacrifice moral and even religious considerations to mere logic and theory. His doctrine of absolute
predestination antagonises the reason and repels the heart.
It is a stumbling block to faith, for it is difficult to believe
in and trust a God who saves and damns according to His
good pleasure and logically consigns unbaptized infants to
perdition. His doctrine of original sin which ascribes the
guilt of Adam's posterity to the guilt of Adam himself
tends to obscure the fact that sin can only be a thing of
the individual will. His representation of human nature
as thereby wholly corrupt and the will as wholly impotent to
the good, apart from grace, is equally ill-balanced. If
man is the victim of the divine determination and wholly
subject to evil, what becomes of moral responsibility ?
Augustine, indeed, retains freedom of choice. But his
attempt to vindicate human freedom in the face of " the

Martin Luther Vol. I

Preface   iii

"A variety ..... of it, without ....
Instrument . . . . - . his advent.

necessity to sin " on the one hand, and irresistible grace on the other, is, as Seeberg points out, little more than a play of words.[51]   Such attempts to evade the rational and moral dilemmas of a too venturesome logic only show that the man was better, in this respect, than his theology.

Little wonder, therefore, that there was divergence from his theology, though there might not be conscious antagonism to it, and the schoolmen, as a rule, professed allegiance to his authority.   At the same time, there was a tendency to tone down his doctrine of absolute predestination by emphasising God's foreknowledge and to make the most of his idea of freedom of choice.   This divergence shows itself in the Semi-Pelagian, or, as Loofs [52] prefers to call it, Neo-Pelagian, trend of the scholastic theology.   By this term Loofs means Pelagian in the mediæval sense, not in the sense in which it was used in Augustine's time.   For the scholastic theologians, even those of them, like Scotus and Occam and his followers, who diverged farthest from Augustine's doctrine of salvation, professed to follow him before all other fathers as their master, and held the teaching of Pelagius to be heresy.   Nevertheless, there is in the scholastic theologians, even the least divergent from Augustine, an element that does not entirely accord with his teaching on grace and free will, and this element becomes more marked in that of the later schoolmen, in whose teaching Luther was trained.

It found expression, in particular, in the scholastic doctrine of merits.   Whilst the reaction from Augustine's doctrine of the impotence of the will is quite intelligible on moral and religious grounds, it took a wrong direction from the religious point of view.   It not only strove to vindicate human freedom on moral grounds.   It sought to construct on this basis, in accordance with the prevailing ecclesiastical tendency to work righteousness, the theory of salvation by merit.   It thereby placed man in a questionable religious relation to God.   So much reward for so much work is practically what the theory amounts to in its more developed

[51] " Dogmen-Geschichte," i. 279.
[52] " Leitfaden," 539 f.

form. The relation between God and man is the relation between master and servant, instead of the filial relation which relies on God's love and mercy for the salvation of the soul, and serves Him, not for reward or for the sake of deliverance from judgment, but in filial fellowship and obedience begotten of faith. The result of this conception was to make of religion a thing of penitential and ascetic works. Augustine, indeed, seemed to have barred the way to such a theory by his insistence on salvation solely by grace freely given. In crowning human merits God crowns His own gifts. Even so, the idea of merit is associated with salvation, and this idea was developed by the mediæval religious spirit and practice until it culminated in the fully-fledged doctrine of merits.

The scholastic theology, while based on Augustine's teaching, was worked out with the aid of the logic and philosophy of Aristotle. The schoolmen applied the Aristotelian dialectic to demonstrate Christian truth. They fitted Augustine into the crucible of the Aristotelian logic and imparted to it the syllogistic form which characterises the thought of the mediæval schools. They imparted to it also the concepts of the Aristotelian ethics and metaphysics, and it was in so doing that their thought took a more or less Neo-Pelagian direction. The theology thus dialectically developed under the influence of Aristotle is a cumbersome and somewhat artificial complex, overloaded with subtle distinctions and far-fetched notions, though evincing great intellectual acumen and resource. It presents a striking contrast to the simpler and more concrete teaching of Jesus and the Apostles. It is still more intricate and far more dialectic, more intellectual and less religious, than the transformation of this teaching in Augustine. Its theoretic presuppositions are not based on real historic and scientific knowledge, and its subtleties, its interminable logic, its labyrinthic minutiæ are often more perplexing and repelling than edifying. Theological jargon run mad is the impression which much of it makes on the modern mind. Augustine might be fanciful and theoretic enough at times. But he was at least a master of expression and wrote lucid Latin. The scholastic theologians were too ponderously pedantic and discursive to think of making themselves intelligible or readable, and their dialectic subtleties have precious little to do with real religion and as little value for the religious life. This was the theological provender on which Luther was reared and which his scholastic training in the Erfurt University had fitted him to digest and even to enjoy.[53] At the same time, it must have proved even to Luther a dreary business at times, though in his case the real interest in this intricate synthesis was not so much the intellectual as the religious one.[54] There came a time when, on religious grounds, he had to unlearn much that he had learned from these theologians whose teaching he had studied, directly or indirectly, and whom he ultimately denounced in his drastic fashion as " Sow Theologians." " I know and confess," he wrote years afterwards (1519), " that I learned nothing (from the scholastic theologians) but ignorance of sin, righteousness, baptism, and the whole Christian life. . . . Briefly, I not only learned nothing, but I learned only what I had to unlearn as contrary to the divine Scriptures." [55]

His early mentors in the scholastic theology were Petrus Lombardus, Occam and his school, and to a certain extent Duns Scotus. Besides these, he turned to the writings of Bernard, Gerson, and Bonaventura in his quest for enlightenment and comfort during his spiritual conflict in the Erfurt monastery.[56]

In their doctrine of salvation the scholastics generally held with Augustine that without the grace of God through Christ men cannot be saved. The grand question was how far the will is, or is not, a factor in the operation of grace and the element of merit is admissible. It was in connection with this question that they developed the

[53] Doctrinam in scholis usitatam quotidic discebat, et Sententiarios legebat, et in disputationibus publicis labyrinthos aliis inextricabiles, diserte multis admirantibus explicabat et . . . facile arripiebat illas scholasticas methodos. Melanchthon, " Vita," 158.

[54] Tamen quia in eo vitæ genere non famam ingenii, sed alimenta pietatis quærebat, hæc studia tanquam parerga tractabat. *Ibid.*, 159.

[55] " Werke," ii. 414.

[56] Melanchthon, " Vita," 159. See also Köhler, " Luther und die Kirchen Geschichte " (1900), 301 f. ; Müller, " Werdegang," 76 f.

doctrine of merits and modified the teaching of Augustine more or less, and in the later scholastic theology the more is characteristic rather than the less. With Bernard and Lombardus, as well as Anselm, Hugo of St Victor, and even Abelard, the modification is only slight. It is confined merely to certain details.[57] In Bernard, in particular, the evangelical-mystic note is very marked. In this respect he has been termed *Augustinus Redivivus*. Christ and the Cross are the foundations of his faith, the love of Christ and mystic union with the transcendental Christ the inspiration and the end of his piety. He gives definite expression to the Pauline doctrine of justification by faith alone, the non-imputation of sin by a merciful God, whilst also accommodating it to the ecclesiastical beliefs and usages of his time and to a certain extent neutralising it by his ascetic conception of the Christian life,[58] which magnifies the religious value of monastic works. Nevertheless, the Pauline element in his teaching is remarkable,[59] and it was not without reason that Luther owned his indebtedness to him.

Petrus Lombardus reflects the Augustinian teaching on sin, predestination, grace, faith, justification,[60] and Luther in studying him would largely assimilate the gist of the Augustinian doctrine of salvation at second hand before turning, as he erelong did, to his own works. Salvation is effected by prevenient and co-operating grace in preparing and energising the good will in those whom God predestinates and elects, and justification is the result of faith and love inspired by grace, which he identifies with the Holy Spirit. This is the Augustinian formula. Only with grace, infusing faith and love, do merits begin, and in the Augustinian sense merits are only God's gifts.[61] " No

[57] It is at most only what Loofs calls cryptic-Pelagian. " Dogmen-Geschichte," 493-494.

[58] See Köhler, " Luther und die Kirchen Geschichte," 330.

[59] For the relative passages in his writings, especially his sermons, see Müller, " Werdegang," 83 f. ; Loofs, " Dogmen-Geschichte," 523-524 ; Ritschl, " Rechtfertigung," i., Pt. II., 111 f.

[60] See the characteristic passages in the four books of the Sentences in Harnack, " History of Dogma," vi. 276-277.

[61] Loofs, " Dogmen-Geschichte," 542.

one can merit the grace of God by which he is justified, although he can merit that he be not utterly cast away." [62] He diverges from Augustine, however, by ascribing to the will itself a certain part in the preparation for grace and by discarding the doctrine of irresistible grace. In thus departing from the Augustinian doctrine of the complete impotence of the will, he follows on the lines of Anselm, Abelard, and even Bernard. Moreover, whilst, like Augustine, associating the notion of merit with salvation, he farther diverges from him in ascribing a certain merit to the will itself, for although merits are said to be due solely to the grace of God freely given, this does not exclude the operation of free will. " There is no merit in man which does not take place through free will." [63] The Neo-Pelagian element in Lombard is, however, but slight and amounts only to what Loofs terms cryptic-Pelagian.

The tendency to ascribe merit in virtue of free will becomes more pronounced in Bonaventura. [64] He attributes a certain merit to man's action inasmuch as, in spite of the fall, he retained the power of disposing himself to the good (*disponat*, *dispositio*). " If man does what in him lies, God gives him grace." [65] This doing what in him lies consists in the assent of the will, the disposing of himself to the good. Even in this initial act grace freely given (*gratia gratis data*, in the Augustinian phraseology) is, indeed, necessary. [66] But the assent is not merely mechanical on man's part. The doing what in him lies does involve active co-operation with grace freely given in the initial act of disposing himself to the good. He thus acquires a certain merit with the aid of grace freely given. This is indeed only a relative or imperfect kind of merit

[62] See the passage in Harnack, vi. 277.

[63] Harnack, *ibid.*, 277. Nullum meritum in homine quod non fit per liberum arbitrium.

[64] Loofs describes his teaching as Neo-Semi-Pelagian, and the same description applies to that of Alexander Hales and Albertus Magnus. " Dogmen-Geschichte," 544.

[65] Si homo facit quod in eo est, deus dat ei gratiam.

[66] See the passages from Bonaventura in Denifle, " Luther und Lutherthum," i. 577-578.

(*Meritum de Congruo*), and it does not suffice to the attainment of salvation. It does not constitute the absolute or all-sufficient merit (*Meritum de Condigno*) which makes acceptable in God's sight. This is due solely to what the schoolmen term " the grace that makes acceptable to God " (*gratia gratum faciens*)—the phrase by which they denote the merit that saves and which is solely the gift of God. Whilst thus striving by this distinction between relative and absolute merit [67] to keep within the Augustinian doctrine of salvation, to find a place for the exercise of free will alongside sovereign grace, Bonaventura really diverges from this doctrine in a Neo-Pelagian direction. He further diverges from Augustine, in his view of predestination, by making God's sovereign decree dependent on His foreknowledge of man's future action, *i.e.*, the exercise of free will.

Thomas Aquinas represents a reaction against this Neo-Pelagian tendency in favour of the Augustinian teaching, though, indirectly at least, he contributed to its development. He teaches the Augustinian doctrine of absolute predestination and irresistible grace and stands nearer to him than Bonaventura. From the point of view of predestination and grace, salvation is wholly dependent on God. From the human point of view, it has another aspect, and Thomas shares the tendency to recognise the

[67] It is difficult to apprehend the distinction between these technical terms, which recur so often in the scholastic theology, and also in Luther's early writings. The distinction is based on what is supposed to have been the original state of man. As created, man possessed natural goodness disposing him to the good and congruous to his nature (*Meritum de Congruo*). To this natural goodness God superadded grace, which as being God's special gift, constituted a higher worthiness (*Meritum de Condigno*), for which he was dependent solely on God. What he could do himself is congruous merit. What he could only do by superadded grace is something that could not otherwise exist, its cause being God. From another point of view the distinction lies in the fact that man as creature cannot make God his debtor. Merit implies the claim of reward, and whilst man may have merit relative or congruous to his capacity as a creature, he cannot have merit in the sense of making the Creator indebted to him. By giving grace which produces merit in the higher or absolute sense God is really debtor only to Himself.

freedom of the will, without which merit cannot be ascribed to human action. The Church belief and practice necessitated, in fact, a theory which could find room for free will in order to find room for merit, and by the aid of the Aristotelian metaphysics he constructed a theory by which grace might be harmonised with free will. This theory is based on the distinction between the soul and its faculties, of which the will is one. Into the essence of the soul God infuses grace, creates a *habitus* or sort of new nature of the soul. This moulding [68] of the soul takes place apart from any act of the will. But as a faculty of the grace-infused soul, the will acts freely, and thus by this abstraction its freedom is preserved and the possibility of merit, as the result of free will, is reconciled with the fact of grace. He indeed, like Bonaventura, speaks of *Meritum de Congruo*.[69] But he differs from him in predicating congruous merit only of the will after being miraculously infused with grace and thus eliminating any power of naturally disposing itself to the good. It was, however, open to his Nominalist critics to modify or reject the abstract notion of a supernatural, metaphysical *habitus* in the Thomist sense, and, by retaining the assumption of the freedom of the will without it, to attribute merit to the action of the will itself. The theory tended in fact to endanger rather than vindicate free will, which becomes the mere agent of a mysterious supernatural power (*habitus*) in the essence of the soul and loses the character of free, responsible volition. It led to a reaction in behalf of the free will as the active principle of the soul, and thus Aquinas, who really strove to check the Neo-Pelagian tendency, gave an impulse to it without intending it.

His theory of infused grace also conditions his teaching on justification by faith. Justification has in it four elements—the infusion of grace, the movement of the will towards God, the inward turning away from sin, the

---

[68] The term used is *informatio*. Hence the theory is called the Information Theory.

[69] Videtur enim congruum est homini operanti secundum suam virtutem deus recompenset secundum excellentiam suæ virtutis.

forgiveness of sin.[70] The second element—the turning of the will to God—is where faith comes into the operation. As the result of infused grace the will turns to God in faith. Justification is thus said to be by faith, and in the Commentary on Romans he emphasises faith in the propitiatory death of Christ and faith in Christ in the Pauline phraseology.[71] At the same time, his conception of faith is rather that of Augustine than of Paul. Justification is a process in which faith is completed by love. Its formula is " faith formed by love " (*fides per caritatem formata*).[72] It begins with faith operated by grace (*gratia operans*) which moves the will to God and is not merited by man. This is the first part of the process.[73] But this faith must perfect itself in love through co-operating grace (*gratia co-operans*), and thus justification is the result of faith and love, of grace and works. This is not the Pauline, but the Augustinian teaching, with the addition of a conception of merit, due to the action of the will as the organ of the grace-infused soul (*habitus*) of which Augustine knows nothing. Here again it was open to Nominalist opponents to stress works rather than grace, love rather than faith, to make justification a thing to be earned rather than accepted.

The Neo-Pelagian doctrine of salvation appears most strongly in the later schoolmen—Duns Scotus, Occam, and his followers D'Ailly and Biel. Scotus minimises the corrupting effect of original sin, which did not essentially deprive man of the natural goodness with which he was created. It was no *corruptio naturæ*. It consisted not in the corruption of his nature, but only in the loss of the supernatural gift of righteousness, which God is supposed

[70] These elements are only formally distinguished. They are not in reality successive, but simultaneous. Justification is operated by God instantaneously and the first element—the infusion of grace—really involves the other three. Tota justificatio impii originaliter consistit in gratiæ infusione. Loofs, 564.

[71] See Denifle, " Quellenbelege über justitia Dei und Justificatio," 142, for relative passages.

[72] Hence the distinction between *fides informis*, imperfect or unfinished faith, and *fides formata*.

[73] Ipsa fides quasi prima pars justitiæ est nobis a deo. Denifle, *ibid.*, 140.

to have added to his natural goodness. Of this loss he made himself guilty by his sin, and original sin consists in this guilt. But his nature remains substantially good, and though there is thereby induced a certain concupiscence, it is not concupiscence in the Augustinian sense, not the total depravity of human nature and the consequent impotence of the will, but only a proneness (*pronitas*) to the immoderate use of the things of sense. He can, in virtue of his natural goodness, even love God above all things. He retains the power of free will. With Duns the freedom of the will is a fundamental conception. God is sovereign, unconditioned will (*potentia absoluta*), of which the universe is the expression. He could have willed everything to be otherwise than it is. He has, for instance, willed the plan of salvation to be what it is and the Church as its instrument. Even morality has no other basis than God's will, which makes an action to be good or bad. There is no inherent necessity in what exists. Arbitrariness, the power to will a thing so, or otherwise, belongs to the conception of absolute will. This conception might seem to render salvation and even morality a mere arbitrary device and make both uncertain and unreliable. Such might be the case, if the conception was logically carried out. But Scotus and his followers were not logical in this respect. They were believing Christians and orthodox churchmen,[74] and they found arguments to show that God's absolute, arbitrary will does not necessarily involve scepticism as to redemption and the moral order of the world. The possibility of God's willing anything otherwise does not invalidate or render doubtful what He has actually willed (*potentia ordinata*). God has willed what is, in accordance with His wisdom. It is, therefore, to be accepted as binding on man. This belief thus safeguards the existing order.

To the human will, in its own sphere, Duns also ascribes the essential quality of freedom, which makes man the

[74] Für ihn (Scotus) war die Kirche ein Staat, der zu seinem Bestand der positiven Gesetze und Ordnungen bedarf. An diesen zu rütteln lag ihm fern. Er lässt sie durchaus als solche gelten, hier schweigt die Kritik. Seeberg, " Duns Scotus," 52 (1900). For the identical attitude of D'Ailly, see Tschachert, " Peter von Ailli," 317 (1877).

master of his own actions.   He, therefore, accepts predestination only in the contingent sense and discards the Augustinian
doctrine of the impotence of the will to do good.   It can of
itself turn to God without grace and thus merit grace con-
gruously.[75]   With the aid of this earned grace it attains
to the higher merit (*de condigno*).   In the first case the
merit is man's own ; in the second it is the merit of grace
which his own has, however, made possible.   But all merit
is, in the ultimate resort, only what God is pleased to account
or " accept " as such (*acceptatio dei*).   For it, too, depends
on God's absolute will.   It is only in as far as, in the exercise
of His sovereign will, God is pleased to accept as meritorious
both what man does and what God Himself contributes
by His grace, that eternal life is attained.   It is thus through
this " acceptation " that the divine factor in salvation really
comes in.   But whilst this acceptation might make salvation
ultimately depend on God's will, the merit which God is
pleased to accept is attributable to man's act as well as to
grace, and the doctrine is therefore Neo-Pelagian, though
Duns disclaims the teaching of Pelagius.[76]

The Nominalist Occam, Duns' pupil, and his followers,
D'Ailly and Biel, reflect the same tendency.   Occam, too,
teaches the Scotist doctrine of God's sovereign will in its
extreme form and emphasises the essential freedom of the
human will.   In virtue of this freedom man can do what he
wills.   He has retained his natural goodness and can, even
without grace, achieve the good after, as well as before,
the fall.   This good includes even the acquired virtues of
faith, hope, and love.   He rejects, indeed, the Pelagian
doctrine that man, in virtue of his natural goodness, may even
avoid all sin and merit eternal life absolutely (*de condigno*).
By reason of sin, grace is necessary.   But by cultivating the
good, by doing what is in him man attains the congruous
merit which enables him, by means of the higher merit
obtained by the aid of grace, to effectuate his own salvation.
He further shares Duns' view of merit as due to " the
acceptance " willed by God, and teaches the non-imputation

[75] Voluntas disponit se de congruo ad gratiam.   See the passages in
Harnack, " History of Dogma," vi. 309.
[76] Seeberg, " Duns Scotus," 319 f.

of sin (*non imputare*) in the divine act of forgiveness, which also takes place because it pleases God so to do.   There is, indeed, in the Occamist teaching, as in that of Scotus, an attempt to keep within the traditional teaching on sin and grace and even harmonise it with that of Paul.   " Everywhere in words," says Harnack, " by means of extremely forced distinctions, Augustinianism is defended, but in reality it is discarded.   The position which was not disputed even by Thomas and Augustine that we are not justified unwillingly (*inviti*) receives from Nominalism a Pelagian interpretation, and the other position that eternal life is the reward for the merits one acquires on the basis of infused grace is so understood that the accent falls on the will and not on the merit of Christ." [77]   Grace is, indeed, emphasised as necessary to salvation.   Whilst the will is free, evil is very potent, as actual experience proves.   Whilst aided by the general divine influence (*generalis dei influentia*) which God as the first cause of all things exercises on human nature, the will is exposed to the evil influence which the devil and the flesh exercise over it.   It needs the help of grace to attain eternal life.   Nevertheless, the fact of free will and the consequent capacity of man to contribute to his salvation, to earn it in co-operation with grace, are explicitly recognised.   The difficulty of doing the good does not invalidate the fact of freedom to do it, which is essential to the conception of will, and of which the fall did not deprive man.   " Liberty," says Biel, " is an essential of the will and the difficulty of eliciting a good act does not lessen its liberty." [78]   Again, the merit of Christ, in addition to any merit of man, is essential to salvation, to the divine " acceptance " and the " non-imputation " of sin by God in forgiveness.   But it is not the sole merit.   " Although," says Biel, " Christ's suffering is the principal merit, on account of which grace is conferred, it is, nevertheless, not the sole and total meritorious cause.   For it is manifest that there always concurs with the merit of Christ a certain

[77] " History of Dogma," vi. 310.

[78] Libertas est essentialis voluntati et voluntas omnes actus suos elicit. Difficultas itaque non opponitur libertati in eliciendo, sed facilitati. See the passage in Scheel, ii. 357.

operation of merit on the recipient of grace." [79] " The human will," he says further (always assuming the general influence of God, without which it can do nothing at all), " can by its own natural power love God above all things. The sinner is able to remove the impediment to grace, because he is able to cease from consent to sin and from sinful acts, yea to hate sin and to will not to sin. By the removal of the obstacle, and by the good movement towards God elicited by his own free will, he can merit *de congruo* the first grace (*prima gratia*) in turning to God." [80]

This Nominalist teaching has undoubtedly a Pelagian ring, though even the Nominalists disclaimed the imputation of Pelagianism. Nor is the Nominalist conception of the divine acceptance by the non-imputation of sin genuinely Pauline. For if acceptance is the act of God, it presupposes the meritorious action of man, and non-imputation has not the same meaning as in the Pauline doctrine of justification by faith through the non-reckoning of sin. With Occam and Biel, as with Augustine and Aquinas, justification is the result of real righteousness, of faith formed by love, whilst, in contrast to Aquinas, this righteousness is not due to infused grace. It has in it the element of human merit, preceding as well as resulting from grace.

Such then was the final outcome of the reaction from the Augustinian doctrine of salvation. It erelong produced a counter reaction in its favour of which Ægidius Romanus, a member of the Augustinian Order, Bradwardine, and Wiclif in the fourteenth century, and John of Wesel and Wessel Gansfort in the fifteenth, were the chief exponents. But in the Erfurt monastery it was the Nominalist doctrine that prevailed, and as a student of the scholastic theology Luther assimilated and continued to profess this doctrine until the study of Paul taught him to reject it. He accepted the freedom of the will and its capacity to do the good, even to love God above all. He professed in his early exposition

[79] See the passage in Loofs, " Dogmen-Geschichte," 615.

[80] *Ibid.*, 615. Occam also holds that man can love God above all by his natural power. So also D'Ailly, although man cannot do so in accordance with the intention of God without grace. See the passages from D'Ailly in Tschachert, " Peter von Ailli," 323-324.

of the Psalms (1513-14) the Nominalist view that to him that does what in him lies God gives grace and that he can thus prepare himself to merit this grace *de congruo*.[81] He accepted the current view of the sovereign will of God, of acceptation and non-imputation, of merits and of justification as expounded by his Occamist teachers.[82] He shared, too, their characteristic teaching on the superiority of faith to reason. For whilst Occam and his school, following Scotus, rationalised the doctrine of sin and grace in a Pelagian direction, they exalted revelation and faith above reason as the source of religious knowledge, and the authority of the Church as the guardian of this knowledge. They questioned the scholastic method of applying reason to the demonstration of Christian truth. Scotus saw that much of this scholastic demonstration was untenable from the rational point of view, and based theology on revelation and ecclesiastical authority, though making lavish use of a subtle dialectic in reasoning out his own ideas. The truths of religion can be known only as far as they are revealed, or contained in ecclesiastical tradition. An assertion may, in fact, be true in theology which is false in philosophy, and vice versa. He and the Nominalists thus contributed to undermine the whole scholastic system, apart from revelation and ecclesiastical belief, and emphasised an implicit faith and ecclesiastical authority. In this respect Luther also followed them, and their destructive criticism of the scholastic system, their emphasis on faith *versus* reason was not without its influence on his ultimate recourse to the Scriptures as the sole and adequate source of Christian faith and on his characteristic exaltation of faith above reason. In both respects he owed something to his Occamist training. He might, too, have learned from them to question the

---

[81] Hinc recte dicunt Doctores quod homini facienti quod in se est, deus infallibiliter dat gratiam, et licet non de Condigno . . . tamen bene de congruo. " Werke," iv. 262.

[82] Nam prius didiceram Meritum aliud esse congrui, aliud condigni, facere hominem quod in se est ad obtinendam gratiam, posse removere obicem, posse non ponere obicem gratiæ, posse implere præcepta dei quoad substantiam facti, licet non ad intentionem præcipientis . . . voluntatem posse ex puris naturalibus diligere Deum super omnia. " Werke," ii. 401.

Augustinian doctrine of the total depravity of human nature and thus have saved himself from burdening his later religious teaching with this one-sided dogma. The scholastic reaction against this extreme doctrine was, as we have noted, natural and inevitable, and Luther in his later attack on this reaction, under the influence of Augustine, did not give due consideration to the moral difficulty presented by the dogma of the enslaved will and the utter corruption of man's nature. The motive of the schoolmen in modifying the Augustinian doctrine might, in part at least, be the desire to make theology square with the Church practice. But the moral motive was also behind the tendency to vindicate human responsibility, which the doctrine of absolute predestination and man's total depravity seemed to endanger. Luther did not squarely face this side of the problem. He sacrificed human freedom to Augustinian determinism and pessimism. He threw away the saner and more rational conception of the schoolmen along with the lumber of the scholastic theology in its Nominalist form, which he found a real obstacle to a right relation to God. He rightly revolted against its assumption of an arbitrary God, which endangered moral values, its imperfect sense of the power of evil over the heart and the will of man, its proneness to predicate of human effort more than, from the standpoint of a lofty moral and religious ideal, it was capable of achieving, its erroneous and huckstering conception of salvation by merit. These features of the system proved to be stumbling blocks in his path to an assured salvation, a true relation to God. What he had learned on these subjects as a student of theology, he wrote in 1519, contributed to "the torture of conscience" [83] from which he suffered so direly in the attempt to reconcile the teaching of his Occamist professors with his personal experience of sin and his high moral and religious ideal. He wrongly, however, included Thomas Aquinas among the Pelagians of the Nominalist school who led him astray. Thomas, of whose teaching he had little first-hand knowledge,

[83] "Werke," ii. 401. Interim mihi sufficit quod carnifex illa conscientiarum theologastria cui totum debeo, quod mea conscientia patitur.

was certainly not a Pelagian in the Occamist sense and did not, as he assumes,[84] teach the Scotist and Occamist doctrine of the freedom of the will.

IV. THE SCHOLASTIC THEOLOGY—DOCTRINE OF THE CHURCH AND THE SACRAMENTS

As in the case of Augustine, the scholastic theologians accommodated their doctrine of salvation to the teaching and practice of the Church, and thereby intensified the sacerdotal element in this doctrine. The Church, through its priesthood and sacraments, is the medium of the divine grace, and Luther's scholastic studies made him familiar with this conception of the Church and the sacraments, as expounded in the schools. The specific conception of the Church as elaborated by the theologians, in accordance with existing ecclesiastical institutions, is the sacerdotal, hierarchic one. The religious conception of it as the community of the faithful, the mystic body of Christ, from whom grace is imparted to its members, finds, indeed, expression. This double conception, to which Augustine had given shape, continued to exist side by side. But practically the mystic body is the hierarchy which, as the dispenser of grace in the sacraments, is essential to the Church and supersedes the priesthood of believers, the community of the elect, though the other conception may be formally recognised in theology. Moreover, as the Church is the body of Christ, it must be a unity, and of this unity the Papacy is an essential element. The Pope, as " the first and greatest of all the bishops," is the head of the Church on earth, and without this head its unity is impossible. In him as the successor of Peter, Christ's vicar, is incorporated the power of the whole Church (*plenitudo potestatis*), and from him the hierarchy derives its powers and functions. He is the absolute ruler of the Church. Administration is subject to his supreme control. Under him the hierarchy exercises a delegated divine

---

[84] " Werke," ii. 394. Certum est enim Modernos (quos vocant) cum Scotistis et Thomistis in hac re (id est libero arbitrio et gratia) consentire.

authority over the faithful and performs its sacerdotal function. In matters of faith his decision is binding on the whole Church, and it belongs to him as absolute disposer of the grace of the Church to dispense it, by means of indulgences, for instance, in unlimited degree. Obedience to him is necessary for salvation, and Boniface VIII. in formally decreeing this dogma was only repeating what Aquinas had propounded.[85] Heresy is inadmissible and incurs excommunication by the ecclesiastical authority and death at the hands of the civil power, which in things spiritual is subject to the ecclesiastical, as the representative of God on earth. The Pope is, in fact, invested with supremacy over the State. Princes are bound to obey him, and in the case of friction between Church and State he may punish them with excommunication and interdict, and even deprivation of their authority.

These high claims were only gradually developed, and there was not lacking throughout the Middle Ages a current of antagonism to them. They were challenged by the emperors in their long conflict with the Papacy in vindication of the independence of the civil from the ecclesiastical power, and by the hierarchy in defence of their episcopal rights. In the early fourteenth century, for instance, Marsiglio of Padua and Occam stood forth as the champions of the imperial claim in the conflict between the Emperor Ludwig IV. and Pope John XXII., and in doing so attempted to reduce the Papacy to the level of a limited monarchy and to revive the democratic conception of the Church. Occam, in this respect, did not stand alone, and Wiclif later in the century followed in his footsteps in vindicating the rights of the Church as the community of believers against both the secularised Papacy and hierarchy. The Great Schism called forth on the part of the hierarchy itself a determined attempt in the first half of the fifteenth century to assert itself against the absolute papal power by maintaining the principle of the superiority of a General Council to the Pope, which was declared and decreed by

[85] See the passages in Mirbt, " Quellen zur Geschichte des Papstthums," 143-144.

the Council of Constance. The attempt was carried farther in a democratic direction by the Council of Basle, which championed the rights of the lower clergy, as well as the episcopal order, to a voice in the government of the Church. Both Councils failed to substantiate these contentions and the Papacy emerged unscathed from the ordeal which began with the Great Schism. Biel and other Occamists of the second half of the fifteenth century do not seem to have shared the ecclesiastical tendency of their master, and Luther appears in his early period, on his own confession, as a thorough-going papalist.

A sacrament is defined by the earlier schoolmen, following Augustine, as " the visible sign of invisible grace." The prevailing ecclesiastical tendency was, however, to emphasise the efficacy of the sign or sacramental rite as conveying grace in itself, and this tendency dominates the sacramental theory of the theologians from Hugo of St Victor onwards.[86]

For Lombard and Aquinas the sacraments are not merely significative of grace. They are the instrumental cause of it (*causa instrumentalis*), though its ultimate cause (*causa principalis*), according to the latter, is God in Christ, from whom grace is derived. Despite this reservation, they are held to cause grace to those receiving them. They are both sign and cause; and in this respect they are unlike the sacraments of the Old Testament, which were signs only, *i.e.*, a prefiguring of the grace to come through Christ. The sacramental rite thus of itself possesses an inherent efficacy, and its symbolic significance is more or less displaced by the magical element in it. The sacraments effect what they symbolise (*efficiunt quod figurant*). They not only signify; they contain grace. They sanctify intrinsically, *ex opere operato*.

Against this conception Duns [87] and Occam represent a reaction in favour of a more spiritual and symbolic view, though in practice, in regard to the sacrament of penance at least, they really augment the effect *ex opere operato*.

[86] Harnack, " History of Dogma," vi. 200 f. ; Loofs, " Dogmen-Geschichte," 567 f.

[87] For Duns, see Seeberg, " Duns Scotus," 345 f.

They deny that they have an intrinsic supernatural virtue, and, in accordance with their conception of God as omnipotent will, assert that the sacraments owe their efficacy to the ordinance or appointment of God, who has willed by this means thus to confer grace on those receiving them. God is the cause of their gracious effect, and grace works along with the sacraments rather than inheres in them. In this respect they contributed to prepare the way for the more spiritual view of the Reformers.

On the other hand, whilst it was contended that there was an intrinsic virtue in the sacraments—that they convey grace *ex opere operato*—there was considerable diversity of opinion as to the conditions under which the effect is produced. The effect is generally stated to be the sanctification of the soul, the end eternal life. But the disposition of the recipient also has a part in the application of sacramental grace, and it is generally admitted that the effect depends on the disposition of the recipient more or less according to the respective view of the subject. One section held that the disposition is practically inoperative. It is of formal, not of positive significance. The effect in this case is purely *ex opere operato* and nothing in the recipient causes, *i.e.*, merits, the imparting of saving grace. Others, though their number was few, contended that, without repentance and faith wrought in the soul by God, the sacraments were altogether inoperative, and that saving grace is entirely the work of these. This view discards the notion of an *ex opere operato* effect and approximates closely to the Reformation view. Others, again (Lombard, Aquinas, etc.), assume the necessity of a good disposition (*bonus motus interior*), *i.e.*, a sincerely religious spirit that aspires for grace and feels real contrition, and thus merits sacramental grace. In this case the grace is *ex opere operato*, but the meritorious disposition of the recipient contributes something to its efficacy (*ex opere operante*). Still others (Scotus and the Nominalists) require only the absence of a bad disposition (unbelief, contempt of the sacrament, mortal sin), and in the case of the sacrament of penance are satisfied with the lower form of attrition (the fear of hell) in the recipient, which the sacramental grace transforms into the equivalent of contrition, and thus magically confers on him a merit which he does not really possess and which is not the result of real contrition and faith.   Here the effect *ex opere operato*, which the Nominalists rejected in the sense of intrinsic virtue in the sacrament, becomes, in practice, in an extreme form a magical influence, and the magical influence thus culminates, in as far as this section is concerned, in a downright swindle.   To say that grace only works along with the sacrament and not intrinsically (*ex opere operato*) may be forcible argument.   But to say that grace, working along with the sacrament, transforms magically a low moral motive into a high one, makes a merit of what is not a merit, is scholastic " humbug."   It is a glaring instance of that tendency in the scholastics to pervert reason into a mere instrument of intellectual juggling, which is so irksome and unedifying to the modern student.   And this appears to have been the predominant tendency in both Church and school in the later scholastic period.

The sacraments are seven in number, though the number was for long uncertain.   Every ecclesiastical rite was regarded as, in a sense, sacramental, and Bernard specifies ten of these as sacraments.   Abelard and Hugo of St Victor fix the number at five, Lombard at seven, and this number was accepted by Aquinas and the theologians of the thirteenth century.   It was only in the fifteenth, however, that the Council of Florence definitely declared in favour of this number, and Pope Eugenius IV. sanctioned it (1439).[88]   The sacraments thus authoritatively enumerated were baptism, confirmation, orders, the Eucharist, penance, extreme unction, and marriage.   Of these the first three impart an indelible character to the soul, and may not be repeated.   All are assumed to have been instituted by Christ.   They are valid if properly performed by the priest, *i.e.*, in exact accordance with the ritual, and their validity does not depend on the moral character of the celebrant, who acts not in an individual capacity, but as the servant of the Church (*ex parte ecclesiæ*), though a bad priest incurs

[88] Mirbt, " Quellen," 162-165.

mortal sin. They are necessary to salvation, because man is led only by means of sensible things to those which are above sense and, moreover, needs in his sinful, spiritually diseased state the healing of this spiritual medicine. The passion of Christ does not of itself suffice and is applied in a certain fashion (*quodammodo*, the *how* being unexplained) to man in the sacraments. In this way they tend to displace Christ Himself, or at least to duplicate His work of redemption, and to interfere with the direct appropriation by faith of the benefit of His death. Personal faith in the Redeemer seems to be a secondary matter.

Each sacrament has its material and form,[89] and its specific function. Baptism takes away the guilt (*culpa*) of original sin and of actual sin, previously committed and present (*peccata præterita et præsentia*), and remits the eternal punishment or penalty (*pœna*), though not the temporal punishment, *i.e.*, the evil effect of sin experienced by the sinner in this life. It does not eradicate concupiscence, the sinful tendency, which still remains as a slumbering flame of sin (*fomes peccati*). But it enables the baptized person to keep it in check. Hence the distinction between sinful and innocent concupiscence. " Although concupiscence," says Lombard, " remains after baptism, nevertheless it does not dominate and reign as before, but is mitigated and diminished by the grace of baptism, so that it is no longer able to dominate unless one surrenders his powers to the enemy in yielding to it." [90] Theoretically, it is equivalent to regeneration, for in baptism the recipient receives along with the remission of guilt and penalty operating and co-operating grace (*gratia operans et cooperans*). In fact, however, it is only the initiation of the process of regeneration, justification. As a rule it must be administered by the priest and only in case of emergency by a deacon or a layman.

In confirmation, which is performed only by the bishop,

[89] The material relates to the elements of which it is composed, *i.e.*, in baptism the water, in confirmation the anointing oil, in the Eucharist the bread and wine, etc. The form relates to the words of the formula used by the priest.

[90] See the passages in Harnack, " History of Dogma," vi. 228.

the baptized believer receives a farther instalment of grace, the power to grow in grace and wage a lifelong warfare against the sinful tendency. In the Eucharist the bread and wine are transmuted by the priest into the body and blood of Christ during the rite of the Mass which precedes it. By this miracle the substance of the elements is transubstantiated, leaving only the accidents (colour, shape, etc.) as the outward and visible form and covering of the body and blood. This miracle is made plausible, though certainly not comprehensible, by the use of the Aristotelian distinction between substance and accident. It is also based on the Realist, in opposition to the Nominalist conception of ideas as having a real existence in objects apart from the mind conceiving these ideas. The ideas of the body and blood of Christ in the bread and wine can thus denote an objective, and not merely a subjective, nominal reality. The miracle further involves the substantial presence of Christ in each of the elements, and therefore the partaking of the bread alone suffices for the laity (communion in one kind), whilst it belongs to the function of the priest to partake of the wine in behalf of the congregation.[91] The miracle farther involves the extraordinary notion that Christ in partaking of the bread at the institution of the supper must have eaten Himself! Nay, an animal, by a mischance in eating the bread, may partake of the actual body of Christ! This monstrous assumption is the crassest production of the mediæval theologians. It introduces into religion a gross materialism, and viewed in the light of the adoration of the host is sheer idolatry. No wonder that even in that age of childish miracles there were many doubters, and that some sought to escape from these puerilities by suggesting a less miraculous explanation. The doctrine of transubstantiation had in fact long been a subject of dispute from the time of Ratramnus and Radbertus in the ninth century, and Berengar and Lanfranc in the eleventh, and it was only made an article of faith by the Fourth Council of the Lateran in 1215. Even so, it

[91] This not only increases the priestly dignity, but it is safer, ensuring that the wine may not be spilt.

continued to encounter opposition not only among the sects
(notably by Wiclif and his followers) but among the theologians of the Nominalist school, who shared their doubts
and suggested a less crass form of belief, whilst submitting
to the received conception as an authoritative doctrine of
the Church. Being a Realist doctrine it was not in favour,
on this account, with the Nominalists. Occam, John of
Paris, D'Ailly and others preferred that of impanation or
consubstantiation, by which the body and blood are present
in the wine and bread, but the latter are not transubstantiated into the former. With this Nominalist teaching
Luther became acquainted as a student of theology, and,
as he tells us himself, it deeply impressed him. " When I
was a student of the scholastic theology I was greatly struck,
on reading the commentary of Cardinal D'Ailly on the
' Sentences,' with the remark that it was much more
probable and would lessen the belief in superfluous miracles,
if one were to regard the bread and wine on the altar as
real bread and wine and not merely their accidents, if the
Church had not determined the contrary." [92] It was, he
adds, this teaching that ultimately enabled him to discard
transubstantiation in favour of the real presence in the
elements in the sense of impanation.

Not only does the priest " make the body of Christ."
He offers Christ anew for the sins of the congregation, and
also as a means of preserving it and the souls in purgatory
from evil. This repetition is based on the assumption that
Christ, in instituting the supper, at the same time offered
Himself and instructed the disciples to renew the offer in
connection with the memorial celebration of His death.
Though Pope Gregory the Great in the sixth century
declared in favour of the repetition, the sacrificial view was
only authoritatively stated by the Fourth Lateran Council
in the beginning of the thirteenth. This became the
generally accepted view of the schoolmen, though Lombard
was disposed to favour the memorial conception of the
rite (*Recordatio*) and Aquinas justified it only on the
ground of the practice of the Church.

[92] " Werke," vi. 508.

Forgiveness of actual sins is obtained by means of the Sacrament of Penance, which consists of three parts—contrition, confession, and satisfaction. These constitute what is called the material of the sacrament, whilst the absolution given by the priest is spoken of as its form. Contrition is real penitence, sorrow for, detestation of sin, prompted by love to God, and Abelard, Lombard, and, on the whole, Aquinas emphasise this as an essential condition of absolution. Alexander of Hales and Bonaventura, and, later, Scotus and the Nominalists discriminated between contrition and attrition, between real repentance and the mere fear of the consequences of sin. According to this theory, the penitent, who may be actuated only by the fear of hell, may nevertheless receive the benefit of the sacrament, which by the infusion of grace changes attrition into contrition, and thus becomes valid in his case for the remission of guilt. This view, which was elaborated by Scotus and the Nominalists, tended to make salvation easier for the ordinary Christian and was influenced by this consideration. It was widely held in the fifteenth century, and in some cases in rather a gross form, as the work of Paltz, one of Luther's teachers in the Erfurt monastery, shows. It certainly tended to demoralise religion and to make the sacrament far too much a popular device for escaping hell and ensuring heaven by priestly intervention, without the essentially religious spirit. " Very few indeed," says Paltz, " are truly contrite ; therefore very few would be saved without the priests. All, however, are able in some fashion to have attrition,[93] and such the priests are able to help and by their ministry (the Sacrament of Penance) to make contrite and consequently to save them." Auricular confession to the priest is the second essential, and only in case of necessity may it be made to a layman. The penitent must confess all his sins, venial as well as mortal, as far as he can remember them, though it is only with mortal sin that the Sacrament of Penance is concerned. Confession once a year was made by the

[93] Possunt autem omnes aliquo modo fieri attriti. See the passages from Paltz's " Cœlifodina " in Harnack, " History of Dogma," vi. 251.

Fourth Lateran Council obligatory and the priest was strictly enjoined to observe absolute secrecy.[94] It is followed by absolution on the part of the priest, who performs this part of the sacrament in virtue of the divine authority, as possessing the power of the keys, of loosing and binding conferred on him at his ordination. The priestly absolution was held by Abelard and Lombard to be only declaratory, forgiveness being the prerogative of God alone. " The priests," says Lombard explicitly, " remit or retain sins in so far as they judge and show that they are remitted or retained by God." [95] Their real power extends only to the imposition or abatement of penitential works, ecclesiastical penalties. Aquinas, on the other hand, ascribed to the priest more than this declaratory power, and taught that, in virtue of the power of the keys, he is the instrumental cause of forgiveness (*causa instrumentalis*). Whilst this became the dominant view, Duns and his school limited the part of the priest to that of moving God by his absolution to fulfil His covenant (*pactum*). Others, such as Wiclif in the fourteenth century and Wessel Gansfort [96] in the fifteenth, vigorously protested in favour of the older view that the priest only declares the remission of sins and that God alone absolves. In absolution the guilt and eternal punishment of sin are remitted, but not the temporal punishment which still accrues in this life for sin, and for this satisfaction must be made to an offended God and as an insurance against the day of judgment. Hence the imposition by the priest as a condition of absolution, which the penitent must undertake to fulfil, of certain penitential performances (prayers, fasting, alms, and other good works). By these the penitent may also add to the stock of merit thereby accruing to him. The Sacrament of Penance thus gave practical shape to the conception of salvation as something to be earned, merited, and its practical efficacy is rendered more certain by the intercession of the Virgin and the saints. Satisfaction might also be made by means of indulgences. The penitent

[94] Mirbt, " Quellen," 135.
[95] Loofs, " Dogmen-Geschichte," 585.
[96] Miller and Scudder, " Wessel Gansfort," i. 145-146, 217-218; ii. 187 f. (1917).

might, for instance, contribute to some ecclesiastical scheme, might buy an indulgence issued for this purpose, or he might pay a sum of money in lieu of going on a pilgrimage to Rome, or elsewhere. In such cases he could at the same time contribute to the remission of the temporal punishment for sin to which he was liable. He might also, according to the more popular view, even benefit the souls of his relatives and friends in purgatory, who were liable to make satisfaction for such sins as had not been adequately atoned for in this life. For whilst the Sacrament of Penance closed the gates of hell, it did not apply to such temporal punishment as purgatory. Luther, as we shall see, had made himself familiar with the scholastic theory on this subject.

For the dying and the gravely sick there is the Sacrament of Extreme Unction, the anointing with oil of the sick person for the healing of the soul, and also, if expedient, of the body. That of ordination confers on the priest the power to loose and bind, to perform the miracle of transubstantiation, and offer Christ anew for sin. It invests him with an indelible character and an official jurisdiction, on the exercise of which depends the efficacy of the religious life. Priestcraft is of the essence of mediæval Christianity.

CHAPTER IV

LUTHER'S SPIRITUAL CONFLICT (1507-1512)

I. HIS " MARTYRDOM " IN THE MONASTERY

DURING the first two years of Luther's life in the monastery, *i.e.*, up to his ordination as priest in the spring of 1507, there is little trace of an acute spiritual conflict.[1] In his letters to his friend Braun and his old teacher Trebonius, and in the interview with his father on the occasion of his first Mass, he appears as the confirmed votary of the religious life and maintains his " confidence in his own righteousness " against his father's doubts and reproaches.[2] These early utterances reveal nothing abnormal in his spiritual experience. He had given himself wholeheartedly during these two years to the pursuit of the life of evangelical perfection and had evidently experienced no serious doubts or misgivings as to this pursuit. But the confident spirit evinced in the interview with his father was not permanent, and during the next half-dozen years he was subject to periodic fits of religious depression, so acute at times that he even despaired of his salvation. This experience he later describes, in recurring passages in his writings, as a spiritual martyrdom, from which he was only delivered by the complete renunciation of his confidence in his own righteousness, which had cost him dire suffering, for a righteousness, not his own, which justifies before God.

---

[1] In a letter of 1530 he says, indeed, that when he became a professed monk he was always sad and miserable. Cum primum in monasterium essem profectus (professus !), evenit, ut semper tristis et mœstus incederem, nec poteram tristitiam illam deponere. Enders, viii. 159. This generalisation must not be taken too literally, in view of other early utterances, which show that up to 1507, at least, he was not always oppressed by sadness.

[2] Enders, i. 1-2 ; xvii. 84 ; " Werke," viii. 574 ; *cf.* " Documente," 20.

He had entered the monastery with the conventional conviction that the monastic life—the life in obedience to " the evangelical counsels," as it was called—was the surer way to attain the gracious acceptance of God, than the life in obedience to " the evangelical precepts "—the life of the ordinary Christian in the world. Salvation is, indeed, attainable by the ordinary way of obedience to the latter. The evangelical precepts, or positive commands of the Gospel, were, in fact, obligatory on all Christians, and involved the regulation of the individual Christian life in accordance with the Gospel and the ordinances of the Church, especially the Sacrament of Penance, with confession and satisfaction for sin in the form of penitential works. Without the grace obtained through this sacrament, salvation is impossible, and the ecclesiastical regulation of the ordinary Christian life in accordance therewith demanded the life of self-denial and satisfaction for sin by almsgiving, fasting, etc. Only in this way could the ordinary Christian render himself acceptable before God, and ensure himself against the day of judgment. In principle there was no difference between the life in obedience to the evangelical precepts and that in obedience to the evangelical counsels to which the monk submitted himself. Both were based on the idea of striving, with the aid of grace available through the sacraments, to merit acceptance with God. The difference was only relative. But the life in obedience to the evangelical counsels was regarded as a higher form of the Christian life and a surer way of attaining salvation. The monk thereby undertook to do more than was required of the ordinary Christian. He gave himself exclusively and freely to the service of God, took upon himself the yoke of Christ in its heaviest form, freed himself from the hindrances to which the ordinary life in the world was exposed, and could thereby attain to a higher merit and thus more surely achieve his salvation than the Christian, who was content to live in accordance with the Gospel precepts and the ordinances of the Church.[3]

[3] Denifle contests the assumption by Luther and his Protestant biographers that the aim of the monastic life was to ensure the attainment of salvation. It was only a method of attaining more surely the

This was the theory with which Luther began his monastic career, and his confidence in this theory appears unshaken at the end of the first two years of his experience of the monastic life. The theory erelong, however, failed to verify itself in practice. It not only failed to yield the expected spiritual results—to realise his striving to find a gracious God. It proved in his case a hindrance in his quest for an assured relation to God, and the sense of this failure resulted in recurring fits of spiritual misery and conflict. Not that he flinched under the monastic yoke of Christ, or wavered in his determination to bear it. It was the vocation of the monk thus to endure. For this he had renounced the life in the world and he submitted himself with wholehearted zeal to the discipline of his Order. In the fervour of his devotion he certainly did not spare himself. He took a meticulous part in the common daily religious exercises, fasted, kept vigil, meditated and prayed in his cell, went begging in the streets of Erfurt and in the neighbouring villages, and gave himself in addition to hard study. At a later period the spiritual and physical strain of these years appeared to him as a veritable " martyrdom." In numerous passages of his writings he repeatedly speaks of his intense devotion and asceticism. Some of these, especially the later of them, are, indeed, of doubtful authenticity, and are, in some cases, manifest additions or amplifications of his editors.[4] But the testimony of what are incontestably his own utterances is very explicit, and so consistent that there can be no reasonable doubt as to the rigorous self-discipline to which he subjected himself. " It was," he says, " a hard and rigorous life." [5]   A. V. Müller, who knows the monastic life by experience, reckons that the ritual exercises occupied six hours a day, besides the time

highest form of the Christian life, the life of evangelical perfection. " Luther und Lutherthum," i. 399.   This contention is, however, unfounded and the assumption is in accordance with the fact that the monastic life was regarded as a means—the surest way—of attaining salvation, or, as Luther put it, " a gracious God." Scheel, " Luther," ii. 363.

  [4] For instance, " Werke," xl. 135 ; xliii. 536 ; xlv. 670. See Scheel, " Luther," ii. 365-366.
  [5] " Werke," xvii., Pt. I., 309 ; " Documente," 43 (1525).

given to private prayer and meditation, and that he spent almost half of the year in fasting and watching, with only one spare meal a day on these fast days.[6] In view of this fact Luther's description of his life as a " martyrdom " is, even from the physical point of view, no exaggeration, apart altogether from the mental and psychic strain of intense religious devotion. It is in the light of this physical and psychological strain that we must read his utterances on the subject. " I was an earnest monk," he tells us in one of these reminiscent passages, " lived strictly and chaste, prayed incessantly day and night." [7] " I kept vigil night by night, fasted, prayed, chastised and mortified my body, kept obedience and lived chastely." [8] " For almost fifteen years I wore myself out in self-sacrifice, tormenting myself with fastings, vigils, prayers and other very burdensome tasks, with the idea of attaining to righteousness by my works." [9] " Certain it is, I was a pious monk and observed the rule of my Order so strictly that I venture to say that if ever a monk could have gained heaven through monkery, I should certainly have got there. This all my fellow-monks who have known me will attest." [10] He even exceeded the prescribed devotions and ascetic routine, and acquired among his brethren the reputation of a virtuoso of the religious life. " I was so deeply plunged in monkery, even to delirium and insanity. If righteousness was to be got by the law, I should certainly have attained it. I was a wonder in the sight of my brethren." [11]

This testimony does not rest merely on his own assertions. It is confirmed by Flacius, who tells us that he had heard in 1543 from one of Luther's fellow-monks that he had lived a pious life amongst them and had observed the Rule most conscientiously and zealously.[12] His intense asceticism threatened, in fact, to seriously undermine his

---

[6] " Werdegang," 27 f.
[7] " Werke," xxxiii. 561 ; " Documente," 43 (1531).
[8] " Werke," xxxiii. 574 ; " Documente," 42 (1531).
[9] " Documente," 38 (1532).
[10] " Werke," xxxviii. 143 ; " Documente," 37 (1533).
[11] " Werke," xl., Pt. I., 134 (1535).
[12] Grisar, " Luther," vi. 207 ; cf. iii. 286.

health, and he ascribed the bodily infirmity from which he suffered later to these years of excessive bodily mortification. " If it had lasted much longer, I would have martyred myself to death with watching, praying, studying and other performances." [13] His ideal was to emulate the ascetic life in its most intense form, of which he read in the lives of the saints. " As a monk I often longed with all my soul to be brought into touch with the life and conversation of some holy man. Meanwhile at all events I cherished the fancy of such a holy man who, living in the desert, abstained from food and drink and lived only on the roots of herbs and cold water. And the idea of these monstrous saints I drew not only from the books of the mediæval sophists, but even from the fathers." [14]

Such passages might be amplified in proof of the consuming zeal with which he gave himself to the monastic vocation. Even if we leave out of account those which are ascribable to his editors or reporters, and which show a tendency to exaggerate his rigorous self-discipline, there is evidence enough in his own testimony to substantiate the fact.[15] Some of his modern biographers have not been sufficiently careful to discriminate between the two and have too readily accepted the exaggerations of this second-hand testimony. On the other hand, Denifle has gone to the other extreme and asserted that Luther's version of his monastic experience is the fabrication of an apostate monk. His account of his excessive self-mortification, his martyrdom in the quest of a gracious God is untrue. It is a myth which he deliberately concocted and foisted on the world long after he had broken with the Roman Catholic Church. This excessive asceticism is, further, not in harmony with the directions and instructions which he received from his preceptor in this matter. It is in flat contradiction to the constitution of the Order, which enjoined " discretion " in the application of the prescribed discipline. The Rule of the Order was comparatively moderate in its demands. It

[13] " Werke," xxxvii. 143 ; " Documente," 37 (1535).
[14] "Werke," xl., Pt. II., 103 (1535).
[15] A. V. Müller has, I think, shown that the traditional account is substantially true to fact. " Werdegang," 27 f.

expressly forbade all excess in fasting, etc., injurious to health.   Moreover, the end of the monastic life was not the attainment of salvation by ascetic works, as Luther pretends, but the higher spiritual life in conflict with the flesh and in security from the snares of the life in the world. Luther himself continued to commend, even after his so-called enlightenment, the discipline of the monastic life from which he says he suffered so direly, and it was only from 1530 onwards that he ventured to impose his lies about it on his credulous adherents.   Up to 1530 he has nothing to say of this martyrdom.   It was only from this year onwards that he concocted and continued to propagate this lying tale in order to glorify himself and defame the Church and its institutions.   Luther, it seems, discreetly waited before setting it forth till 1530, when we are to suppose that his fellow-members of the Augustinian Order, who could have contradicted him, were all dead.[16]

In this fashion Denifle proves to his own satisfaction that Luther's later utterances on his " martyrdom " in the monastery are a deliberate falsehood.   He makes no attempt to discriminate critically between his own testimony on the subject and the exaggerations of his editors or reporters. Luther deliberately misled the latter, and both he and they, under the influence of religious animus and with a supreme indifference to truth, were the propagators of a libellous legend.   This thorough-going conclusion certainly shows that the animus is not all on one side.   It is grotesquely pre-judiced and is certainly not an unbiased interpretation of the evidence.   It has proved too gross a dose of passion and prejudice for reasonable Roman Catholic writers to swallow.   It is, for instance, not the case that these so-called lying utterances date only from 1530 onwards.   Five years earlier Luther speaks of " the hard and rigorous life " which he lived as a monk.[17]   In other earlier passages he refers explicitly to the earnest endeavours he made to attain by his monkish works to an assured relation to God, to the misery of conscience he endured in seeking by penitential exercises

[16] " Luther und Lutherthum," i. 353 f.   Grisar, " Luther," vi. 187 f., practically repeats Denifle.
[17] " Werke," xvii., Pt. I., 309.

to reach this certainty. The earliest of them, in which he refers to his penitential sufferings, go back to the years 1515 or 1514, and these indications have a retrospective bearing.[18] We can, in fact, from his letter to Staupitz in 1518, carry the evidence back to the early years of his intercourse with his Vicar-General—to the year of his sojourn at Wittenberg in 1508-1509.[19] Such passages directly or indirectly afford convincing evidence of the painful zeal with which he disciplined himself to this end.

Nor was it the case, as Denifle contends, that the monastic life was conceived on moderate lines and that excessive asceticism was rather a breach than a fulfilment of its discipline. " Discretion " was, indeed, to be observed in the application of discipline. But the principle of it was self-abnegation in a measure beyond that of the evangelical precepts, and in the monastic literature of the fifteenth and preceding centuries the current conception of it was that of " a martyrdom." Moreover, Luther had been warned on his reception of the heavy yoke he was taking on himself. He was quite aware that he was bound minutely to observe the Rule, and that any infraction of it constituted guilt (*culpa*).[20] To him this was a very real source of disquiet. The observance of the Rule depended to a certain extent on individual temperament. The monk who was satisfied with mere routine might get through without undue suffering. Luther knew of such easy-going brethren who shirked whenever they could.[21] But those who, like him, took this routine very seriously, might easily strain it into a martyrdom of soul and body. He had made the acquaintance of such at Magdeburg and Erfurt, for instance. Such examples, he tells us, were often before his mind,[22] and in his efforts to emulate them he certainly did not spare himself. When he became district vicar of his Order at Wittenberg, he insisted on strict observance, even when he might reason-

---

[18] " Werke," i. 30-31 ; " Vorlesung über den Römerbrief," ii. 102, 109, 273 ; Enders, i. 29 (1516), 196 (1518).

[19] Memini, Reverende Pater, jucundissimas et salutares fubulas tuas, etc. Enders, i. 196 ; *cf.* " Werke," i. 540.

[20] Müller, " Werdegang," 21.   [21] " Werke," xxxiii. 574.

[22] *Ibid.*, xxxviii. 105 ; xlii. 504 ; l. 612.

ably have allowed dispensation in the case in question.[23] There can, in fact, be no reasonable doubt that in his later as well as his earlier utterances on this subject, he was substantially telling the truth, though he did not view this martyrdom at the time in the later light of his evangelical standpoint, when it appeared to him as a perversion of the truth and even of blasphemy against the Gospel.[24]

To a Roman Catholic critic like Denifle such " martyrdom " is incredible, if only because it seems to call in question the working of an institution which the Church in its infallible wisdom has ordained. Such an institution must work according to plan, and if in Luther's case there was anything abnormal, it was due either to a perverse misapprehension of the Rule, or, as Denifle prefers to conclude, to sheer lying about his excessive self-discipline. Its observance required only a balanced and salutary devotion to the religious ideal and anything beyond this is simply incredible. But not only was this not the current conception of the monastic life. The assumption fails to take account of the fact that the Rule might not be the norm of practice in every case. It does not reckon with the personality of the individual. In the religious sphere it is artificial to assume a regular average of performance, apart from character and temperament. Luther with his highly-cultured mind, his intensity of thought, imagination and feeling, his sensitive conscience was evidently very unlike the normal type of monk. It is, therefore, not improbable that his monastic experience was not of the common order. His subsequent career certainly marks him as an original personality. To measure such a man by the conventional standard betrays the narrow formalist. Luther legends there are in plenty invented by both his friends and his enemies. This one is due to mere prejudiced carping.

Equally strong is the evidence that all this monastic devotion produced in Luther the sense of failure and gave

[23] Enders, i. 87-88.
[24] On Luther's " martyrdom," see Scheel, " Luther," ii. 110 f.; Müller, " Werdegang," 30 f.; Strohl, " L'Évolution Religieuse de Luther," 81 f.

rise to an acute spiritual conflict. In numerous passages of his writings, both early and late, he speaks of this phase of his monastic experience and even his most prejudiced critics can hardly gainsay his testimony on this head, though they may ascribe it to wrongheadedness and presumption, or even to moral and spiritual degeneration. The fact of a crisis of some kind is unquestionable. Luther did pass through a painful experience that transformed his conception of religion and ultimately brought about a religious revolution.

II NATURE AND CAUSE OF THE CONFLICT

What is the true explanation of this spiritual conflict ? What led to it and with what was it specifically concerned ?

In considering this question the personality of Luther— the temperament, the moral and mental mould of the man —must be taken into account. Temperament certainly made its contribution to it. Temperamentally, he seems to have been high-strung, emotional, sensitive, quick-tempered, impetuous, imaginative, impressionable. In a word, one of those intensive natures which, whatever the sphere and the object of their activity, live at high pressure. This is the impression we derive from his recorded experience as a monk as well as from his writings generally. The religious fervour of the monk reflects not merely the overmastering power of faith on mind and soul. It is partly at least the self-expression of the man, of the temperamental qualities which this faith transforms and directs. The intense quest for a gracious God, the unremitting pursuit of evangelical perfection in its highest form was temperamental as well as religious. To this end he made a whole-hearted use of the conventional method, submitting himself whole-heartedly to the " martyrdom " of the monastic life. " It availed me nothing," he tells us again and again. " I tried hard, but I came no farther forward." [25] The result of this sense of

---

[25] " Documente," 33. Tentabam multa, confitebar quotidie, etc. Sed nihil prorsus proficiebam. See also *ibid.*, 30, 35, 36 ; " Werke," xxxiii. 574-575 ; xxxvii. 661, etc.

failure was to such an intense nature a terrible perturbation of soul. It gave rise to fits of depression proportionate to the intensity of the effort. The average monk might be spared such acute experiences, or might get over the sense of failure by the ordinary means of confession and penance. The high-strung, impressionable temperament of Luther was less manageable under the sense of failure. These fits of depression bordered on despair at times. " To speak of myself," he wrote to a friend in 1516, in reference to these experiences, " with what great miseries have I been tormented." [26] That there was in such experiences a temperamental element is evident from the fact that they were recurrent, if intermittent, and that they were not confined to his spiritual conflict in the monastery. They occurred at intervals in later life, even long after he had succeeded in his quest for a gracious God. Melanchthon [27] and others of his friends speak of these later attacks from personal knowledge, and Luther himself made no secret of them. One explanation is that his excessive devotion in the monastery induced a nervous disorder which occasionally manifested itself in these terroristic experiences. Luther certainly attributed the disordered digestion from which he later suffered to the overstrain of these years of asceticism and spiritual trial, though he says that it was due less to the asceticism than to the psychic struggle which he endured in the monastery.[28] It stands to reason that the continuous self-mortification, the intensity of the daily round of devotion, the hard study, the lack of sufficient diet and bodily exercise should have had a detrimental effect on nerves and imagination. But apart from this overstrain, the temperamental element does seem to have predisposed him to recurring acute crises of this kind, whatever the character of the strain, or even when there was no ostensible strain at all. Melanchthon says that he was liable to sudden fits of terror at the thought of an angry God, and implies that they were recurrent from his student days onwards. His knowledge of the early period of Luther's life is

[26] Enders, i. 31 ; cf. " Lectures on Romans," ii. 102, ut prope desesperent.
[27] " Vita," 158.   [28] " Tischreden," i. 199.

evidently vague, but as far as he speaks of his later life
his testimony is decisive, and we know from other sources
that Luther did suffer from such attacks even after the
discovery of his specific doctrine of justification by faith
had delivered him from the misery incident to his quest,
as a monk, for a gracious God. One of these fits at the
thought of an angry God certainly drove him into the
monastery. This particular instance may be explained by
the physical fright induced by the imminent danger of
death during the thunderstorm. At the same time there
does seem to have been in him a temperamental strain
which suggests a nervous imagination, combined with a
morbid tendency to introspection. The terrible experience
of the thunderstorm may have induced this liability to sudden
terroristic fits. Such an experience might well make its subtle
effects felt in this way in the after-life of a man of his high-
strung temperament, and it would not be far-fetched to look
in this direction for an explanation of the abnormal element
which undoubtedly entered into his religious experience.

It is, however, a mistake to seek to explain his spiritual
conflict in the monastery exclusively from this point of view,
as Hausrath, Grisar, and other recent writers are disposed
to do. According to these writers, his conflict was a case
of neuropathy pure and simple. The cause was not really
spiritual, but physical—the result of the intense asceticism
which adversely affected his digestion and his nervous
system, already predisposed by his harsh upbringing to
terroristic fits. Hausrath goes the length of saying that
this fitful perturbation amounted to mental derangement
(psychosis).[29] This is one of those generalisations which,
while containing a certain element of truth, fail to take
account of all the facts of the case. There is, at all events,
no real evidence for the assumption that the harsh experience
of his early life made him a confirmed neurotic. What
evidence there is tends rather to disprove this assumption.
The strain of the monastic life had, indeed, on his own

[29] " Luther's Leben," i. 109. Ebstein, a competent medical authority,
vigorously protests against this assumption. " Luther's Krankheiten "
(1908). Grisar, whilst accepting the " pathological " theory, also rejects
Hausrath's assumption. vi. 172 f.

testimony, an adverse effect on his physical health. But it does not warrant the conclusion that his spiritual struggle was therefore a case of disordered nerves. Whilst Luther was certainly high-strung, he combined with an intense temperament a strong will and a potent intellect, and these are hardly the qualities of a confirmed neurotic. Moreover, the neuropathic theory assumes that his neurotic condition was chronic and that the years of spiritual conflict in the monastery were one long nightmare of impaired vitality. Here again the evidence is not in accordance with the theory. It is not borne out by the testimony of his early letters. In one of these written in 1509 he explicitly tells us that he was quite well, though he was overstraining himself in the study of philosophy.[30] He is found taking his share in the priestly duties performed by ordained monks in the village chapels in the neighbourhood of Erfurt, and he tells us that he had the utmost difficulty on one of these occasions in keeping from laughing at the rustic accompaniment of the village precentor. " For I was not accustomed to such organ playing (*orgeln*)." [31] After all, these fits of depression were only incidental. The temperamental element is, indeed, discernible in his religious experience. But it was only one element in the spiritual conflict of these clouded years in the monastery. This conflict was certainly far more than a case of disordered nerves. It was specifically religious, and any explanation of it that ignores the whole personality of Luther—the moral and mental as well as the temperamental mould of the man—is one-sided and misleading.

He evidently carried with him into the monastery a very sensitive conscience. The minute regulation of the monastic life tended to aggravate this sensitiveness and foster the thought of transgression. It involved an ever-alert attention to a prescribed course of conduct, constant self-examination and confession, anxious concern about the state of the soul. Moreover, the solitary life tended to

[30] Enders, i. 6. Quod si statum meum nosse desideres, bene habeo Dei gratia, nisi quod violentum est studium, maxime philosophiæ. *Cf.* i. 1-2 ; xvii. 84 (1507).
[31] " Tischreden," iv. 14.

aggravate this anxious introspection, to foster melancholy, to magnify the sense of guilt for sins of omission or commission in the observance of the Rule. His worst spiritual trials, he tells us, came to him at night, when he was alone and the devil had a free hand with him. " Never am I less alone than when I am alone," he said, quoting from St Bernard the old classic saying.[32] He knew from experience the morbid effects of the solitary life, the melancholy, the over-anxiety even about trifles which it tends to foster. This tendency was, in fact, one of the pitfalls of the monastic life. " Whoever is inclined to the spirit of sadness," he later warned his students, " let him see to it that he is not alone." [33] " The monks have long said that a melancholy head is a bath (*balneum*) prepared by the devil." [34]

The sense of transgression was all the more active in his case, inasmuch as he took the exact performance of all that the Rule prescribed very seriously. " I vowed to keep the whole Rule," [35] and he seems to have understood the obligation in a literal sense. He was not prepared to accept a less exacting interpretation, though he was familiar with such, and might at times find a passing consolation in these.[36] The whole Rule and nothing less was for him the indispensable condition of the life of perfection. The transgression of it was sin and might even involve mortal sin. This painfully conscientious observance might at times inspire him with an exalted sense of his worthiness. But the thought of transgression would suddenly overwhelm him and his self-confidence would vanish in a fit of nagging misgiving. " Although I readily listened to the flattering appreciation of my own works (on the part of the Prior and the Brethren) and allowed myself to be esteemed a marvellous fellow (*wunderthäter*), who could make of himself a saint in such outstanding fashion, and devour death and the devil, I nevertheless failed to stand the test of

---

[32] " Werke," iii. 481.   [33] " Tischreden," i. 48.   [34] *Ibid.*, i. 198.
[35] " Werke," viii. 633. Ego vovi totam regulam. According to Müller this meant that every infraction was regarded as sin, and Luther was taught the Rule in this sense. " Werdegang," 21-22.
[36] " Werke," viii. 635; *cf.* " Tischreden," ii. 65; v. 213.

even a small attack of death or sin. When such a trial came, I fell straightway and found no help either in my baptism or my monkery." [37]

His anxiety on the score of the formal observance of the Rule was, however, only a comparatively secondary element in his spiritual conflict. Conscientious scruples, painful self-examination of this kind were part of the monastic burden and were accepted as a matter of course. The recurring moods of dejection which they fostered were common enough in such an atmosphere, and Luther's experience in this respect was not singular. It was incidental to the monastic life, though it might be more acute in his case than in others, as we learn from a letter written long afterwards to a young correspondent, who suffered from fits of religious depression and whom he warned to flee solitude.[38] The real root of his conflict lay deeper—in his keen consciousness of sin in the ethical sense. Under the microscope of his sensitive conscience, sin and the sinful tendency (concupiscence) were terrible realities. Sin is not a mere weakness of human nature. Luther envisages the problem not from the human standpoint, but in the light of his conception of an absolutely righteous God. His conception of God and His perfect righteousness (*justitia*) conditions his conception of sin. Sin is the antithesis of this righteousness and the antithesis is absolute. On the one hand, a perfectly righteous God who requires the perfect fulfilment of the law, which is the expression of His righteousness. On the other, sin which, in virtue of the sinful tendency, renders such fulfilment impossible and induces the sense of guilt, condemnation before God. The conception of God and man's relation to Him is the legalist one which, as in the case of Paul, proved for Luther the great stumbling block until he found deliverance in the discovery of justification by faith in the Pauline sense. For, in virtue of the misapprehension of the Pauline teaching, this conception underlay the current doctrine and practice of the Church in as far as God was represented, in the legalist sense, as judge, and as this representation found expression in the

[37] "Werke," xxxviii. 148.   [38] Enders, viii. 159-160.

idea of satisfaction for sin and meritorious works, as an insurance against the day of judgment. It was this legalist conception, in which he had been nurtured and which formed the principle of the monastic life in particular, that lay at the bottom of these spiritual *Anfechtungen* in the monastery in his quest for a gracious God and the higher life. For him, as for Paul, the thought of God's righteousness, the law, sin and the experience of the sinful tendency were the great difficulty. The divine righteousness and the law as the expression of it gave a desperate significance to the fact of sin and the sinful tendency. In the face of this righteousness sin means guilt; the sinful tendency, " the law of sin in the members," raises in acute form, for him as for Paul, the question of the possibility of the fulfilment of this righteousness after the legalist method. The guilt and the power of sin was for both the haunting problem. For Luther's spiritual struggle was a repetition of that of Paul under changed conditions. For Paul, the Pharisee, the problem was concerned with the works of the Jewish law; for Luther, the Christian monk, with the works of the new law into which the Gospel of faith, in which Paul found deliverance, had been transformed.

As in the case of Paul, Luther's keen consciousness of sin and the sinful tendency did not necessarily imply the domination of sensual desire. Concupiscence is not merely the lusts of the flesh in their grosser form. It denotes the disposition of the heart and the will to evil, which survives the taking away of original sin by baptism and conditions and impairs the moral and religious life. Luther was not, in fact, like Augustine, the slave of the sexual instinct, as some of his critics and detractors would have us believe.[39] His experience of the sinful tendency was, in this respect at least, not that of Augustine, and he tells us in his notes on the Psalter (1513-15) that it was impossible for him to

[39] See Grisar, i. 26-28, for the contemporary charges of which he was the object after he became famous as a Reformer. Preserved Smith in his article on " Luther's Early Development " too readily accepts the erroneous view of Denifle on this subject. *Journal of American Psychology*, xxiv. 370 f.

understand this frame of mind.[40]   Concupiscence denoted
for him sins of the spirit rather than the flesh.   He explicitly
mentions under this head anger, pride, luxury.[41]   Specifically it means what is involved in self-love, selfishness.
Denifle has grossly misrepresented him in identifying it
with the lusts of the flesh, and his theory that the sensual
tendency ultimately led him to a sense of moral bankruptcy
and induced him to take refuge in the doctrine of justification
by faith alone is utterly misleading.   It is not shared by
reasonable Roman Catholic writers like Kiefl, who have
rightly discarded the theory of Denifle and his followers
Grisar, Paquier, Cristiani as untenable.[42]   His temptations
did not lie in this direction.   Melanchthon bears witness
to his habitual abstinence in the matter of food and drink.[43]
" When I was a monk," he himself says explicitly, " I was
not much troubled with sexual desire." [44]   After sixteen
years of the monastic life he could remind his father that his
fear lest he should not be able to keep his vow of chastity
had been utterly groundless.[45]   His confessions to Staupitz,
he further tells us, " were not concerned with women, but
with the real (spiritual) difficulties (*die rechten Knotten*)," [46]
with God's righteousness, with sin and penitential satisfaction for sin, with the weakness of the human will in doing
the divine will, with the impossibility of loving God above
all things, with the difficulty of transforming the passions
into this perfect love by the complete control of self, with
the problem of acceptance with God and the certainty of
salvation, and of predestination in its bearing on this
certainty.

In later years Luther often recalled the heart-searching
experience of this conflict in the quest for a gracious God.
These reminiscences, which date from an early period, best
convey the character and the severity of this spiritual
experience.   The lack of the power, if not the will, to

[40] " Werke," iii. 549.   [41] *Ibid.*, iv. 207.
[42] See Strohl, " L'Évolution Religieuse de Luther," 20 f.
[43] Valde modici cibi et potus, etc.   " Vita," 158.
[44] " Tischreden," i. 47.
[45] " Werke," viii. 573 ; sed nequaquam posito mei timore.
[46] " Tischreden," i. 240.

believe in the face of these recurring questionings was one
of the most trying features of it. " I believe," he wrote
in his Commentary on the Psalms in 1513 in reference to
Isaiah xxxviii. 14 (O Lord, I am oppressed, undertake for
me), "that there are many now—and I speak from my own
suffering and that of many others—who experience this
prophecy. Because they know right well all that is to be
believed, but they find it so difficult to believe and assent
to it that they seem to be oppressed, as in a terrible dream,
and are sore of heart, nor are they able to raise their souls
to the Lord. They are, indeed, eager and ready to believe,
but they know not how." [47] Another feature of it was the
consciousness of the vain confidence in his own righteousness, when measured by the standard of God's righteousness
in the juridical sense. "Some," he says in the Commentary on Romans (1515), "the devil urges to seek with
foolish labour to be pure and holy without sin, and whenever
they feel that they sin and any transgression overtakes
them unawares, he so terrifies them with the thought of
judgment and troubles their conscience that they almost
despair." [48] In such a mood the words *justitia Dei*
sounded like the knell of doom in the criminal's ear. "To
speak of myself, the term *justitia* became so loathsome to
me that it would not have caused me so much suffering
if some one had laid violent hands on me. And yet this
word is ever on the lips of the juridical theologians, than
whom there is not in this world a more ignorant and un-
skilful set of people in this matter, with their chatter about
the intention of the good, etc. For I have found in myself
and many others that when we esteem ourselves righteous,
God laughs at our righteousness." [49] The thought of the
law as the expression of the divine righteousness and of its
non-fulfilment would at times overwhelm him with the sense
of his guilt before God, and even afterwards when he had
learned to interpret the term righteousness in the evangelical
sense, the old racking doubt would anon return. "The
law," he says, "was the most terrible misery, the thing,

[47] "Werke," iii. 423.
[48] II. 102, edited by Ficker (1908).   [49] *Ibid.*, ii. 273.

as Paul says, that kills. The law is no joke. As a young man it meant to me sheer death." [50] In his later reminiscences he speaks again and again of the terror with which this thought inspired him. This may seem to us a case of ill-regulated imagination. But the fear of God was a very real factor in the religion of the age, because its conception of God was associated with the idea of retribution. This fear was no mere synonym for piety. It was an experience in which the sense of moral responsibility, culpability, mingled with that of awe in the presence of absolute righteousness. Calvin shared it with Luther, and this element enters into the religious life of every one who takes the thought of God seriously. " Without the fear of hell," he said in a sermon of 1513 or 1514, " no one is or ought to be unless he is absolutely perfect." [51]

" These words ' just ' and ' justice ' were as a thunder-bolt in my conscience. Forthwith I was struck with terror at the sound of them. Just—therefore He will punish." [52] They conjured the thought of God and Christ as judge and shook his confidence in his own merits. The doctrine of merits by which, in virtue of satisfaction and other works, the Church insured the sinner against the day of judgment broke down utterly in the face of this conception. " In our time," we read in a letter of 1516, " the temptation of presumption makes itself powerfully felt in many and especially in those who strive with all their might to be righteous and good. Being ignorant of the righteousness of God which is freely and abundantly given us in Christ, they seek to increase their good works so that they may attain the confidence of standing in the presence of God embellished with their own virtues and merits, which is an impossibility. You were among those who cherished this opinion, yea error, and so was I. But now I fight against it, though I have not yet completely overcome it." [53] " Those who, depending on their own powers, seek to justify themselves and ensure salvation by the works of the law rise up against Christ, the future adamantine judge,

---

[50] "Tischreden," i. 240.   [52] "Tischreden," ii. 176 (1532); cf. iii. 226.
[51] " Werke," iv. 664.   [53] Enders, i. 29.

with but very meagre resources. I advise them first to
count the cost and then they will find that they are not
able to face the ordeal." [54]   It availed not to resort to the
intervention of the saints or redouble his self-mortifications.
" We fled from Christ as from the devil," he says in his
later drastic fashion, " and ran to the Virgin Mary and
St Barbara, for we were taught that every one must appear
before the judgment seat of Christ with his works and his
order." [55]   " Often was I horrified at the name of Jesus,
and when I regarded Him on the Cross, it was as if I had
been struck by lightning, and when I heard His name
mentioned, I would rather have heard the name of the
devil, for I laboured under the belief that I must seek by
my good works to make Christ my gracious friend and
thereby reconcile an angry God." [56]   " When I first read
in the Psalms and ever afterwards, ' In Thy righteousness,
deliver Thou me,' I was terrified and felt anxious at these
words, ' the righteousness of God,' ' the judgment of God,'
' the Word of God,' for I understood the righteousness of
God not otherwise than as a strict judgment. How then
could He deliver me according to His strict judgment ?
In that case I should be eternally lost." [57]

The text that especially troubled him was Romans i. 17.
" This passage always stuck in my mind. For I was unable
to understand otherwise the word righteousness, wherever
it might occur in Scripture, than in the sense that God
was righteous and would judge righteously." [58]   God's
righteousness was always associated in his mind with God's
justice, in considering this passage. He could not conceive
of it otherwise than as something innate in God, which
must necessarily condemn the unrighteous. He thought of
it in the philosophical or juridical, not the evangelical
sense,[59] and was unacquainted with, or did not pay
particular attention to the patristic or even the mediæval

---

[54] " Werke," ii. 504 (1519).
[55] Ibid., xlvii. 109-110 ; " Documente," 27 (1538) ; cf. 31.
[56] " Documente," 24-25 (1539).
[57] " Tischreden," v. 26 (1540).
[58] Ibid., v. 234-235 (1542).
[59] See, for instance, " Werke," xl., Pt. I., 41, 407, 410 ; xl., Pt. II., 7.

exegesis of the passage, which explained it as the righteousness by which God makes us righteous,[60] *i.e.*, in His forgiving mercy in Christ. He was misled by the dominant conception of God as one who requires from us satisfaction for sin and whose justice must be propitiated, through the Sacrament of Penance, by our works and merits. God was thereby conceived under the retributive aspect,[61] which overshadows the conception of Him as infinite love and mercy, revealed in Christ. Here also the scholastic theology, in its tendency to accommodate itself to the teaching and practice of the Church, misled the perplexed student, who was bent on finding a solution of the problem of his personal salvation. To attain the assurance of salvation in the face of a retributive God, who demanded perfect righteousness in the sinner, seemed an utterly hopeless pursuit to one whose moral and religious ideal was so high. "'The Righteousness of God revealed in the Gospel' (Romans i. 17). Long did I seek and beat against this passage, which was expounded as the righteousness by which God is formally just and condemns sinners. For thus all the doctors," he erroneously continues, "with the exception of Augustine, interpreted the passage—the Righteousness of God, that is, the wrath of God. As often as I read it, I wished that God had never revealed the Gospel. For who can love an angry, judging, condemning God?"[62] "I was long in error and knew not what to make of this passage, because I could not discriminate between the law and the Gospel, and believed that Christ differed in nothing from Moses, except in the matter of time and perfection."[63] He farther failed, he says, to distinguish between the righteousness of God in the active sense (*justitia activa*), which cannot but condemn, and the righteousness of God in the passive sense (*justitia passiva*), which is equivalent to His mercy and leads Him to justify

[60] Denifle, "Luther und Lutherthum," i. 424, and see his "Quellen belege."

[61] On this point see Holl, "Gesammelte Aufsätze," i. 2 f.

[62] "Werke," xliii. 573 (between 1540 and 1542).

[63] "Tischreden," v. 210 (1542-43).

the sinner. Until he grasped this distinction the whole Scripture was for him full of darkness. [64]

Confession, contrition, and satisfaction, as prescribed in the Sacrament of Penance, failed to reassure him in his chronic perturbation at the thought of a retributive God. The term penitence, like the term righteousness, caused him infinite heart-searching, as he later reminded Staupitz. "Formerly," wrote he to Staupitz in 1518, "there was not to me a bitterer word in Scripture than Penitence, although I sedulously feigned it in the presence of God and sought to profess a love which was both factitious and forced." [65] Here, too, fear was the uppermost feeling—the fear that the satisfaction rendered by penitential works for both present and past sin might be insufficient. Had he done enough to make his contrition effective for the remission of these sins ? How could he be sure that he was truly contrite ? Was he capable of the absolute hatred of sin which true contrition implies ? Hence the recurring doubt and fear on this ground in spite of official confession and absolution. "By this doctrine I was, in truth, so misled by the scholastic teaching that scarcely with great effort by the grace of God was I able to transform the word penitence into one of joy. For if we wait till we are sufficiently contrite we shall never experience this joy. This I very often found to my great grief in the monastery. I conformed to this teaching, but the more I was contrite, the greater my misery, the more conscience rose up against me ; nor was I able to accept absolution and the other consolations which they to whom I confessed imparted. For I reflected, Who knows whether such consolations are to be trusted ? " [66] In the face of this doubt he found it hard to understand how sin could be taken away in the Sacrament of Penance, as the scholastic theologians taught. "I, poor fool, was unable to perceive how I ought to repute myself a sinner like others and prefer myself to no one when I was contrite and confessed. For I thought that after contrition and confession all sin had been taken away

[64] "Werke," xliv. 485, and many other passages to the same effect.
[65] Enders, i. 196.   [66] "Documente," 37-38.

and purged even inwardly. But if, as they say, we ought always to remember past sins, then, thought I, they are not remitted—which nevertheless God promises to those confessing. And thus I fought with myself, not knowing that there is indeed true remission, but not the taking away of sins unless in the hope that they are to be taken away, *i.e.*, by the grace of God, whereby they are not imputed." [67]

The Sacrament of Penance, with its doctrine of satisfaction, aggravated the thought of Christ as judge. " Under the Papacy they inculcated on us that Christ would come as judge, and although they read the Gospel daily, they proclaimed Him as judge and insisted that we should make satisfaction for our sins. To this end they established the saints and Mary as intercessors. Formerly we were thus subject to judgment and the thought of the Son of God was a cause of terror. If we had known better we should not have gone into the monastery. When I beheld Christ, I seemed to see the devil. Hence the invocation, O Mary, pray for us to thy Son and assuage His anger. Even yet I have trouble daily before I can seize hold of Christ. So strong is the habit of former years. It is an old, evil, rotten tree that has rooted itself in me, for it is a doctrine according to reason that he who commits sin shall make satisfaction for it. This is natural law—if I sin, it behoves me to make satisfaction. Thus I lose Christ, the Saviour and Consoler, and make of Him the jailer and hangman of my poor soul. Anew we obtain light. But even when I became a doctor I was ignorant of this." [68]

To these perplexing questions was added the problem of predestination, which had for him not merely a speculative but a religious significance. His lecture notes on the Sentences show that his mind was preoccupied with this problem, [69] and in his exposition of Romans he refers explicitly to the mental and spiritual suffering which it caused him. " Let me here give a word of warning," he says in his comment in the ninth chapter. " Let no one rush into these speculations, whose mind has not been

[67] " Römerbrief," ii. 109.
[68] " Werke," xlv. 86 (1537).   [69] *Ibid.*, ix. 57-58.

purified, lest he fall into an abyss of horror and desperation, but let him first purify the eyes of his mind by meditation on the wounds of Christ. For neither would I discourse of these things unless the order of lecturing and necessity compelled me." [70] Long afterwards he reminded Graf Albrecht of Mansfeld of his perturbation over this problem. " I also was so entangled in these speculations and trials that if Dr Staupitz, or rather God through Dr Staupitz, had not helped me out of them, I would have been over-whelmed and long since in hell. For such devilish thoughts, in the case of the weak, make people despair of God's grace. Or they become so bold and reckless that they scorn and rebel against God and say, ' Let it come as it will, I shall do what I like, since it is all lost labour.' " [71] As lecturer on the Sentences, he shared the Occamist doctrine that the divine decree by which God predestines and elects to salvation is conditioned by His foreknowledge and leaves room for the exercise of free will.[72] Salvation is both necessary and contingent. It is necessarily effected because God has decreed it. It is contingent because it depends on the exercise of man's will. But Luther could not see how this necessity and contingency could be reconciled. The contingency seemed to render the whole thing un-certain. " The theologians say that the elect are necessarily saved (*i.e.*, in virtue of the divine decree). But they also say that it depends on our will whether we are saved or not. Thus I formerly understood the doctrine." [73] The result was a speculative difficulty which tended to render salvation uncertain even from the speculative point of view, and the uncertainty was aggravated by the fact that, from the religious point of view, Luther was by no means sure of the power of the will, even with the aid of grace, to do its part in making the divine decree effective. Moreover, the Occamists also taught that God decrees and accepts in virtue of His absolute, arbitrary will, and this element of arbitrariness tended to increase the feeling of uncertainty. Not only does salvation depend, in the ultimate resort, on

[70] " Römerbrief," ii. 226.   [72] " Werke," ix. 57, 62, 71.
[71] Enders, xiv. 189 (December 1542).   [73] " Römerbrief," ii. 209.

the arbitrary exercise of God's will. This arbitrariness seems to render all moral values and all moral effort of questionable validity. How could anyone be sure that he is not the plaything of arbitrary omnipotence? How could he commit himself unreservedly into the hands of such a God? The haunting doubt on this ground was the most terrible element in his spiritual conflict, the darkest of the clouds that enveloped his soul. It was fitted at times to rouse a feeling of rebellion against, even hatred of God; nay, to cast doubt on the existence of God. At such moments his faith in the teaching of the Church seemed to be built on the sand. As a student of theology Luther's powerful intellect would not be satisfied with the mere acquisition of knowledge. He sought to probe to the foundation of things, and this intellectual activity exposed him to trials of this kind, of which the average monk could have no experience. This experience was all the more acute inasmuch as his intellectual search for truth was at the same time a religious quest—the quest for a gracious God and the higher life.

In the presence of this problem both mind and heart seemed hopelessly baffled. He endured the torture of the damned. Happily, it was only incidental and, in its incidental form, only of a few minutes' duration at a time. His realistic belief in the devil and his works gave a fearful reality to this experience. When he reflects on this problem during many a sleepless hour, it is the devil that takes the other side and plies him with his cunning arguments and drives him to utter desperation. These grotesque interviews have for the reader their comic side. "I never heard an argument of man which moved me. But the devil—he can bring arguments. He has often argued with me so that I did not know whether God existed or not." [74] "The evil spirit drives the poor soul to search into God's secret counsel, whether it is foreknown or not. Here the devil exercises his most cunning arts and powers, bringing poor mortals to seek a sign of God's will and makes them impatient and suspicious of God, so that they almost long for another

[74] "Tischreden," i. 238 (1533).

God. . . . This is to struggle with hell when we are tried with the thought of our foreordination." [75] " All discussions concerning predestination," he says later in reference to these satanic encounters, " are to be shunned. Staupitz used to say, ' If you wish to dispute about predestination begin from the wounds of Christ, and then your trouble will cease.' But if, on the contrary, you proceed to reason without this safeguard, you will lose Christ, the word, the sacraments, and everything else. I forget all that Christ and God are when this thought comes upon me and rush to the conclusion that God is a miscreant. We must hold fast to the word, in which God is revealed and salvation is offered to us, if we trust in Him. But at the thought of predestination we forget God. The *laudate* ceases and the *blasphemate*[76] begins." " I have known a man " (meaning himself), he wrote in 1518 in the " Resolutions " on his ninety-five Theses against Indulgences, " who asserted that he had often suffered these pains of hell at a very brief interval of time, so great and so infernal that neither tongue could speak nor pen describe them, nor one who has not experienced them can believe, so that if they were completed, or lasted half an hour, yea six minutes, he would utterly perish and all his bones would be reduced to ashes. Then God appears fearfully angry and along with Him the whole creation. There is no flight, then, no consolation, either within or without, but accusation on all sides. Then he wails forth this verse, ' I am cast away from before Thine eyes ' ; nor does he dare to say, ' Lord convict me not in Thy wrath.' At such a moment the soul cannot believe that it can be redeemed." [77] In such moments Luther reached the nadir of his spiritual misery. No one could write such a confession who had not plumbed the very depths of spiritual despair. Even long after his discovery of a gracious God, as his letter to Welskamp in January 1528 shows,[78] he was not unfamiliar with this paroxysm at the

---

[75] " Werke," ii. 688 (1519).

[76] " Tischreden," ii. 582 (1532) ; *cf.* ii. 113. [77] " Werke," i. 557-558.

[78] Enders, vi. 173. Verum est hanc tentationem esse multo gravissimam et mihi etiam ab adolescentia non incognitam. . . . Ego alios salvos feci, me ipsum non possum salvum facere.

thought that he might be predestined to damnation. The thought of predestination evidently became to him the thorn in the flesh, and the tendency to morbid introspection, of which there was a strain in his nature, threatened at such moments to upset the balance between reason and imagination.

At first sight one is apt to conclude that all this perturbation of soul over sin, the law, righteousness, penance, predestination in the quest for a gracious God was due to a misapprehension of the teaching of the Church on these subjects. This is the view of Roman Catholic writers who complain that Luther has misunderstood and misrepresented this teaching. His spiritual conflict was the result of imperfect knowledge or wilful disregard of the received doctrine on grace, faith, and works, and was therefore needlessly self-inflicted. The fact seems to be, however, that he was well acquainted with this teaching, and that in spite of this knowledge he found in it neither peace of conscience nor assurance of salvation. He knew well enough that the Church did not teach that he could find a gracious God in virtue solely of his own efforts. The scholastic theology emphasised the impossibility of fulfilling the law and rendering oneself acceptable to God in virtue of one's natural powers without grace. Dependence on grace is a fundamental of the religious life, and only on this basis can anyone merit acceptance with God by a life of active goodness and penitential satisfaction. His early lecture notes on the Sentences show that he shared the current teaching on works and grace.[79] He held, too, the scholastic doctrine of infused grace by which sin is expelled, and without which works have no validity for salvation and man cannot do what is pleasing or meritorious in God's sight.[80] He was also familiar with the doctrine that salvation depends on the merits of Christ, that God's saving grace cannot be merited by the sinner, and that faith is a necessary condition of the appropriation of these merits, by which saving grace becomes effective in the justification of the sinner. Even the Occamist teaching that God gives grace to

---

[79] " Werke," ix. 88 ; cf. viii. 620.   [80] Ibid., iv. 665,

him who does what he can presupposed the factor of grace
in the doing of such works. Works, merits, justification,
faith, the co-operation of the will in well-doing imply the
underlying condition of grace. Even for the Occamists who,
on this understanding, emphasised the human factor in
salvation, salvation ultimately depended on " the acceptation " of God, who is pleased to reckon as meritorious works
done with the aid of His grace.

Luther's conflict was not the result of scepticism as to
the traditional teaching of the Church. He assumed the
truth of this teaching and fervidly rejected any divergence
from it as heresy.[81] The Occamists, in fact, emphasised
the supreme importance of faith as the indispensable condition of the knowledge of God, revelation as against reason,
and as an Occamist Luther magnified faith above reason
and devoutly believed in the received scheme of salvation.
To him faith was the supreme element in the religious life
long before he discarded the ecclesiastical for the Pauline
doctrine of justification by faith, though he felt the difficulty
of absolute assurance of salvation as the result of faith.[82]
For ten years, he tells us, he submissively received the
teaching of the Pope, of the Councils, and the schools,
even if parts of it seemed absurd from the rational point
of view. His principle was that of Solomon, " Trust not in
thine own understanding." [83] Even when doubt assailed
him he would ask himself whether his own presumption
was not the root of his soul trouble. " Should you alone
be wise ? Can it be that no one experiences this trial
but me ? " [84]

Such reflections only served to increase the poignancy
of his experience, for to one who accepted the traditional
teaching with such fervour of faith doubt seemed equivalent
to damnation. His trouble, in fact, arose not from any lack
of confidence in the received teaching of the Church on grace
and works, but from his acceptance of this teaching. For,
along with the doctrine that works without grace are unavailing for salvation, the Church by its doctrine of merits

---

[81] " Documente," 11-12, 26, 34.   [83] " Werke," viii. 45.
[82] " Werke," iii. 423.   [84] " Documente," 29 and 42.

taught that salvation must be earned by means of these works. Its retributive conception of God conditioned its doctrine of salvation. God, Christ is the perfectly righteous judge, before whom the sinner must give an account of his works. In order to appease (*placare*) this righteous judge, he must make satisfaction for sin by penitential and other works, and by these he must sedulously strive to add to his stock of merit to this end. Luther's fear of this righteous judge was, therefore, no mere product of a nervous imagination, though this element might enter into and aggravate it. It was the natural result of the ecclesiastical conception of a retributive God who will demand an account of actual sin committed after baptism, and will weigh the merits and demerits of the sinner as well as the merits of Christ and the saints, to which he may appeal in his behalf. Grace, salvation may not be merited by his own works apart from faith and grace given in and through Christ. But faith and grace presupposed, the sinner has to reckon with the question whether these works will suffice for his justification at the great ordeal at the bar of a perfectly righteous judge.

This is where the thought of God's perfect righteousness, the law came in to perturb the conscience and cloud the soul. What if God were not propitious to him and how could he be sure of finding a gracious God? Had he been sufficiently contrite, rendered sufficient satisfaction for sin?[85] How could he attain to that perfect love of God which the self made so difficult to realise? How escape the danger and the guilt of mortal sin? How, in view of the Occamist conception of free will, overcome the will to evil and bring it, even with the aid of God's grace, to do only the good,[86] and this from the pure love of God? How to hate sin and repent of sin with a hatred commensurate with the perfect love of God and eliminate from this hatred the lower fear of hell (attrition)? How to attain the ideal of the religious life in pure devotion to God and to the service of God, unalloyed by the imperfection of the flesh in conflict with the spirit? How, as the result of this

[85] "Werke," i. 321 ; "Römerbrief," ii. 109.
[86] Sed nos faciliter malum et difficulter bonum. "Werke," ix. 71.

quest for a gracious God, this striving for the highest life, to attain the certainty of acceptance with God, the confidence, the full assurance of faith ? It must be remembered that Luther as a monk was bound to concern himself with these questions. His vocation demanded that he should constantly examine and cross-examine himself in this fashion. These questions were, therefore, not necessarily the obsessions of a neurotic mind.

At the root of all his disquietude was, more particularly, this lack of certitude. " Oh when wilt thou become truly pious and do sufficient to attain to a gracious God ? " was the recurring question.[87] In spite of his fervid belief in all that the Church taught on these problems, this assurance failed him and at times the consciousness of this over-whelmed him with doubt and even despair of his salvation. " My trial," he says, " was that I thought that God was not propitious to me." [88] His sensitive conscience could not find a lasting panacea in the Sacrament of Penance, or the Mass, or the pursuit of monastic virtue. " The more I desired to come to Christ by this method, the farther He seemed to recede from me. After confession and the Mass I was never able to attain peace of mind, because my conscience could not derive a firm consolation from such works." [89] Equally ineffective was the infusion theory by which sin and the fear of God and hell were supposed to be expelled. " As the scholastic theologians understood this theory, what other effect could it have than to produce desperation, and disquiet an unhappy conscience ? For so I have almost despaired of God—what He is in Himself and what character He possesses." [90]

The fact was that in spite of the will to believe, the ecclesiastical theory of salvation failed at such times of haunting perplexity to verify itself in experience. " When-ever even a little temptation to death, sin, and doubt came, I fell straightway and found no help in my baptism and my monkery. I lost hold of Christ and His baptism and

[87] " Werke." xxxvii. 661.
[88] "Tischreden," i. 200 ; cf. " Documente," 33 and 42.
[89] " Werke," xliii. 537 ; cf. "Tischreden," i. 226.
[90] " Werke," iv. 665.

was the most miserable of mortals. Day and night I groaned and despaired, so that no one could help me. Thus was I bathed and immersed in my monkery and had a terrible time of it. God be praised that I did not torment myself to death. I would have been long since in hell with my monk's baptism. For I knew Christ no longer in this condition but as a severe judge, from whom I wanted to flee and yet could not escape." [91]

This young monk absorbed in the quest for a gracious God in the Erfurt monastery is a tragic figure. His is by no means a solitary instance of such spiritual struggle within a Church professing to possess the absolute truth and governed by an infallible priesthood. Even under this absolute system there had been many throughout the Middle Ages who questioned and doubted, and even refused to accept current dogma and usage. The scholastic theology, in particular, bristled with problems and incited to subtle discussion, whilst recognising the principle of submission to an absolute external authority as the standard and judge of truth. Those who refused implicit obedience to this authority were persecuted. The mediæval Church sought to ensure such obedience by the penalty of death for heresy. Even so, it had only partially succeeded in enforcing its authority over mind and conscience, as the persistent existence of the mediæval sects shows, and this enforced system of belief was bound ultimately to find its Nemesis in the effective assertion of the rights of both. From this point of view the tragic figure of this young monk is supremely significant, apart altogether from the character and causes of his quest for a gracious God. It is the age of the Renaissance, of a new culture and a quickened intellectual life in which Luther's conflict supervenes. The hour has come and the man, though the man is as yet unconscious of his destiny. In the silent suffering of the Erfurt monastery Luther is forging the new principle and the new conception of religion which will erelong challenge and overthrow the old system of corporate belief and authority. He has not yet reached this stage of his religious

[91] " Werke," xxxviii. 148 (1533) ; cf. xl., Pt. II., 92.

development. But he is on the way thither and will get there in due time.

III. RELATIVE APPEASEMENT

Luther's utterances on this subject cannot be explained away as a later misrepresentation under the influence of his breach with Rome and his revulsion from the monastic system. There is, indeed, a tendency to exaggeration in his later reminiscences. He was prone to use strong language in the expression of his feelings and his opinions. He felt strongly and spoke impulsively. Over-emphasis and drastic utterance were innate traits of his nature, and this tendency was undoubtedly intensified by the great change which radically transformed his religious stand-point and brought him into active antagonism to the scholastic theology and the Church. His " Table Talk " and the controversial writings in which he speaks of his monastic experience cannot, therefore, always be taken in the literal sense. His reporters sometimes misunderstood him or amplified his sayings in the light of their own conceptions. They altered or added in accordance with later preconceived beliefs, and their representations are thus more or less inaccurate and misleading. At the same time, due allowance made for exaggeration or misrepresenta-tion, there is no real ground for the conclusion that his conflict in the monastery in the quest for a gracious God and the higher life is pure romance or distortion. The evidence for this conflict is, as we have noted, by no means based on later inaccurate generalisations. It goes back to the years before he discovered his cardinal doctrine of justification by faith in the Pauline sense, and without the spiritual experience to which it testifies, this discovery would hardly have been possible.

Luther evidently tried his best to find a remedy in accordance with the received teaching and practice of the Church. He made sedulous use of the confessional and sought instruction and comfort from his confessor and his teachers. And not without effect for the time being at least. It is a mistake to assume that he derived no comfort or spiritual profit from his experience of the monastic life. He believed firmly, in spite of incidental doubts and misgivings, in the conventional piety, and, on his own testimony, he had his seasons of confidence in his own righteousness.[92] His confessor did his best to reassure him and not altogether in vain, though he sometimes got impatient with his oversensitiveness and bluntly rebuked him. " You are a fool," he once told him. " God is not angry with you, but you are angry with God." [93] He also speaks appreciatively of the help afforded him by his preceptor, to whom on one occasion he communicated his doubts about the efficacy of the Sacrament of Penance. " What dost thou, my son? Dost thou not know that the Lord Himself commands us to hope? " This was, indeed, a word in season. What he needed in these hours of depression was a more optimistic view of God and self. Such a view was not lacking in the devotional literature which he read and in the scholastic theology which he studied. Along with the retributive conception of God, some of the scholastics taught the hope of individual salvation on the ground of practical experience of God's grace, which justified the confidence that God would accomplish the work He had begun in the soul (*certitudo spei*).[94] Among those whose works Luther particularly studied, Biel taught the importance of personal faith (" particular faith ") in the sense of the hope, the confidence that God will ultimately accept the sinner.[95] It was with this " certitude of hope " that his preceptor sought to exorcise the pessimism and dejection which paralysed the will to believe.[96] " By this one word, ' commands,' " says

[92] " Tischreden," iii. 103. Ita ego fui præsumptuosissimus monachus justitiarius. Postquam missificassem et orassem, satis præsumptuosus videbar. See also " Werke," xxxviii. 147-148 ; xl., Pt. I., 137 ; xliv. 260 ; xlvii. 460 ; " Documente," 20, 36.

[93] " Tischreden," i. 47.

[94] See Seeberg, " Dogmen-Geschichte," iii. 430-432 (1913).

[95] Scheel, " Luther," ii. 151.

[96] Fides firmat intellectum, ne discredat, spes autem firmat affectum, ne diffidat, in the words of Bonaventura. See Seeberg, " Dogmen-Geschichte," iii. 431.

Luther, "I was so encouraged that I felt I could rely on absolution. Though I had often before heard it pronounced, yet, impeded by my foolish thoughts, I judged that I could have no confidence in it, but heard it as if it did not apply to me." [97]

Melanchthon, who says that he derived his information from Luther himself, also tells of these efforts to dispel his doubts by encouraging him to hope in his personal salvation. An old monk, he relates, often comforted him by emphasising personal faith in this sense and reminding him of the clause in the Creed, "I believe in the forgiveness of sins." He pointed out to him that the words were to be understood in a personal, and not merely in a general sense, and quoted one of St Bernard's sermons to this effect. Melanchthon adds that Luther was not only greatly comforted by such admonitions, but that he found in the words of St Bernard an insight into the Pauline doctrine of justification by faith. [98] It seems, however, very doubtful whether Melanchthon rightly understood the import of the incident to which Luther referred. Luther did not owe his discovery of the doctrine of justification by faith in the Pauline sense either to St Bernard or to one of his fellow-monks. In his Commentary on Romans he quotes the passage in question from St Bernard's sermon without any reference to the service rendered him by the aged monk in bringing it to his notice. Whilst he read Bernard's sermons in the monastery and appears to have derived a relative help for his troubled soul from his teaching, [99] this teaching appeared to him, afterwards at least, to lack consistency as far as the apprehension of the Gospel was concerned. [100] The incident of which Melanchthon speaks, seems, as Scheel believes, to have referred to the question of predestination, not to that of justification. What the old monk apparently did was to encourage him, in the midst of his perturbations over this dogma, to believe that he was personally among the number of the saved, in virtue

[97] "Documente," 38.
[98] "Vita," 159.
[99] See Müller, "Werdegang," 83 f.
[100] "Tischreden," i. 436 ; cf. "Werke," xlvi. 782.

of the remission of sin through Christ.[1] Certain it is that when Luther later in the " Table Talk " mentions his obligation to a certain Augustinian monk, the obligation had reference to this problem. " If," he warned him, " anyone wishes to think of predestination and does not consider Christ apart from these swathing bands, as He is set forth to us in His words, he must perforce fall into desperation." [2]

There can be no doubt, in view of these testimonies, that Luther did find at least a relative mitigation of his soul trouble in the mystic-evangelical element in mediæval thought, as represented by St Bernard and Gerson. That he was familiar with the writings of Bernard, Gerson, and Bonaventura, we know from his own testimony. His Commentary on the Psalms shows that he had read Bernard's sermons.[3] The writer to whom, in the period of his *Anfechtungen* in the monastery, he owed most was, however, not Bernard, but Gerson.[4] He rated Gerson most highly among all the doctors who have treated of this subject. It was not without reason, he says, that he was termed the *Doctor Consolatorius*.[5] He esteems him superior to even Augustine and Bernard, because, unlike them, he knows the temptations of the spirit (*de pusillanimitate spiritus*) and not merely those of an intellectual or bodily character. He teaches from experience, and therefore he found him most helpful in mitigating the haunting anxiety caused by a sensitive conscience and the dread of predestination, even although he did not, like Paul, understand how to counteract the fear of the law by the righteousness [6] of Christ. Gerson seems to have helped him by showing that distrust of self and all its works, humility and suffering constitute the condition of the operation of God's mercy

---

[1] " Luther," ii. 137-138.

[2] " Tischreden," iii. 521.

[3] Müller· (" Werdegang," 83) concludes from this fact that these sermons were to him a Vade Mecum in the monastery.

[4] Scheel does not attribute much influence to Gerson in this early period. Köhler also thinks that his influence only made itself felt later.

[5] " Tischreden," v. 213.

[6] *Ibid.*, i. 496 ; ii. 65.

and goodness. Only such does God save as turn to Him in their impotence, doubt, and fear.[7] William of Paris also contributed, though in a less degree (*aliquid*),[8] to console him in his spiritual misery. On the other hand, he could make nothing of Bonaventura's reasonings on the mystic union of the soul with Christ by means of the will and the intellect. He was unable by force of will and intellectual abstraction to reason himself out of his spiritual trouble into the higher plane of mystic speculation. " Bonaventura drove me frantic." [9]

The strange feature of his case was that, in spite of wise and friendly counsel, followed by intervals of relaxed tension and even seasons of self-satisfaction and exaltation, these fits of depression persistently recurred. This was the thing that seems to have perplexed his confessor and his teachers, who at times frankly avowed that they could not understand this chronic sinister experience.[10] Worse still, Luther himself did not know what was wrong with him. He did not realise that what was fundamentally wrong with him was the attempt to achieve his salvation by the legalist method after the monastic fashion. Like Paul he was striving to attain the highest moral and religious life in accordance with the conventional method, and the result was the same in both cases—the sense of failure and the misgiving and misery which this involves. Even Staupitz, who took a special interest in him, and to whom he gratefully acknowledges his obligations, was at times at a loss what to make of it.

His intimate intercourse with the Vicar-General of his Order seems to have begun in the autumn of 1508, when he was transferred from Erfurt to the Augustinian monastery at Wittenberg to continue his theological studies and to

---

[7] See the passages from the writings of Gerson, Bernard, and William of Paris, which Müller thinks proved serviceable to Luther. " Werde-gang," 77 f. ; see also Köhler, " Luther und die Kirchen-Geschichte," 301 f. *Cf.* Boehmer, " Luther im Lichte der neueren Forschung," 61-62 (5th edition, 1918).

[8] " Tischreden," ii. 65.

[9] *Ibid.*, 1. 302.

[10] " Documente," 24 ; " Tischreden," ii. 62.

lecture on Aristotle's Ethics [11] at the university, for which
the Emperor Maximilian, at the request of the Elector of
Saxony, had granted a charter of foundation in 1502.
Staupitz became the first Dean of the Theological Faculty
and, along with Martin Pollich, its first Rector, had given
the Elector the benefit of his counsel in its organisation.
Its constitution, which the jurist Christopher Scheurl recast
in 1508, and the courses of instruction were of the conventional mediæval type. The assumption that its foundation
was the outcome of a set policy in favour of the new culture
against the old scholastic system [12] seems to rest on no
substantial evidence, though humanist studies found a place in
its curriculum, and ultimately, with the advent of Melanchthon,
the university stood in the front rank as a centre of humanist
culture. The Elector's chief motive was to secure for the
electoral dominion the benefit of a territorial university, as
an offset to that of Leipzig in the Duchy of Saxony, not to
create a rival, on exclusively humanist lines, to the older
seats of the scholastic learning. Humanist sympathies were,
indeed, discernible on the part of some of the members of
the Arts Faculty, but the scholastic spirit and method at
first dominated the curriculum. Still less does there seem
to have been a set intention to introduce a distinctive
evangelical tendency into the Theological Faculty.[13] The
foundation of a Chair of Biblical Study does not necessarily
betoken a spirit of innovation in theology. Such instruction
was not unknown in other German universities, and the
Theological Faculty at Wittenberg professed the Scotist and
Thomist theology before Trutvetter came from Erfurt in
1507 to represent the Occamist school of thought.

As at Erfurt, the Augustinian monastery at Wittenberg
was closely connected with the university. The professorship of Scripture and the lectureship in Ethics were founded

[11] Melanchthon (" Vita," 160) and most of Luther's biographers
wrongly say that he lectured on the Physics. He lectured on the Physics
later to the monks of the Augustinian monastery at Wittenberg after
his final transference thither. Oergel, " Vom Jungen Luther," 110.

[12] Paulsen, " Geschichte des gelehrten Unterrichts," i. 108.

[13] So Oergel, " Vom Jungen Luther," 97. Scheel (" Luther," ii.
182 f.) contests this view.

by the Elector in connection with the monastery and formed part of the university curriculum. It was to this lectureship that Luther was called in October 1508. He thus became for a year the colleague of his Vicar-General, who occupied the Chair of Biblical Exegesis. Whether he was directed by Staupitz himself or by his Order to take upon himself this office is not clear.[14] According to Luther himself his transference from Erfurt to Wittenberg was the result of a " sudden " resolution, apparently on the part of his superiors, and may have been due to an urgent request for assistance on the part of Staupitz.[15] At all events it proved to be a momentous step in his early career, since it brought him into close touch with one who, on his own confession, exercised a marked influence on his early religious development. That Staupitz had already a particular interest in him and that his object in bringing him to Wittenberg was to help him in his spiritual conflict, as the biographers generally assert, is merely conjecture. He is supposed [16] to have been attracted by the pensive young monk during his visits as Vicar-General to the Erfurt monastery. He seems, however, to have been rarely at Erfurt during Luther's first years in the monastery, and what evidence there is tends to show that it was during the year 1508-09 that he first came into close contact with him.[17]

From Luther himself [18] we learn that this year was a very arduous one. He devoted himself with characteristic zeal to the preparation of his lectures, though he much preferred the study of theology to that of philosophy.[19] He attended, in addition, the theological courses in the university necessary for the degree of Biblical Bachelor

[14] Müller thinks that he was directed by a Chapter of his Order held at München in October 1508. This is only a conjecture. Melanchthon says that he was requested by Staupitz, " Vita," 160. But his knowledge of this episode is rather vague.

[15] Enders, i. 5.

[16] Oergel, " Vom Jungen Luther," 107-108, and others.

[17] Müller contends, on insufficient grounds, that Staupitz and Luther were not intimately acquainted before 1512, and that it was only after his second transfer to Wittenberg that their close relations commenced.

[18] Enders, i. 6.

[19] *Ibid.*, i. 6.

(*Baccalaureus Biblicus*) which he acquired in the spring of 1509, and which obliged him to lecture on a portion of Scripture, whilst continuing his instruction on Aristotle's Ethics. The study of the Sentences followed the taking of the degree of Bachelor, and in the autumn he had passed the prescribed test in this subject and was preparing to deliver his introductory lecture on the first book of the Sentences, when he was summoned to return to the Erfurt monastery.[20] Besides this strenuous intellectual work he had to perform the religious duties of his Order, and we can well believe that, as he wrote to his friend Braun, he had scarcely a moment to spare for correspondence.[21]

Luther gratefully acknowledged at a later time the spiritual profit which he derived from Staupitz.[22] The Vicar-General, though a protagonist of the strict observance of the Rule, was by no means a martinet in his dealings with his monks. As Luther in later years reminded him, he could tell a pleasant tale at meal times as well as edify his hearers with his more serious table talk.[23] He was quick to note the careworn face of the young lecturer and student of theology and would inquire across the table the cause of his depression.[24] In response to Luther's confession of his soul trouble he would tell him that such trials were divinely sent for his spiritual good. Luther thought of St Paul's thorn in the flesh and of the strength made perfect in weakness, and accepted the fatherly exhortation as the voice of the divine Paraclete.[25] In the confessional as well as in these familiar talks he undoubtedly derived enlightenment and comfort from his sagacious and kindly superior. In so far as his depression was the fruit of a too active imagination, he would tell him, as his Erfurt confessor had done, not to magnify every peccadillo into a transgression. When his torment was caused by brooding over the problem of predestination he would remind him of the wounds of

---

[20] Enders, i. 18, 23.
[21] *Ibid.*, i. 4-5.
[22] "Tischreden," i. 244; iv. 231. *Cf.* Enders, i. 196; iv. 231; xiv. 189.
[23] Jucundissimas et salutares fabulas tuas. Enders, i. 196.
[24] "Tischreden," i. 240.
[25] *Ibid.*, i. 240 ; *cf.* ii. 13.

Christ and tell him to view the divine decree in the light of the actual salvation available through Christ.[26]   It was the mystic-evangelical message of Bernard and Gerson, who found in the Cross the great reassurance in the face of doubt and trial, the guarantee of God's mercy and goodness. When he lamented the weakness of his will to achieve the highest good, he would comfort him with his own similar experience in the attempt to realise the life of evangelical perfection.   He seems, in fact, to have frankly acknowledged the futility of seeking to attain to the perfect love of God by the legalist method and told his penitent that he had ceased to keep up this pretence and thus try to deceive God. "Formerly," said he, " I confessed daily, and daily resolved that I would serve God perfectly.   Daily I failed until I determined to renounce the attempt to keep up this lie in the sight of God, and await the hour that God will meet me with His grace.   Otherwise it is all lost labour." [27]   The whole penitential practice was, he further pointed out, based on a mistaken principle.   Penitence ought to spring from the love of God and His righteousness, not to be regarded as the means of attaining them by penitential works.   This was an impossible undertaking and could only foster the sense of failure with resultant self-torment and misery.   The love of God is rather the beginning than the goal of true penitence.   " These words," Luther afterwards gratefully wrote to him, " stuck in me like a sharp arrow and I began to compare the word penitence (penance) with the scriptural passages which treat of repentance, and lo ! it became a most delightful exercise.   Everywhere the words were a joy to me.   They were so clearly favourable to this joyous meaning that, whereas before there was almost no word in Scripture bitterer to me than this word penitence, which I feigned in the presence of God and sought to express in a forced and fictitious love, now (*i.e.*, at the time of writing, May 1518) none has to me a sweeter and more pleasing sound." [28]   Though he did not at the time fully grasp all that this principle connoted and, as he adds, only learned

---

[26] " Tischreden," i. 512 ; ii. 227.
[27] *Ibid.*, ii. 665-666.   [28] Enders, i. 196-197.

the full meaning of the term with the aid of St Paul, it undoubtedly contributed materially to assuage the torment of conscience which the Sacrament of Penance had caused him. It was not without reason that he wrote long afterwards (1542), " If it had not been for the help of Dr Staupitz, I would have been submerged in the sea of doubt and been long since in hell." [29]

At the same time the mitigation of his spiritual trouble was only relative. To Staupitz, as he later wrote, he owed it that the light of the Gospel began to shine in the darkness of his heart. But it was only a beginning, and he did not owe to him the discovery of his doctrine of justification by faith. Staupitz, it must be remembered, parted company with Luther when this doctrine ultimately carried him into antagonism to the Church whose teaching he shared. Like his other confessors and teachers, he failed at times to understand what was wrong with him. Luther was searching for the certainty of acceptance with a righteous God, for the confidence that would stand the test of the retribution associated with the traditional conception of God as lawgiver and judge. His difficulty with the law and the divine righteousness in the juridical sense remained. To this problem Staupitz could only give the conventional solution, for he too believed in the Church's doctrine of merits. In this respect he was, therefore, no pioneer of the gospel of faith *versus* works, in which Luther ultimately found the solution of the problem of " a propitious God " for which he was seeking.[30] " I learned my theology not all at once," he says. " I had to search deeper and deeper, and to this my trials brought me in the end." [31] It is therefore premature to conclude with Seeberg [32] and Jundt that he had already in 1509, as the result of the teaching of Staupitz, discovered the Gospel.

The sadness which Staupitz had partially mitigated persisted, therefore, whenever this thought recurred. This was one of " the knotty points " (*die rechten Knotten*) which

---

[29] Enders, xiv. 189.   [30] " Tischreden," i. 240.   [31] *Ibid.*, i. 146.
[32] " Dogmen-Geschichte," iv. 68-69; *cf*. Jundt, 57-58. See also Strohl's criticism of Seeberg's view, " L'Évolution Religieuse de Luther," 120 f.

even Staupitz could not unravel. " I cannot understand
it," he would reply. "This," says Luther, "was a fine
kind of consolation. When I tried another confessor the
result was the same. To put it briefly, no confessor would
have anything to do with the matter. Then, thought I, no
one experiences this trouble but only you. And then I
felt like a dead man." [33]

[33] "Tischreden," i. 240 ; ii. 62, 403.

CHAPTER V

THE DISCOVERY OF THE GOSPEL (1509-1513)

I. LECTURER IN THEOLOGY AT ERFURT

ON his return from Wittenberg in the autumn of 1509, Luther had some difficulty in obtaining the degree of *Sententiarius* from the Erfurt Theological Faculty, which seems to have resented his association with the rival university.[1] The delay was not due, as Oergel[2] thinks, to his distaste for the theology of Lombardus and his consequent hesitation to acquire a title which obliged him to lecture on the Sentences—the standard text-book of the scholastic theology. Such an assumption is disproved by his own testimony. His letter to Braun in March 1509 shows that he preferred the study of theology, " which searches out the kernel of the nut and the marrow of the wheat and the bones," to that of philosophy.[3] In his lecture notes on the Sentences he expresses his deep appreciation of their author, and in his " Table Talk "[4] he repeatedly speaks of him as the master of theological method and the best of the exponents of the scholastic theology. He threw himself whole-heartedly into his task and took great pains in the preparation of his lectures. This is evident from the notes on the margin of the books which he used for this purpose. Happily these books ultimately found their way to the municipal library at Zwickau, and their discovery in 1889 has thrown light on his studies and his theological standpoint during the years (1909-11) in which he was occupied with the preparation and the delivery of these

[1] Enders, i. 23. Fui quidem a facultate vestra (Erfurt) cum omni difficultate admissus et susceptus.

[2] " Vom Jungen Luther," 114.

[3] Enders, i. 6.

[4] " Werke," ix. 29 ; " Tischreden," i. 85 ; ii. 515-517 ; iii. 542-543.

lectures.[5] From these marginal notes we learn farther that his studies were not confined to these books. They show a wide range of additional reading, including the works of Occam and his followers D'Ailly and Biel.[6] Nor did he limit his attention to the leading exponents of the theological school to which he himself belonged. He was more or less familiar with the writings of Scotus, Hugo of St Victor, and St Bernard.[7] With the writings of a number of the Fathers, besides Augustine, he seems to have had more than a second-hand acquaintance as his references to some of those of Chrysostom, Jerome, Ambrose, Hilary, Dionysius, Leo the Great, and Gregory the Great show. He rates the authority of Augustine very high,[8] though he tends to interpret him in the Occamist sense,[9] and later confesses that until he read his works on the Pelagian controversy he did not realise his superior merits, at least as an exegete, to Jerome.[10]

He shows an intimate knowledge of the Scriptures in the Vulgate version (*nostra translatio*) and appeals to it as the standard authority.[11] Another evidence of the conscientious labour bestowed on these lectures is the use made of the "Biblia cum Glossa," published at Basel in 1508, as

[5] These marginal notes have been edited by Buchwald in vol. ix. of the Weimar edition of his works (1893). They are not the actual lectures as delivered by him, which have not survived, but only the preparatory material of them. They consist of a collection of the minor works of Augustine (" Augustini Opuscula Plurima " in one volume), of the " De Civitate Dei " and the " De Trinitate," and of the " Sentences " of Lombard, which were available in the monastery library at Erfurt. Annotated copies of Anselm's " Opuscula " and Tauler's " Sermons " were also among the collection in the Zwickau library. But these notes belong to a later time. In the case of Augustine's " Opuscula " Luther himself has noted that he was utilising this volume in 1509. The notes on Augustine may indicate, as Neubauer asserts, that he also gave a course on Patristic before going on to lecture on the " Sentences." " Luthers Frühzeit," 111 (1917).

[6] "Werke," ix. 33, 34, 37, 40.   [7] *Ibid.*, ix. 12, 43, 69.

[8] *Ibid.*, ix. 39, maxime illustrissimo jubari et nunquam satis laudato Augustino.

[9] *Ibid.*, ix. 9.

[10] Enders, i. 65-64. See Scheel, " Luther," ii. 219-220.

[11] "Werke," ix. 63, 67.

well as the older Commentary of Nicolas of Lyra, in the interpretation of Scriptural passages.[12] He even has recourse to the original Hebrew text for the explanation of certain Old Testament words and passages and for this purpose uses the commentary of the mediæval Hebraist, Paul of Burgos, and the Hebrew grammar and dictionary of Reuchlin.[13] He evidently had at hand, too, the mediæval Greek manual known as the Catholicon, and inserts some Greek words in these marginal notes.[14] But his Hebrew at this stage was very rudimentary and his Greek purely ornamental. Apart from the passages in Reuchlin, he could probably make nothing of the Hebrew text. His knowledge of Greek seems not to have extended much beyond the alphabet, and his use of Greek terms apparently represents nothing more than a rather helpless tribute to the new Greek learning. Whilst he valued the Latin classics and shows familiarity with them,[15] he does not seem as yet to have had any practical appreciation for the critical humanist method, and his respect for the Vulgate was by no means affected by his friendship with humanists like Lang, whom he had known as a student at Erfurt and with whom he kept in touch, and with Lang's humanist friend Peter Eberbach.[16] His resources were still too scanty to provide him with the philological apparatus necessary to make him a competent or independent Bible critic. He could only read Justin Martyr in the translation of Pico Mirandola,[17] though the fact that he mentions the great Italian humanist does reveal an interest in humanist literature.

Within scholastic limits, however, he does exercise the critical faculty in quite a remarkable degree. His duty as lecturer was to examine the text of the Sentences word for word and to comment on the more difficult passages, and he sought to obtain a reliable text [18] by comparing the various editions of his author. His capability as a literary critic is evidenced by the conclusion at which he rightly

---

[12] "Werke," ix. 90.

[13] *Ibid.*, ix. 26, 33, 67 ; *cf.* Enders, ii. 379.

[14] *Ibid.*, ix. 25, 27, 68.

[15] *Ibid.*, ix. 6.

[16] Scheel, ii. 230-231.

[17] "Werke," ix. 27.

[18] *Ibid.*, ix. 67, etc.

arrives from a comparison of the style of a work ascribed to Augustine ("De Cognitione Veræ Vitæ") with that of his authentic writings, that it was not written by him.[19] On the other hand, he decided in favour of the Augustinian authorship of the "De Spiritu et Anima" by a comparison of its contents with passages in others of his works.[20] Whilst cherishing a profound admiration for his author and showing due respect towards the scholastic theologians and the Fathers, he permits himself to differ from them on occasion. He does not, for instance, share the view of Lombard on original sin and concupiscence.[21] He pronounces an opinion of Duns Scotus to be erroneous and very near to heresy,[22] and does not hesitate to criticise the theologians of his own school of thought.[23] He ventures to assert his own view on the procession of the Spirit from the Father and the Son against that of many distinguished doctors of the Church, and not only claims that he has Scripture on his side against their " human reasons," but boldly says with Paul, " If even an angel from heaven, i.e., a doctor of the Church, teaches otherwise, let him be anathema."[24] In such instances we have already a foretaste of the later Lutheran appeal to Scripture as the supreme authority and his self-assertive style in dealing with opponents. So, too, in the drastic language in which he defends his Order against the humanist Wimpfeling, he already shows a tendency not to measure his words against an obnoxious adversary. He roundly calls him " a garrulous barker and envious detractor of the glory of the Augustinians, who needs the application of the surgeon's knife to open his mole's eyes ! "[25] " A pig can never teach Minerva " is another temperamental saying in reference to those who would pit their human wisdom against theology,[26] though this saying was a current one in the schools and is not peculiar to Luther. He can evidently with difficulty restrain an impulsive and cutting retort when his feelings are rasped. Such outbursts are, however, few in number and they were by no means

---

[19] "Werke," ix. 6.
[20] Ibid., ix. 14.
[21] Ibid., ix. 75.
[22] Ibid., ix. 43.
[23] Ibid., ix. 54.
[24] Ibid., ix. 46.
[25] Ibid., ix. 12.
[26] Ibid., ix. 65.

exceptional in scholastic controversy. Personalities were in fact part of the controversial game in those days of scholastic disputation, and these specimens hardly justify the assertions of later Roman Catholic opponents (Cochlaeus, Oldecop, Dungersheim) that as a young monk he was given to contention and quarrelling. These seem to be part of the malicious gossip that gathered round Luther in his later conflict with Rome and are not to be taken very seriously. They are, in fact, contradicted by other contemporary testimonies to his exemplary conduct as a monk.[27] Generally speaking, the style of these notes is didactic and matter of fact, whilst enlivened by occasional flashes of strong feeling. Both the manner and the matter of the lectures are of the conventional scholastic type. They show no material departure from the scholastic method and the scholastic theology. Luther is a keen and painstaking exponent of the Occamist school of thought, and if he shows an occasional tendency to independent judgment, he maintains his respect for the traditional teaching in which he had been nurtured.[28]

As an Occamist, he emphasises faith as against reason, revelation as against philosophy. But this emphasis is not to be regarded as an anticipation of his later distinctive teaching on saving faith. It is his tribute to the Occamist principle which, in reaction from the scholastic method of seeking by the aid of the logic and philosophy of Aristotle to prove the truth of Christian doctrine by reason, taught that revelation is the sole source of theological truth and that faith is the indispensable condition of its authority.[29] Hence the emphatic expression of his dissent from the philosophising doctors and their mentor Aristotle,[30] though as a budding theologian he by no means eschews the conventional scholastic disputation, and seems to tackle with zest the current problems of the schools. " Philosophy," he says with reference to the doctrine of the generation of the Son, " has brought forth many monstrosities (*multa monstra*), and but for it we should easily solve many things which are now

[27] See Grisar, " Luther," i. 22, who, however, is too inclined to believe the gossip of these later opponents.

[28] " Werke," ix. 39, 65 ; *cf.* 18.

[29] *Ibid.*, ix. 92.

[30] *Ibid.*, ix. 24, 44.

impossible of solution." [31] The philosophers dispute about words and lose themselves in a labyrinth of error.[32] These errors, he adds contemptuously, are concocted out of " the dregs of philosophy." [33] In this mood Aristotle is " a rancid philosopher," " a chatterer " (*fabulator*),[34] and he falls foul of those who have the impudence by their sophistries to bring him into accord with the Catholic faith.[35] Only the Word of God, not philosophy, can teach us concerning the things of God, and the foolishness of the Gospel is far superior to the wisdom of the world.[36] Whatever is added to faith is " a figment of man," the mere smoke of earth that impedes the light of heaven, and is the cause of so much diversity of opinion among the doctors.[37] The distinction between the natural and the supernatural is for him absolute. " What nature has not been able to understand, the truth of Scripture and faith can attain." With the word in hand, he will defy, yea anathematise all the doctors of the Church.[38] Already, even as an Occamist, the infallible believer in the word in revelation *versus* philosophy is on the way. Philosophy can at most take a very modest and humble place beside theology, and to this extent he is willing to make use of its service. He does, in fact, himself philosophise all through these notes, though evidently on the understanding that the Occamist position is recognised, and as the result of his reflection on the doctrine of transubstantiation, for instance, he was already, under the influence of D'Ailly's teaching, tending towards a more rational view of the Real Presence in this sacrament.[39] The Realists, as the opponents of his school, are teachers of error.[40] Porphyry and the Neoplatonists are accordingly subjected to energetic criticism, and Augustine, in spite of his Neoplatonism, is made to side with Occam. As against the subtleties of the scholastic theology, there was no little justification for this onslaught

[31] " Werke," ix. 57.

[32] *Ibid.*, ix. 24, 29.

[33] *Ibid.*, ix. 16, 45.

[34] *Ibid.*, ix. 23, 43.

[35] *Ibid.*, ix. 23, 27.

[36] *Ibid.*, ix. 29, 56.

[37] *Ibid.*, ix. 62, 65.

[38] *Ibid.*, ix. 46.

[39] He later recalls this fact in the " De Captivitate Babylonica." " Werke," vi. 508.

[40] IX. 21, 83 ; *cf.* 55.

in favour of faith on what was deemed philosophy in the Middle Age. But it savours too much of the Occamist partisan. It is also to a certain extent the fruit of imperfect knowledge, and the depreciation of reason in itself as the source of the higher knowledge, even in theology, is distinctly unenlightened.

The notes on the Sentences afford at least a passing glimpse of the theology which Luther professed as lecturer. It is difficult to obtain from them an exact idea of his theological position at this period and the specialists are by no means agreed on the subject. Scheel contends that they contain substantially little more than the commonplaces of the Occamist school to which he belonged, and that they show little or no indication of his later specific evangelical teaching.[41] Loofs [42] and Holl [43] are inclined to question this view to a certain extent. Seeberg [44] and Müller [45] strongly contest it and are of opinion that not only had he already diverged in important respects from the Occamist teaching, but had essentially grasped, though not developed, his distinctive principle of justification by faith. To me it seems that the evidence tends largely to support the contention of Scheel, though he has expressed it rather too positively and seems to ignore too much the evidence on the other side. The lecturer on the Sentences is substantially an exponent of the Occamist theology in which he had been trained, whilst appreciating, and to a certain extent striving to assimilate, that of Lombardus and Augustine, whom the Master of the Sentences professed to follow. The works of Augustine had begun to influence his theological thinking, as the notes on these works and the frequent citations from them in the course of his lectures show. At most, however, he seeks to combine his teaching with that of his own Occamist teachers, and there is as yet no radical breach between them and their disciple. He shares, for instance, the current Occamist distinction between

[41] " Luther," ii. 235 f., and " Entwicklung Luthers " (" Schriften des Vereins für Reformations-Geschichte," 1909-10), 125 f.

[42] " Leitfaden," 690-691.

[43] " Gesammelte Aufsätze," i. 159 f.

[44] " Dogmen-Geschichte," iv. 69-71.   [45] " Werdegang," 106 f.

faith as intellectual assent, mere belief (*fides acquisita*, or *informis*, acquired by an act of the intellect) [46] and infused faith, which is the gift of supernatural grace and, united with love and hope, justifies the sinner, enables him to appear worthy in the sight of God.[47] To attain this worthiness is the true way of salvation. Justification is still conceived in the conventional sense of faith working by love.[48] Whilst noticing various interpretations of Romans i. 17 he is still ignorant of the later evangelical signification of "the righteousness of God," and limits his comment merely to the words "from faith to faith." [49] Similarly, with the Occamists he questions the Thomist notion of a supernatural disposition (*habitus*) infused into the essence of the soul as an unwarrantable metaphysical assumption, borrowed from Aristotle. Justifying grace, which operates love, is, he holds with Lombard, against the Aristotelians, inspired or infused by the Holy Spirit, and is not a metaphysical quality.[50] He farther shares the Occamist doctrine of merits *de congruo*. Whilst ascribing to grace all merits in the sight of God,[51] and holding with Augustine and Lombard that God in the justification of the sinner crowns only His own gifts,[52] he recognises the freedom of the will to do the good and thus acquire a relative merit (*meritum de congruo*). The will is free [53] to choose the good, though it is naturally inclined to evil in virtue of the sinful tendency (concupiscence) due to the fall, which exercises a tyranny (*tyrannus*) over human nature and makes it difficult, nay impossible without grace (*per se*), to do the good.[54] Occamist is also his doctrine of original sin which, he holds, in opposition to the Master of the Sentences, consists not in concupiscence, but in the loss of original righteousness, involving guilt (*culpa*) which is taken away in baptism, whilst concupiscence remains in the struggle of the flesh and the spirit, as the punishment (*pœna*) of original sin.[55]

---

[46] "Werke," ix. 90, 92.
[47] *Ibid.*, ix. 90, 91.
[48] *Ibid.*, ix. 72.
[49] *Ibid.*, ix. 90.
[50] *Ibid.*, ix. 42-43.
[51] Totum deo tribuendum, ix. 71.
[52] *Ibid.*, ix. 72.
[53] *Ibid.*, ix. 31.
[54] *Ibid.*, xi. 71, 73. Sed nos faciliter malum et difficulter bonum.
[55] *Ibid.*, ix. 73 f.

In the notes on this subject, the keen sense of sin, the struggle with "the law of the members," the emphasis on prevenient grace and the dependence of weak human nature on its operation in counteracting the power of sin seem to reflect the teaching of Augustine rather than the Occamists, though he does not yet share Augustine's conception of irresistible grace.[56] The quest of a gracious God, the problem of justification in the face of the divine righteousness does not, indeed, find explicit expression. But the keen consciousness of sin, the sensitive conscience, the high ideal of the moral and religious life which ultimately led to his specific doctrine of justification are already discernible,[57] and the reference to Christ as " our life, our righteousness, and our resurrection through faith in His incarnation "[58] seems to show that he was already concerning himself with this train of thought, even if he had not yet apprehended it in the later evangelical sense.   There is at least a half conscious departure from Occamism in this respect in the notes on Augustine and on Lombard, who professed to follow him as his master.   The independent expression of his religious aspirations is already beginning to make itself felt, tentatively at least, and the tendency to test and criticise in accordance with these aspirations might ultimately lead to startling results.   Even at this early period Luther bids fair to break new ground in religion and at the same time make history.   Otherwise, however, there is little trace of his personal religious experience in these notes.   According to his later retrospective testimony he had been during these years passing through a soul-searching conflict in his quest for a gracious God.   Of this conflict there is no explicit sign.   The reason seems to be that he had as yet discovered no definite and distinctive solution of the problem of his personal salvation that would have led him to reject the theology which it was his business as lecturer to expound, and in which these notes show that he professed belief.   He does not, in fact, seem aware that

---

[56] Gratia non necessitat, sed inclinat. " Werke," ix. 62.

[57] On this subject see Holl, " Gesammelte Aufsätze," i. 160 f.

[58] " Werke," ix. 17, 18. See Loofs, " Leitfaden," 691, and Hirsch, " Initium Theologiæ Lutheri in Festschrift für Kaftan," 160.

there was any other solution, because he has not learned to understand Paul in any other than the traditional sense. So long as he remained an Occamist in theology these notes would naturally reflect the belief of his school. Moreover, an official course of lectures on a received text-book was hardly fitted for the intrusion of personal religious difficulties, which were more in place in the confessional than in the lecture room. The only echo of them is the emphasis on the struggle of the flesh and the spirit and the keen consciousness of the power of sin—the law of the members.

II. THE MISSION TO ROME

During this period Luther was not only busied with his lectures as *Sententiarius*. He was employed by his brethren in representing the interests of the monastery in the negotiations for a combination of the Observantine with the Conventual section of the Augustinians in the province of Saxony and Thuringia. As Vicar-General, Staupitz had zealously furthered this project in association with the General of the Order at Rome, and in September 1510 it was formally sanctioned by a Bull of Union.[59] It aroused the opposition of the Erfurt monastery and Luther was dispatched along with Nathin to represent its objections to the Archbishop of Magdeburg through the Provost of the Cathedral at Halle, Adolf of Anhalt. In this affair Luther was thus arrayed in opposition to his Vicar-General and patron, Staupitz, against the union scheme in behalf of the stricter minority of the Observantine section, which resisted any association with the Conventuals. The deputation to Halle seems to have been ineffective and the Erfurt monastery thereupon resolved to make representations to the General of the Order at Rome on the subject. With this mission it entrusted Luther and another monk in the

[59] The Bull was drawn up and promulgated by the papal legate in Germany in December 1507, but not formally put in force by Staupitz till September 1510. It is given by Böhmer, " Luther's Romfahrt," 161 f.

late autumn of 1510.[60] As a zealous Observant, the task
of championing the more rigorous minority seems to have
been ardently espoused by Luther. It was all the more
welcome inasmuch as he was eager to visit the holy city
and earn the spiritual benefit to be derived from it. He
wished, he says later, to make a general confession at its
shrines of all his sins from his youth onwards, as he had
already done twice at Erfurt.[61]

On coming in view of Rome he dropped on his knees
and devoutly apostrophised " the holy city rendered sacred
by the blood of the martyrs." Of the ancient Rome only
the ruins remained, and the Rome which he saluted was
the late mediæval city, with its narrow, unwholesome
streets clustering near the Vatican, and was as yet only
being tentatively transformed by the influence of the
Renaissance. As the capital of Christendom and the focus
of a great tradition, it was invested with a prestige which
exercised an overwhelming spell over the devoted pilgrim.
But the reality corresponded ill to the ideal of the pious
imagination. A large part of the ancient city was a
melancholy waste. Whilst containing many churches and
monasteries, the Rome of the beginning of the sixteenth
century did not number more than 40,000 inhabitants and
was ill-governed, ill-policed, and not too secure a place of
residence. Under the rule of Julius II. and his immediate
predecessors its moral and religious reputation was very
low. It was rather the centre of a secularised ecclesiasticism
than of anything like real religion, with its swarm of corrupt
papal officials and lax Church dignitaries. The ecclesiastical
intrigue and self-seeking of Christendom were focused in
the curia, where the oppressive and sordid fiscal and
administrative system of the Church had its headquarters.
Pope Julius was more a politician and a soldier than a chief
pastor, and was more concerned in aggrandising his worldly
power by the Machiavelian statecraft of the time than
exemplifying the spirit of Christ. The chief business of
the city was that of finance which flourished in connection

[60] This seems to be the correct date, rather than the autumn of 1509
or 1511. See Scheel, ii. 415-416.   [61] " Tischreden," iii. 432.

with the papal fisc, and it is significant of the mercenary spirit of the capital of western Christendom that banking and its accessories were so distinctive a feature of the seat of the papal government. Its moral condition was deplorable. The courtesan and the prostitute abounded. Luther must have rubbed his eyes over this spectacle. " I would not," he said later, " have missed being in Rome for any amount of money. Had I not seen it with my own eyes, I would not have believed it. For there is there so great and shocking impiety and wickedness. There neither God nor man, neither sin nor shame is regarded." [62] No less shocked was he by the state of religion. " At Rome I found many very unlearned persons " (among the priests).[63] Many of them did not understand the Latin language.[64] He was pained by the irreverent formalism of the services and the unabashed scepticism that underlay much of it. The priests hurried through the Mass, some of them making a mockery of the solemn rite, whilst the young and devout monk from Erfurt shuddered at their hypocrisy and impiety.[65] He himself celebrated Mass frequently and his conscientious exactitude so bored them that they would tell him to hurry up and have done with it. The pomp, luxury, and simony of the cardinals and other high dignitaries, who appropriated and misspent the revenues of the Church to the utter detriment of religion, shocked him.[66] Some of them were openly addicted to sensual vice.[67] The personal impressions which are reflected in some of these and other passages of his later writings evidently stamped themselves deep on his memory. They are also discernible in the sustained and scathing indictment of papal Rome in the " Address to the German Nobility " in 1520.[68] They are by no means peculiar to Luther, who was only giving expression to the feeling current among all serious-minded observers of the condition of things at Rome. He quotes, in fact, the

[62] " Tischreden," iii. 451-452. For details on the deplorable condition of Rome at this period see Böhmer, " Romfahrt," 99 f.
[63] Ibid., iii. 451-452.   [64] Ibid., iv. 193.
[65] Ibid., iii. 313 ; " Werke," xxxviii. 212.
[66] " Werke," vii. 729 ; cf. 732 and xliii. 421 ; " Römerbrief," ii. 302.
[67] " Werke," xliii. 57.   [68] Ibid., vi.

saying of Cardinal Bembo, that in Rome were to be found the dregs of the whole world. He refers, too, to the denunciations of Ægidius, the General of his own Order at the time of his visit, of Ludwig the Minorite, and others, and quotes the current distich, " If you wish to live piously, depart from Rome. There, everything is allowed except to be virtuous." [69] It is certain that these impressions were not the fruit of mere fault-finding, for Luther was and remained for years to come a devout son of the Church and subject of the Pope. His own testimony on this point is decisive. [70]

Oldecop professes to know that Luther learned Hebrew from a Jew at Rome, and being " a wild young blood," hit upon the idea of laying aside the monk's cowl and devoting himself to study for ten years. To this end he petitioned the Pope, who rejected his crave. [71] This malevolent gossip, whose author otherwise makes wholly unfounded statements, needs no refutation, though it does duty in Grisar's work [72] as historic evidence. Luther spent only a few weeks in Rome (December 1510 to January 1511) and his time was taken up with the business of his Order and with the pious duty of visiting, praying, and saying Masses at the shrines of the apostles and saints. [73] He tells us that he did not fail to take advantage of the opportunity to gain the benefit of the grace to be derived from this devotion. He ran like a fanatic from one church to another in the hunt for the indulgences applicable to this life and the next, which were thus obtainable. [74] As an ardent monk, his main interest in Rome was naturally the religious one, and neither here nor at Florence does he seem to have been much impressed by the architectural and artistic splendours of Italy. His outlook was the limited one of the devotee, to whom religion is everything. He shared the superstitious reverence for the relics of the saints and the

---

[69] " Tischreden," iii. 345.
[70] See, for instance, " Werke," i. 69 ; ii. 72-73.
[71] " Documente," 5-6.
[72] " Luther," i. 35-36.
[73] " Tischreden," iii. 434-435.
[74] " Werke," xxxi. 1, 226 ; " Documente," 43.

credulity which it fostered, though he learned later to criticise it in no measured terms.[75] The Roman churches were rich in these fabulous remains. In the Catacombs, where " many hundred thousands of martyrs " [76] had found a resting place, he found an additional stimulus to his piety. He took advantage, too, of the chance to obtain the advantage of indulgence for others. The wealth of grace was available for those in purgatory, and so convinced was he of the reality of this privilege that " he was truly sorry that his father and mother still lived, for now he could have got them safely out of purgatory with his Masses." [77] He could do this service for his grandfather at least, and he tells us that for this purpose he climbed the *Scala Sancta* at the Lateran, saying a Paternoster at each step. It was only when he arrived at the top that the doubt occurred to him, " Who knows whether it is true ? " [78] Even the plenitude of grace, which Rome was supposed to impart, could evidently not prevent the recurrence of the misgivings which had haunted him in the Erfurt monastery. This experience must have brought home to him the fact that something was still lacking in his quest for a gracious God.

He must have lost some illusions at Rome. But it was only later, under the influence of the breach with the Pope, that he became fully conscious of the fact. " Whoever went to Rome and brought money with him obtained the forgiveness of sins. I, like a fool, carried onions there and brought back garlic." [79] Among his disappointments was the rejection of the petition of which he was, along with another monk, the bearer. The failure of his mission did

[75] " Werke," xlvii. 816-817.   [76] *Ibid.*, ii. 72.
[77] *Ibid.*, xxxi. 1, 226 ; " Documente," 43.
[78] Luther's account occurs in a sermon of 15th September 1545. The discovery of this version of the incident effectively disposes of the story related by his son Paul to the effect that, whilst he was ascending the steps, the words of Habakkuk ii. 4, " The just shall live by faith," sounded in his ear, and that he then discovered the Gospel according to Paul. " Documente," 2. The son was only eleven years old, and though he says that he had the story from his father, he must have misunderstood what Luther said. Luther's own version of the incident as given above is decisive.
[79] " Werke," xlvii. 392.

not, however, betoken the defeat of the party he represented ; for Staupitz, in view of the opposition to his policy within the Observantine section of the Order, erelong (1512) gave up the union project and thereby put an end to the controversy.[80]

Before its conclusion Luther, probably in the late autumn of 1511, had betaken himself once more to the monastery at Wittenberg. The accommodating policy of Staupitz, who was prepared to abandon the union, seems to have convinced him of the inadvisability of prolonging the quarrel and to have alienated him from the recalcitrant majority of the Erfurt brethren. His friend Lang, who had also become a monk, shared his view, and the friction which ensued sufficiently explains their resolve to get themselves transferred by Staupitz to Wittenberg, without ascribing, with Grisar, ulterior motives for this step. The fact seems to have been that the controversy had become by this time largely an academic one, and that Luther had good reason to dissent from the meticulous spirit of the majority of his brethren at Erfurt. What Cochlaeus calls "his desertion to Staupitz"[81] rests on the later gossip of some of his former fellow-monks, and Grisar's ascription of ambitious motives is purely gratuitous.[82] In view of Staupitz's conciliatory attitude, there was very little to fight about, and Luther appears to have become impatient of these internal bickerings at Erfurt and to have sought a more congenial environment in the Wittenberg monastery.[83]

His transference evidently did not impair his reputation outside Erfurt, for at a meeting of the Order at Cologne in May 1512, at which he was present along with Staupitz, he was nominated sub-prior of the monastery at Wittenberg and directed to prepare himself for the theological doctorate.[84] This official disposition was evidently due to Staupitz, who bore him no grudge for his former opposition to his union

[80] Böhmer, "Romfahrt," 60 f.
[81] Ad Staupitium suum defecisse.
[82] "Luther," i. 38.
[83] See Böhmer, "Romfahrt," 64 f. ; Scheel, "Luther," ii. 302 f.
[84] Enders, i. 7 ; cf. "Tischreden," iii. 611, where he speaks of his visit to Cologne.

policy and, in view of his zeal and ability, had destined him to be his successor in the Chair of Biblical Literature in the university. He was by no means happy at the prospect of this promotion and it was only with the utmost reluctance, and in deference to the insistence of his superior, that he gave way.[85] Instead of being actuated by ambition, as Grisar would have us believe, it is clear from the evidence of his own letters at the time, as well as his later declarations, that he shrank from the responsibility which the doctorate and the professorship involved.[86] Equally reluctant was he to assume the office of preacher which the degree of doctor also involved. Once more Staupitz was inexorable in spite of the fifteen reasons which he adduced to the contrary. The Vicar-General told him that he also had at first shrunk from the ordeal of holding forth in the pulpit, and made fun of his plea that this ordeal would kill him in three months' time. " In God's name, then, be it so. Our Lord God has very important business on hand in heaven and has great need of you up there." Therewith he laughed him into the pulpit of the refectory of the monastery, where he gave his first trial sermons.[87]

On the 4th of October (1512) he was admitted to the degree of Licentiate in Theology and a fortnight later graduated as Master and Doctor, Andreas Bodenstein von Karlstadt, the Dean of the Theological Faculty, officiating as Promoter, and the Elector himself, at Staupitz's instigation, providing the fifty gulden in payment of the graduation fees.[88] On the 22nd he was admitted a member of the Senatus Academicus. The Erfurt brethren, whom he had invited to the ceremony, did not respond to the invitation. They still resented his transference to Wittenberg and they

---

[85] Enders, i. 24.

[86] Ibid., i. 7-8, 24 ; " Tischreden," ii. 379 ; iv. 13, 129-130. Multi stupebunt meum doctoratum anno ætatis meæ 28 compulsum a Staupitio.

[87] " Tischreden," iii. 187-188.

[88] Luther's receipt for the money has been preserved and disposes of the story that Staupitz had taken the sum out of a fund destined for the education of a monk of the Nürnberg monastery, and thus defrauded the monk of this benefaction. See Scheel, ii. 431. This is only one of the many inventions of Luther's enemies relative to the earlier period of his life.

regarded his promotion to the doctorate in another university as an aggravation of his offence. His old teacher Nathin accused him of breaking his oath of allegiance to the Erfurt Theological Faculty. In the course of an acrimonious correspondence, of which only two letters have survived, Luther denied that he had taken such an oath as would have bound him to graduate doctor at Erfurt and have justified the reproaches of his old teacher. He had acted in good faith and had only allowed himself to become a candidate for the Wittenberg doctorate under pressure from his superior. If he had been aware that he was under an obligation to graduate at Erfurt, he would have been in a position to adduce this obligation as an insuperable reason for withstanding Staupitz's unwelcome proposal. In these circumstances the Erfurt Faculty, to which he had in his letter of invitation given notice of his intention to graduate, was blameworthy in not apprising him of their claim on him. Ultimately he apologised for any offence of which he had unwittingly been guilty and begged the Faculty to forgive whatever he had unwittingly done amiss. The correspondence proves rather the ill-will of the Erfurt brethren, especially of Nathin, towards him than any intention on his part to slight his old university, to which with evident sincerity he expresses his respect and gratitude.[89]

III. The Great Illumination

The doctorate was the mediæval hall-mark of his proficiency to expound the Scriptures. The study of the Bible had formed an integral part of his theological course, even if it was overshadowed by that of the scholastic theology. It was, theoretically at least, the standard authority, and to the Occamist school in particular revelation was the grand source of theological truth. Luther did not need to become an evangelical reformer to value it as the highest source of truth. Its interpretation was, however,

[89] Enders, i. 17-19, 23-25.

conditioned by the authority of the Church and the accumu-
lated tradition which the Church sanctioned, and only on
this condition was he at liberty to expound it. At this
stage he could conscientiously subject himself to this
condition, which his oath as doctor bound him to respect.
The day might come when, as the result of his quest for a
gracious God, conscience might drive him to view his
obligation in a different light.

On his own testimony, he had not yet made the great
discovery that radically affected his religious outlook. He
later tells us explicitly that when he became a doctor he
was ignorant of the Gospel in the Pauline sense.[90] He
was still haunted by the thought of God's righteousness,
still impelled by the striving to attain by his good works
the confidence of his acceptance with God.[91] Staupitz had
lessened his difficulties with the Sacrament of Penance.
But he had not essentially solved for him the problem of
his relation to God in the face of the divine justice or
righteousness, which involved the idea of retribution for
actual sin. For the solution of this problem he was still
searching after he became doctor of theology and professor
of the sacred Word. Böhmer concluded from the reference
to the cardinal passage in Romans i. 16-17, in the notes on
Lombard, that he had already made his great discovery
during his first sojourn at Wittenberg in 1508-09.[92] But
there is nothing in the notes on this passage to show that
he had hit on his later characteristic interpretation of it,
and in the fifth edition of his " Luther " Böhmer discarded
his earlier inference.[93] Seeberg, on the contrary, still,
though for different reasons, prefers the earlier date. He
ascribes his enlightenment to the influence of Staupitz,
who during his first sojourn at Wittenberg had explained to
him the true significance of repentance. He assumes that
this explanation must have led him to the apprehension of
Romans i. 17 in the Pauline sense.[94] The conclusion by

---

[90] " Werke," xlv. 86.   [91] Enders, i. 29.
[92] " Luther im Lichte der neueren Forschung," 47, second edition.
[93] *Ibid.*, 40.
[94] " Dogmen-Geschichte," iv. 62 f.

no means necessarily follows, and the notes on Lombard certainly do not tend to warrant it. Luther nowhere ascribes to Staupitz, who shared the traditional conception of the divine righteousness, his new insight into the Pauline teaching on the subject. Moreover, it is rather far-fetched to explain away Luther's assertion that when he became a doctor (*i.e.*, October 1512) he was still ignorant of the Gospel, by saying that the term doctor means, in this instance, an academic teacher, not the doctor's degree, and refers to the commencement of his academic teaching in 1508-09.[95] O. Ritschl also connects the new insight into the passage in Romans i. with the discussions with Staupitz in 1508-09.[96] But the reasons he gives for this conclusion are likewise only inferential and are equally unconvincing. Grisar, on the other hand, founding on the preface written by Luther to his works in 1545, puts it as late as 1519.[97] In this preface he tells us [98] that in this year he began a second course on the Psalms, after he had become more expert as an exegete through his previous expositions of the Epistles to the Romans, Galatians, and Hebrews, and the Psalms. He then refers to the fact that he had previously been seized with the ardent desire to understand the teaching of Paul, but that the words " righteousness of God " in Romans i. 17 had long been an obstacle to such an understanding, and that it was only after long meditation that he began to perceive the true meaning of the passage. He does not, however, say that the discovery took place in the year in which he returned to the exposition of the Psalms, *i.e.*, 1519. The mention of this second exposition carries his mind back to his previous courses on the Pauline epistles, and this again recalls the difficulty he had once experienced in understanding Paul, which evidently lay still farther back. What he says on this subject is evidently a reminiscent parenthesis which refers, not to the year 1519, in which he began his second course on the Psalms, but to the absorbing quest for the true

---

[95] " Dogmen-Geschichte," iv. 71.

[96] " Dogmen-Geschichte des Protestantismus," ii. 9 f.

[97] " Luther," i. 374. What he discovered was, according to Grisar, the assurance of salvation.   [98] " Documente," 16-18.

meaning of the passage in Romans i., which preceded not
only it, but his previous courses on the Epistles and the
Psalms. He is not concerned to give the exact date of
the discovery in which this quest had ended, and merely
adds that, by this discovery and his subsequent experience
as an exegete, he was better fitted to expound the Psalms a
second time. Grisar's conclusion that it did not take place
before 1519 is thus due to a misapprehension of the source
on which he founds it.[99]

In other passages of his writings Luther frequently
referred to the subject. Though he does not in any of
them give the exact date of this experience, he explicitly
says that it took place in the room in the tower of the
monastery at Wittenberg, which served as his study, after
long and intense meditation. " The meaning of these
words (*justitia Dei*)," he tells us in several passages of the
" Table Talk," " the Holy Spirit imparted to me in this
tower." [100] It was only, however, as he further tells us in
the preface to the 1545 edition of his works, after he had
spent days and nights (evidently over a lengthy period) in
intense meditation on the passage in Romans i. that " by
the mercy of God " this sudden insight came to him. In
October 1512, when he took his doctor's degree, he was

[99] Scheel, whilst rejecting Grisar's conclusion, thinks that Luther's
memory was at fault and that he confused his second with his first exposition of the Psalms, ii. 436. This is highly improbable. Loofs shares his
opinion (" Leitfaden," 689). The explanation given in the text seems
to me to be the true one, and is supported by Seeberg, " Dogmen-
Geschichte," iv. 67-68, and Böhmer, " Luther," 38-39, though Seeberg
thinks that he made his discovery as early as 1508-09. Holl also concludes that the discovery must have preceded the first exposition of the
Psalms and places it between the summer of 1511 and the spring of
1513, " Aufsätze," i. 162-163. Hirsch (" Initium Theologiæ Lutheri,"
160) accepts the year 1513, whilst holding that he had already at an
earlier period an inkling of what he then fully grasped. Müller, on
questionable grounds, concludes that he only made his discovery when
preparing his lectures on the Epistle to the Romans at the end of 1514,
" Werdegang," 128-130.

[100] " Tischreden," iii. 228. Cum semel in hac turri et hypocausta
specularer de istis vocabulis ete, die schrift hat mir der Heilige Geist in
diesem Thurm offenbaret. *Cf.* ii. 177 ; iv. 72-73 ; v. 26 ; " Werke,"
xliii. 537 ; xliv. 485-486.

still engaged in the absorbing quest, for by his own testimony this illumination had not yet dawned on him. Before the autumn of 1512 the evidence does not warrant us in placing the incident. This is the *terminus a quo* for what, in speaking of this illumination in the 1545 preface, he calls " his spiritual rebirth," " his entrance into paradise through the open gateway " of this new insight.[1] On the other hand, his first course on the Psalms, which he began in the summer of 1513,[2] furnishes explicit evidence that he was already, before its commencement, in possession of this new insight. This is the *terminus ad quem*. It must, therefore, have taken place in the interval between the autumn of 1512 and the summer of 1513.

His great difficulty had been the retributive conception of God, which the phrase " righteousness, or justice of God " implied. Hitherto, as he tells us in the 1545 preface, he had been accustomed to conceive of the justice or righteousness of God in the sense in which it was used in the schools, *i.e.*, in the philosophic sense (*philosophice*) as " the active justice (*justitia activa*) by which God is just and punishes sinners and unjust persons." [3] There can be no doubt that this was the usual, if not the only, sense in which the term was used by the scholastic theologians,[4] and that it was the one that had hitherto haunted Luther's mind and sensitive conscience. In the mediæval commentaries of Lyra and others on the passage in Romans i. the righteousness of God was indeed interpreted in the sense of the righteousness by which God justifies the sinner (in the mediæval sense of justification), and the notes on the Sentences of Lombard [5] show that Luther had

---

[1] Hic me prorsus renatum sensi esse et apertis portis in ipsum paradisum intrasse. " Documente," 17.

[2] Böhmer, " Romfahrt," 14.

[3] " Documente," 17. Usu et consuetudine omnium doctorum doctus eram philosophice intelligere.

[4] Müller, " Werdegang," 130 ; Seeberg, iv. 67.

[5] " Werke," ix. 90. Denifle (" Luther und Lutherthum," 388) attempts to discredit Luther's account of his discovery of the true meaning of God's righteousness in the Gospel in Romans i. 17, by adducing a passage in Luther's Commentary on Genesis in which he says that all the doctors, with the exception of Augustine, had interpreted Romans i. 17

read Lyra's comment on the passage, though he does not remark on the term "righteousness," but confines his attention to the phrase "from faith to faith." Obsessed by the thought of God's righteousness in the philosophical or active sense of His punitive justice, this comment had evidently not succeeded in counteracting the current conception in the scholastic theology of a retributive God, who justifies according to the deserts of the sinner (*distributor et judex meritorum*, as Lombard has it) and cannot do otherwise than punish sin. As long as this retributive conception of God's righteousness possessed his mind, the problem could not fail to torture his sensitive conscience. It was only after his second transference to Wittenberg and subsequent to his graduation as doctor that, as the result of persistent reflection, he at last discovered the Pauline solution in the distinction between God's righteousness in the law (*justitia activa*) and in the Gospel (*justitia passiva*).[6]

Such is the import of his own testimony in the 1545 preface, which is the most authoritative deliverance on the subject. Conscious of sin, in spite of his irreproachable life as a monk,[7] perturbed by a reproving conscience at the thought of his sin in the presence of a retributive God, he was unable to trust in the satisfactions by which he sought to placate this God.[8] Not only could he not love a God

in the sense of God's punitive righteousness. This is, of course, inaccurate. Therefore, concludes Denifle, Luther was either ignorant of the mediæval exegesis of the passage, or he was guilty of downright lying in his account of his discovery. But the Commentary on Genesis consists of notes made by a student and published after Luther's death. The passage is evidently an inaccurate version of what he said. What he does say in the 1545 preface and other authentic passages is that he was taught by all the doctors (whom he had read or under whom he had studied is what he means to convey) to understand the passage in the punitive sense. In this he was simply stating the fact that he had been so instructed by the theologians. He does not say in these authentic utterances what the passage in the Commentary on Genesis makes him say, and the conclusion of Denifle, who founds on this passage, is, therefore, baseless. See Scheel, "Entwicklung Luther's," 105 f.

[6] He uses those scholastic terms to express the distinction.

[7] Irreprehensibilis monachus vivebam. "Documente," 17.

[8] Nec mea satisfactione placatum confidere possem. *Ibid.*, 17.

who must needs punish sinners in spite of such (necessarily imperfect) satisfactions. He hated the very thought of such a God and chafed at the phrase *justitia Die* in wrathful rebellion.[9] The reflection that not only in the law but even in the Gospel this punitive righteousness was manifested, threw him into paroxysms of bitter indignation. " Thus I raged and my conscience was agitated by furious storms. I beat importunately at that passage in Paul, thirsting with a most ardent desire to know what the apostle meant." [10]   At last the long-sought insight flashed on his mind as he perceived the connection (*connexionem*) of the clause, " the righteousness of God revealed in the Gospel," with that which follows, " the just shall live by faith." If the second is explanatory of the first, the righteousness of God must be understood not in the active, punitive sense, but in the passive or imputed sense (*justitia passiva*). God does not reveal in the Gospel the righteousness that inexorably demands the punishment of the sinner, but the righteousness which He mercifully gives or imputes to the sinner, and which the sinner receives in faith and is thereby justified in His sight. In other words, he had caught the Pauline distinction between the law and the Gospel, in which righteousness is the gift by which a merciful God justifies the sinner, through faith, as Paul understands it. In this sense God's righteousness is equivalent to God's grace and has nothing to do with the retributive conception of the theologians. The distinction between active and passive justice is, indeed, borrowed from the scholastic theology. Luther makes use of terms familiar to him, and one can hardly imagine Paul himself expounding the passage in the language of the scholastic theology. But, terminology apart, Luther had substantially caught the Pauline meaning of the Gospel of justification by faith and had rescued it from the retributive conception which the theologians associated with it. Henceforth, he says, the whole Scripture assumed for him a new aspect and, read in the light of this new insight, confirmed him in his

[9] Certe ingenti murmuratione indignabar deo. " Documente," 17.
[10] *Ibid.*, 17.

interpretation. " Therefore," he adds, "just as I had previously hated the phrase 'justice of God,' so now I extolled it with equal love as the sweetest of words. And so to me that passage in Paul was the true gate of paradise." [11] He was subsequently confirmed in his new interpretation on reading the " De Litera et Spiritu " of Augustine who, to his joy, expounded the words in the same sense, though he had not fully grasped all that they implied.[12]

The experience which he thus describes was undoubtedly the great turning point of his religious life. It was no mere phantasy of his old age. He speaks of it again and again in numerous passages of his " Table Talk " and other writings as the great deliverance from his long spiritual conflict. It is already reflected in his first course of Lectures on the Psalms, delivered between 1513 and 1515. In his comment on Psalm i. 5 he already, in speaking of the divine righteousness by which we are justified, adduces the reasoning of Paul on this subject, and extols him as the most profound of theologians,[13] of whose teaching the modern theologians are practically most ignorant.[14]   In commenting on Psalm xxxii. 1 he expressly refers to Romans i. 17 and interprets the passage in the sense of his new understanding of it.[15] This interpretation recurs in the comments on other Psalms from Psalm xxxv. onwards.[16] His mind, in fact, was so engrossed with the Pauline teaching on justification that he tends to obtrude it into his exposition at the expense of the historic sense.

The illumination of 1512-13, which is thus based on reliable evidence, marks the second of the two great crises

[11] " Documente," 17.   [12] Ibid., 18.
[13] Disputatio profundissimi theologi. " Werke," iii. 31.
[14] Ibid., iii. 31.   [15] Ibid., iii. 174.
[16] Ibid., iv. 117, 119, 417, for instance.   Hirsch (" Initium Theologiæ Lutheri," 161-165) supposes that the comment on Psalm i. 5 was not in the lectures as originally delivered, i.e., summer of 1513, but was inserted later as the result of the revision of the lectures with a view to publication. It is not till the 32nd or the 35th Psalm that the Pauline conception appears. Hedwig Thomas (" Zur Wurdigung der Psalmen Vorlesung Luther's ") finds no trace of this revision in the original MS. of the lectures, and this supposition is evidently groundless. See Strohl, " L'Évolution Religieuse de Luther," 144-145.

in the religious experience of Luther. The first came to
him when he vowed to become a monk amid the terrors
of the thunderstorm ; the second when, in the solitude of
his cell in the tower of the Wittenberg monastery, he found
in Romans i. 16-17 the answer to the problem, How can I
find a gracious God ? The first and dramatic experience
drove him into the monastery to seek salvation in the practice
of the life of evangelical perfection, in accordance with the
monastic ideal and method. This quest resulted in the
recurring sense of failure, of baffled effort. The second
launched him on his career as the pioneer of a new conception of the religious life and ultimately of a far-reaching
reformation on behalf of this conception, in opposition to
the old one, which he had weighed in the balance and found
wanting. An unforeseen and mysterious evolution had led
him along a way, darkened by doubt, and misgiving, and
fear, to the peace of mind and conscience of which he was
in search, or, as he phrases it, to " the open gates of
paradise." As yet, however, there is nothing to indicate
that this evolution was, in reality, of the nature of a religious
revolution. It was only gradually, as he set himself to
work out the implications of this experience, that he became
conscious of its far-reaching import. He soon realised,
indeed, that the new conception of his relation to God was
out of harmony with the current theology, and felt it incumbent on him to challenge the teaching even of his own school
of thought on the subject. At first, however, he did so
only tentatively. He merely ventured to make use of his
right as an academic teacher to proclaim his views in the
fashion usual in academic discussion. Apart from his
personal religious experience, which is the secret factor at
work behind his professorial teaching, the Lutheran
Reformation, in its earliest phase at least, is largely a matter
of theological controversy carried on by the young professor
from his chair in the usual manner against the scholastic
theology. The issue is a theology based on the Word,
particularly the Pauline teaching, *versus* the theology taught
in the schools under the influence of the Aristotelian philosophy and ethics. The Lectures on the Psalms contain the
first instalment of this new theology, as far as Luther himself

had comprehended the teaching of Paul, as distinctive from that of the schoolmen. In the Lectures on the Epistle to the Romans we have the second and more developed instalment, as the result of progressive reflection on the specific problems to which his closer study of Paul gave rise, and which widened the breach with the scholastic theology. Even so, he is not yet conscious of any radical divergence from the teaching and institutions of the Church, of heresy or schismatic revolt, though, in the Commentary on Romans, the critical, reforming note in regard to ecclesiastical institutions as well as doctrine becomes ever more boldly audible.

CHAPTER VI

THE NEW THEOLOGY AND ITS DEVELOPMENT
(1513-1516)

I. THE LECTURES ON THE PSALMS

IN his exposition of the Psalms Luther used, not the original text, but the Vulgate. His knowledge of Hebrew was still rudimentary, and, judged from the modern standard of adequate scholarship, he was ill-equipped for his task. He himself later regarded the exposition as a performance of no value and not worth printing.[1] At the same time, he made use of the available scholarship in the preparation of the lectures. He consulted Reuchlin's Hebrew grammar and dictionary and his exposition of the penitential Psalms. He used Lefèbre's edition of the Psalter, containing Jerome's version and others, and his "Commentary," published in 1509.[2] Besides the "Commentaries" of Lyra and Cassiodorus and the "Glossa Ordinaria," he made extensive use of the "Enarrationes in Psalmos" and other works of Augustine, as well as the writings of Anselm and Bernard.[3]

The exposition takes the conventional form of reading the text, word for word, with verbal explanations and short and dictated notes on the meaning of certain phrases (*glossæ*), with the addition of oral expositions of the thought of the Psalmist (*scholæ*). He also follows the exegetical method of the time based on the assumption that the words of Scripture contained a threefold or even a fourfold sense

---

[1] Nugæ enim sunt, et spongia dignissima. Enders, i. 27. Letter to Spalatin, 26th December 1515.

[2] Second edition, 1513. His notes on Lefèbre's work, which he made in preparation for his lectures, are given in "Werke," iv. 466 f., and show how extensive was his use of this source.

[3] See the notes on Anselm's "Opuscula," in "Werke," ix. 107 f., which belong to this period.

—the literal or historic, the figurative or allegoric, the moral or tropological, and the prophetic or anagogical sense. He had at his disposal, in Lefèbre's " Commentary," a striking example of this method, of which he makes ample use,[4] in preference to that of Lyra, who emphasised the historic interpretation and whom, on this account, he at this period disparaged. The distinction between the letter and the spirit left room for the most arbitrary interpretation. Christ is made to speak in the Psalms, directly or indirectly, on the assumption that the Old Testament is throughout a prophecy or anticipation of the Gospel The Law in the positive sense is, indeed, distinguished from the Gospel, though the Gospel is still conceived as a new law.[5] But spiritually apprehended, viewed with the eye of faith, which discriminates between the letter and the spirit, it points the way to Christ, is in fact identical with the Gospel.[6] Moreover, he envisages the Psalms under the influence of his own personal religious experience and from the standpoint of the Pauline teaching, as he had come to understand it. The marked tendency to read this teaching into the Psalter further lessens the value of his exposition from the historic point of view. The Commentary really reflects more the thought of Luther, as influenced by Paul, than the thought of the Psalmist. In thus allegorising and reading Paul into the Psalter, he was, indeed, following the method of Paul himself, who found in the Old Testament the testimony to his distinctive Gospel. In so doing he thus does not really misrepresent the Apostle's teaching. Nevertheless, the modern reader cannot help feeling that much of this argumentation, viewed from the historic standpoint, is out of place, and that the exegesis is arbitrary and unscientific. It is as an expression of his own religious thought and experience, not as an objective interpretation of the Psalmist, that it is historically important and so interesting and significant. " Without knowing it," says Kuhn, " he gives us before all the history of his own heart." [7] In it we have

___

[4] He declares his adhesion to this method in his preface. " Werke," iii. 11.   [5] " Werke," iii. 28, 37, 65, etc.

[6] *Ibid.*, iii. 96. Lex autem spiritualiter intellecta est idem cum evangelio. *Cf.* iv. 306.   [7] " Luther," i. 108 (1894).

the first stage of his development under the influence of the
Pauline teaching. The young professor is already in these
lectures the prophet of a new theology. In numerous
characteristic passages he proclaims the Pauline doctrine
of justification by faith as he is learning to understand
it in consequence of his illumination in the monastery
tower

His own religious experience is the main influence at work
in these lectures. At the same time, in the working out of
his theme, he assimilates not a little from Augustine, Anselm,
and Bernard, and his thought is still largely influenced by
the Nominalist theology in which he had been trained.
Hunzinger [8] and others descry in the lectures the marked
influence of the Neoplatonism of Augustine and see in
Luther the disciple, for the time being, of his philosophic
mysticism. This influence has, however, been exaggerated.
Luther seems, indeed, to have been attracted by the Neo-
platonic, mystic element in Augustine's teaching, which
emphasises the distinction between the visible and the
invisible, the sensible world and the eternal, spiritual reality
or essence underlying it. In a number of passages in the
lectures he speaks of the invisible, spiritual world revealed
by God to faith,[9] the hidden wisdom which no philosophy
can discover and is only made known by the Holy Spirit
within us,[10] which to perceive we must believe,[11] which
unravels itself to us by the internal word (*verbum
internum*),[12] and comes to the soul in the higher
apprehension of faith.[13] But in these expressions he is
only stressing faith as the indispensable condition of the
knowledge of God and divine things in the Occamist
rather than in the Augustinian Neoplatonic sense. There
is nothing to show that he had in his mind in such passages

---

[8] " Luther's Neuplatonismus in der Psalmen-vorlesung " (1906) ;
Loofs, " Dogmen-Geschichte," 692 f. ; Braun, " Die Bedeutung der
Konkupiszenz in Luther's Leben und Lehre " (1908). On the other side
see Scheel, " Entwicklung Luther's," 164 f. ; Strohl, " L'Évolution
Religieuse," 166 f.

[9] " Werke," iii. 368.   [11] *Ibid.*, iv. 95.
[10] *Ibid.*, iii. 172.   [12] *Ibid.*, iii. 281.
[13] *Ibid.*, iv. 151, 265. Excessus or raptus mentis, extasis.

the conception of God in the metaphysical sense as the ultimate essence or substance underlying all things, with which the soul may unite itself by spiritual abstraction, contemplation. He had, indeed, as he tells us himself, attempted to find comfort in his spiritual trial in mystic speculations. But he could make nothing of these speculations, and there is no reason to assume that when he wrote these lectures he was a votary of this train of thought. What he had sought was not a philosophic but a personal God with whom he could enter into an assured relation, and what attracted him in the philosophical teaching of Augustine was not the metaphysical but the ethical and religious element in this side of his teaching. It appealed to him as a monk, for whom the terrestrial is of no account compared with the things of the spirit, and of whose religious aspirations it was the appropriate nurture. The distinctive thing in the lectures is not Augustinian Neo-platonism but the evangelical element in his religious thought, which he develops under the influence of his new apprehension of God's righteousness in the Gospel. Here indeed the influence of Augustine is very marked, and the tendency to assimilate his evangelical teaching, in so far as he was acquainted with it, and in opposition to the scholastic theology—already discernible in the notes on Lombard—is now unmistakable. Next to Augustine, he owed not a little to Anselm and Bernard. In the preparation of his lectures he read the " Cur Deus Homo " and other writings of Anselm, and the sermons of Bernard. He was in particular influenced by Augustine's view of the evil effect of sin on human nature and the necessity of prevenient and justifying grace. From Anselm he learned to conceive of justification as the remission of sin, imperfectly grasped by Augustine, who confused justification with sanctification. The influence of Bernard is reflected in the emphasis on humility, springing from the sense of sin, as an essential of the relation of the soul to God.[14] To these and other ideas he imparts the stamp of his personal apprehension and experience—the distinctive note already discernible in his theology.

[14] Jundt, " Développement," 84 f. and 134 f.

At this stage, however, he does not understand how to relate his religious apprehension and experience to the old beliefs. He has not yet made clear to himself the antagonism between this experience and these beliefs, and the lectures accordingly do not unfold a consistent and uniform theology. He is evidently not yet conscious of any essential divergence from the traditional faith and practice of the Church. He remains a devout monk. He venerates the Church and its institutions, though the critical note, especially in reference to the misplaced zeal for external observances, indulgences, etc., is not lacking.[15] He is unconscious of heresy; frequently, in fact, attacks the heretics, and distinguishes between his teaching and theirs.[16] Though he realises the difference between his apprehension of the Pauline teaching and that of the schools,[17] he nevertheless retains much of the Nominalist theology. He follows the scholastic method and makes use of the ideas and terms of this theology. The antithesis between faith and intellect, the idea of the non-imputation of sin by "the pact of God," by which it pleases Him to accept the sinner,[18] the idea of merit and the distinction between merits *de congruo* and *de condigno*, the natural freedom of the will and the ability to prepare for grace by doing what is within one's power,[19] the co-operation of the will and grace,[20] the remnant of good in the soul which impels it to seek God and desire the good (*synteresis, conservatio*),[21] the infusion of grace and the expulsion of sin—all this he retains from the scholastic theology. He even recognises the value of Aristotle's philosophy for theology, if rightly understood and applied.[22] Two voices still utter themselves in him—that of the scholastic theologian and that of the disciple of Paul—and he has not learned clearly to differentiate between them.

[15] "Werke," iii. 61, 155, 171 ; iv. 78, 307, 312. Grisar thinks that he has in view more particularly the extreme Observantine section of his own Order, but the limitation does not necessarily follow.
[16] "Werke," iv. 285, 385, etc.   [17] *Ibid.*, iii. 31.
[18] *Ibid.*, iii. 289.   Non justificarent nisi pactum dei faceret.
[19] *Ibid.*, iv. 262.
[20] *Ibid.*, iii. 259.   Gratia co-operans.
[21] *Ibid.*, iii. 44, 93, etc. ; *cf.* i. 36.   [22] *Ibid.*, i. 28.

At the same time, it is the voice of the disciple of Paul and Augustine rather than that of the scholastic theologian that speaks in his distinctive message concerning the relation of the soul to God and the attainment of salvation. Very noteworthy is the individualist, subjective note in his treatment of this supreme problem. As in Paul, religion is a matter of personal faith, individual experience, of the heart, not of external observance. In the solution of this problem the Church and its institutions recede into the background. To those who are zealous for its observances he quotes the passage in Joel, " Rend your hearts and not your garments." [23] As in Paul, too, God is everything in this solution—God manifesting and making effective His redeeming power and mercy in Christ. From the religious point of view, man, on the contrary, is nothing. He is the slave of sin. For Luther's view of human nature, like that of Paul and Augustine, and in striking contrast to that of Jesus, is very pessimistic, in spite of his recognition of the remnant of good in it.[24] The keen sense of sin, which had given such poignancy to his spiritual conflict in the monastery, is reflected in his conception of humanity. With Augustine he regards man as " a mass of perdition," human righteousness as only sin.[25] Even the infant of a single day is a sinner in the sight of God.[26] With Paul he envisages human nature from the ideal of perfect righteousness, the divine perfection, and he expresses his view of it in very sweeping, nay exaggerated language. " All that is in us and the world is abominable and damnable in the presence of God, and thus he who adheres to Him through faith necessarily appears to himself vile and nothing, abominable and damnable." [27] In the presence of an absolutely righteous God, he stands self-condemned, conscious only of guilt, haunted by the fear of judgment. Here, too, Luther is giving expression to his personal experience in his

[23] " Werke," iii. 61.

[24] *Ibid.*, iii. 535. Oppressi dura servitute. Ita peccator oppressus peccatis, sentiens se cogi a diabolo et membris peccati ad peccandum semper. *Cf.* 215, iv. 383.

[25] *Ibid.*, iv. 343, 383.

[26] *Ibid.*, iii. 284.

[27] *Ibid.*, iii. 462.

search for a gracious God. Salvation, justification begins in self-humiliation, self-accusation, self-detestation, self-judgment.[28] It is preconditioned by the recognition that God only is righteous in the absolute sense, that human righteousness cannot avail in the sight of an absolutely righteous God, and that God is, therefore, just in judging and condemning the sinner. To judge and condemn oneself (*se judicare*) is thus to justify God (*Deum justificare*), *i.e.*, pronounce Him true and just ; whereas to justify self is to judge and condemn God.[29] In view of man's innate sin and God's absolute righteousness, there is no escape from this conclusion. Hence man must discard all self-righteousness if he would become righteous in the sight of God. "The righteousness of God cannot arise within us until our righteousness entirely falls and perishes."[30] In order to do righteous works, he contends against Aristotle and the scholastic theologians, we must first be made righteous.[31] This is the fundamental principle, "the profound theology" (*profunda theologia*) of Paul, which the scholastic theologians have practically, if not theoretically, ignored, and on which he joins issue with them.[32] Even the recognition of this fundamental verity is already an act of faith, the work of God within us, not our own.[33] It is revealed in the Gospel and is not due to our understanding.

Moreover, if self-righteousness could avail for justification, Christ would have died in vain.[34] "We are all sinners and cannot become righteous except by faith in Christ,[35] so that Christ's righteousness may reign in us, whilst through Him and in Him we confide for salvation."[36] To this end He became incarnate, was crucified, and raised for our

[28] "Werke," iii. 29, 31, 345, etc. Nemo per fidem justificatur nisi prius per humiliatatem sese injustum confiteatur, 345.

[29] *Ibid.*, iii. 289-290.

[30] *Ibid.*, iii. 31.

[31] *Ibid.*, iv. 3 ; *cf.* 18.

[32] *Ibid.*, iii. 31 ; *cf.* 283 and 319, where he speaks slightingly of the Scotists and the Occamists.

[33] *Ibid.*, iv. 241 ; *cf.* iii. 174. Nullus hominum scivit quod ira dei esset super omnes, sed per evangelium suum, ipse de cœlo revelavit.

[34] *Ibid.*, iii. 31, 172.   [35] *Ibid.*, iv. 388.   [36] *Ibid.*, iv. 383.

salvation.[37] In view of this absolute dependence on Christ for salvation, the Occamist assumption that the necessity of His death cannot be proved is false. On the contrary, this is the corner-stone of the scheme of salvation. Without His death there can be no remission of sin, no justification, since salvation is impossible by our own righteousness, our own merits.[38] Through Christ alone is sin remitted and God's saving righteousness is manifested and becomes operative in our salvation.[39]

It is in this remission that justification specifically consists. The righteousness of God thereby becomes the saving righteousness revealed in the Gospel. In this sense it is equivalent to His grace, His mercy, which He exercises for the benefit of the sinner through Christ, and by which the sinner becomes righteous in His sight.[40] This becoming righteous in God's sight is effected by way of imputation, which consists in the non-reckoning of sin and the reputing of righteousness to the sinner.[41] In justification he thus enters into a relation to God which he could not possibly attain by virtue of his own righteousness. Self-righteousness being, through man's sinful condition, utterly worthless in the sight of a perfectly righteous God, there can, in fact, be no worthy relation, no real fellowship between the sinner and such a God except by way of the non-imputation of sin and the reputation of righteousness. Imputation is, however, not based, as in the Occamist theology, on the arbitrary will, but on the righteousness of a merciful God, made operative through Christ, though Luther has not yet systematically discarded the Occamist idea.

A further essential of justification is faith on the part of the sinner. God's saving righteousness in Christ is appropriated by faith and by faith alone, and it is not attainable

[37] Propter nostram salutem. "Werke," iii. 176.

[38] *Ibid.*, iii. 172.

[39] *Ibid.*, iii. 174. Hoc autem non fit nisi per Christum ; ergo nemo ex se, sed per solum Christum salvus erit.

[40] Justitia fidei qua justificatur anima quæ est gratia et misericordia, iii. 179 ; *cf.* 226.

[41] *Ibid.*, iii. 175. Quilibet est justus cui deus reputat justitiam, tali enim non imputat peccatum quia reputat ei justitiam.

by human merit.[42] Even faith is God's gracious gift and has no meritorious quality.[43]

Justification is thus, on God's part, the remission, through non-imputation, of sin and the reputation of righteousness by His grace or mercy, and the appropriation of this righteousness by faith, received as a gift and without any merit, on the part of the sinner. It is not, however, identified with the magical operation by which, according to the traditional view, God takes away the guilt of original sin by sacramental grace in baptism. Luther already begins to question this view.[44] Though he does not reject it outright, he doubts whether the new relation of fellowship with God in justification is thus operated by the magical removal of original sin and its guilt. Even in this new relation the fact and power of sin and the need of remission remain, though man is made capable, by the non-imputation of sin and the reputation of righteousness, of fellowship with God.

Luther's characteristic conception of justification, whilst assimilating elements from other sources, is a reflection of his religious experience. It is thus that he solves the problem of a gracious God and disarms the fear of a divine retribution, which had so long obsessed him. The thought of a retributive God is displaced by the thought of a God, who, whilst He must, in virtue of His absolute righteousness, judge and condemn the sinner, longs to save him and has devised the means of his salvation. Luther conceives of God in a new light as One whose very nature leads Him freely to communicate His righteousness to those who, in themselves, have no claim on it.[45] The Gospel, as he now understands it, has transformed the conception of a divine judge into that of the Father God, who in Christ gives and

[42] Justitia quæ in nobis est ex deo per fidem, iv. 241. Fides enim sola justificat, iv. 438 ; cf. iii. 320. Remissionem esse sine meritis, iii. 174.

[43] Fides quæ ex gratia dei donatur impiis, iii. 649 ; cf. iv. 127.

[44] "Werke," iii. 174-175 ; iv. 206, 211. See Loof's "Dogmen-Geschichte," 696.

[45] Hoc est esse deum, non accipere bona, sed dare, iv. 269. Se deum vere probat qui vult sua dare nobis et noster deus esse, nobis benefacere, iv. 278.

gives freely what is His to man. " To benefit another is divine." [46] This evangelical conception has delivered him from the doubt and misgiving, the fear and despair of his quest for God. He now views this tragic experience— the distrust of self, the failure of self-righteousness, the accusation and condemnation of self which had haunted his mind and conscience—as the God-appointed way to God. It is for him, in fact, the only way. To be justified by God we must first learn by this experience to justify God. As the result of this new conception of God and this insight into the meaning of his religious experience, his attitude towards God has changed from fear to faith, from misgiving to trust, from doubt to confidence, from despair to the hope of salvation.[47] *Fides* becomes *fiducia*. Faith is, indeed, intellectual assent—the perception by the individual, inspired by God, of the truth of the Gospel, acceptance of the divine scheme of salvation. But it involves the element of trust, confidence in God's mercy in Christ. Whilst this confidence does not yet mean the absolute assurance of salvation as a present certainty, and salvation is still a thing of hope, it has disarmed the old doubt and distrust of God. Christ has become our peace, where before fear and misgiving reigned in the heart.[48]

In consequence of this faith, this confidence, the whole spiritual life has been transformed. A new dynamic has entered into it. Faith is not merely receptive ; it becomes active in this new life. Whilst justification by non-imputation of sin and reputed righteousness has a judicial aspect, as an act of acquittal for sin it has also its ethical aspect. It is the beginning of a process of regeneration, which God works in the heart and which involves growth in real righteousness. Justification is also vivification, resurrec-

---

[46] Benefacere enim alteri divinum est, iv. 278.

[47] Sic enim Christus in evangelio, " crede," " credite," confidete, iii. 651. Dismissis peccatis anima sit in quiete conscientiæ et fiducia gratiæ dei, iv. 228.

[48] " Werke," iv. 15-16. Justitia nostra Christus est et pax nostra quam deus nobis dedit. Et per illam nos justificavit et ita pacem habemus. See also O. Ritschl, " Dogmen-Geschichte des Protestantismus," ii. 72 f.

tion.[49] Luther thus speaks from his own experience of faith
as the dynamic of a new life. Like Paul, the pessimist has
been transformed into the optimist. Concupiscence, the law
of the flesh, " the law of the members " in Pauline language,
is indeed still operative in the struggle between the flesh
and the spirit, and it behoves all who are in Christ to be
always in a state of compunction for sin.[50] But this
compunction under the sense of sin does not imply that sin
is all-powerful in the justified soul. The conviction of its
power is not a confession of moral bankruptcy, an evidence
of Luther's moral and spiritual collapse, as Denifle perversely
opines. It is only an indication of the new vitality of the
spiritual life, renewed and fructified by faith. Concupiscence
is a very real clog of this vitality, though it does not become
actual sin except with the consent of the will.[51] But the
Cross is the mortification of the old man.[52] Christ has not
only fulfilled the law for us. He imparts the grace which
enables the spirit to overcome the flesh. Justification thus
also means for Luther, as for Paul, the liberation, the
emancipation of the spirit from the power of the flesh, from
the old slavery to sin. From this point of view it is,
in truth, not complete as long as we are in the flesh, since
sin, guilt is unavoidable in this life, and its forgiveness a
life-long exercise of God's mercy in Christ. " Always we
sin and always we are to be justified." [53]

There is thus already something distinctive in Luther's
theology, whilst he does not clearly see all its implications
and has not yet emancipated himself from traditional
doctrine. The old, in fact, not seldom appears alongside
the new and he is not fully conscious of the divergence of
the one from the other. This explains how it is possible

[49] Dimissa sunt ei peccata et resurrexit, iii. 29-30. Vivifica me est
dicere justifica me, da mihi spiritum, da mihi vivam et perfectam fidem
in qua vivam et justus sim, iv. 325 ; cf. 520.

[50] " Werke," iii. 62.

[51] Ibid., iii. 546. In " Werke," i. 55, Luther already (1514 or 1515)
pronounces it to be invincible, experimur omnes invincibilem esse
concupiscentiam penitus.

[52] Ibid., iv. 383.

[53] Ibid., iv. 364. Semper peccamus, semper justificandi.

for Roman Catholic theologians like Denifle, who is followed by Grisar, to find in his teaching at this stage nothing essentially at variance with that of the Church. According to Denifle, he is at most veering towards the downward path which was to lead, in his opinion, to heresy and moral bankruptcy.[54] It was only in his lectures on the Epistle to the Romans that he developed his distinctive heretical teaching.[55] Grisar repeats this contention. " Taken in their context, none of these passages furnishes any decisive proof of a deviation from the Church's faith. They forebode, indeed, Luther's later errors, but contain as yet no explicit denial of Catholic doctrine." [56] This contention overlooks too much the really distinctive evangelical note in these lectures. It may be the case that he is not yet conscious of divergence from the faith of the Church. But he is already to a certain extent explicitly at issue with the scholastic theology, and is virtually at variance with the received faith in his conception of justification as distinctively the remission of sin and the creation of a new relation between the soul and God, in the elimination of the thought of merit and reward from this relation, and in the emphasis that salvation is wholly dependent on God's mercy and grace in the acceptance of the sinner, apart from any reckoning of merits and demerits.

II. THE LECTURES ON ROMANS

Luther began his course on the Epistle to the Romans in the spring of 1515 and continued it till the summer of 1516. These lectures give us a deeper insight into his genius as a religious thinker. In them he develops the distinctive theology which he had read into the Psalms from a direct study of the teaching of Paul himself, on which this theology was based. Unlike the lectures on the Psalms, which were vitiated by the lavish use of a forced and

[54] " Luther und Lutherthum," ii. 438 f.
[55] *Ibid.*, ii. 476-478.
[56] " Luther," i. 74.

artificial method of exegesis, the Commentary on Romans is an attempt to interpret the actual meaning of the text. Though he still recognises the conventional assumption of a recondite, in addition to the obvious meaning of Scripture, he makes a more restricted use of this method and concerns himself mainly with the actual thought of the Apostle. These lectures also mark an advance in the apprehension and discussion of his specific doctrine of salvation. Whilst this doctrine already substantially appears in those on the Psalms, it is worked out in the Commentary on Romans in greater detail and with a firmer grasp of its implications, a keener sense of its divergence from the received theology. The criticism of this theology is wider in scope and more uncompromising in tone. " In the years 1512-17," says Holl, " Luther's creative power displayed itself most powerfully—more powerfully, in fact, than in the period after the Leipzig Disputation." [57] The most striking proof of this creative power is the Commentary on Romans. At the same time, he has by no means emancipated himself from the influence and the limitations of the scholastic train of thought. He makes use of the scholastic terminology, and his interpretation of the Epistle is perforce influenced to a considerable extent by current theological ideas.

Nor is the Commentary an attempt to elucidate the Pauline teaching in the light of the historic environment and the personal religious experience which shaped the Apostle's thought. From this point of view, it does not satisfy the more exacting standard and method of modern exegesis. Luther has no knowledge of, or any particular interest in, the many critical questions which exercise the mind of the modern exegete. His attitude towards the Epistle is primarily the religious, not the critical, historic one. He approaches and interprets it in the light especially of his own religious experience. The scientific study of theology and history was only in its infancy. Humanism was only tentatively applying the critical method, and neither in the university nor in the monastery had Luther been trained in the application of this method. At this stage he accepts

[57] " Aufsätze," i. 91.

the Bible as the literal Word of God or Christ without asking himself whether there might not be a rabbinic element in the thought of Paul or in his reasoning and his method of exegesis. So little does he discriminate in these matters that at this period he implicitly believes in the absolutely authoritative testimony of the Church, as against the heretics at least, and even in the word of a prelate or any good and holy man as the word of Christ, on the strength of the text, " He that heareth you heareth me." [58] Unlike the modern exegete, he uses the Vulgate text, which the Wittenberg printer Grunenberg printed for the purpose of his lectures, and which appears to have been mainly based on the Basle edition of 1509 and to some extent on Lefèbre's edition of the Pauline Epistles (1512).[59]

He endeavoured, however, to fit himself for his task by the study of the best available sources. He made a painstaking attempt to establish a correct Latin text. He has made some progress in the study of Greek and Hebrew since he annotated the Sentences. He derived no little aid in the understanding of original Greek passages from his humanist fellow-monk and colleague, Lang. Besides using Lefèbre's Latin text and " Commentary," he had the advantage of consulting from Chapter ix. onwards [60] Erasmus' edition of the Greek New Testament and his Latin annotations. He evidently realised the value of the new scholarship and availed himself of it to bring out the sense of the text. Lefèbre and Erasmus were authoritative guides for both text and interpretation, and Reuchlin for the meaning of Hebrew words and passages. Whilst continuing to use the " Glossa Ordinaria," Nicolas of Lyra, Paul of Burgos,

[58] Luther's " Vorlesung über den Römerbrief," ii. 88 ; cf. 92 ; edited by Ficker (1908).

[59] Ficker, " Introduction to Römerbrief," 46-49. As in the Psalms, he follows the conventional method of reading and grammatically explaining the text word for word, with glosses or notes on certain words or clauses, and a detailed commentary on important passages or themes (Scholæ).

[60] He had expounded the first eight chapters before Erasmus' edition, which was published in the beginning of 1516, came into his hands.

Lombardus, and other commentators, he frequently disagrees with their interpretation. His predilection for humanist scholarship is unmistakable, and as compared with the lectures on the Psalms, the Commentary shows a conscientious striving, under humanist influence, to improve on the old commentators.

Moreover, there was in Luther's quest of salvation as a monk something akin to Paul's quest of it as a Pharisee, and this affinity of religious experience fitted him to bring to his task an insight into the Apostle's teaching which no mere scholarship could give him. For both, the righteousness of God and the means of attaining it is the great problem. Both had sought the solution of this problem by the legalist method—Paul in the attempt to observe the Jewish law, Luther in the attempt to realise the life of evangelical perfection in accordance with the monastic conception of it. Both had experienced the futility of this quest and the misery which the sense of failure induced. Both had a lofty ideal of the divine righteousness, the same exalted conception of God and the good, the same sensitive conscience, the same sense of sin, alike as moral imperfection and guilt, and as the transgression of a strictly regulated mode of life. Both had been trained in a complex accretion of doctrine and tradition—Paul in Rabbinism, Luther in Scholasticism—in which religion was entangled in a network of speculation and traditional beliefs and practices. Paul the Pharisee and Luther the monk were kindred souls in these respects. Both had, in addition, experienced a deliverance from the bondage of the law, the system of work righteousness. Luther, in fact, owed his deliverance from this bondage to a new religious insight derived directly from Paul, and this insight, coupled with the similarity of their previous religious experience, gave him a key to unlock the mind of the Apostle, though he does not always use the key aright and sometimes misunderstands him. Paul's influence on his distinctive thought is unmistakable. On no one else was the Pauline influence so powerfully exerted during the long interval between his day and that of the great Reformer. Luther was shaped in the mould of Paul. He is the greatest of his disciples.

The Commentary shows, indeed, the continued influence
of the scholastic theology. Just as Paul reasons out his
conception of Christianity with the aid of ideas and terms
derived from rabbinism, so Luther's thought is conditioned
to a considerable extent by those of scholasticism. But as
in the case of Paul, the antagonism to the dominant system
is equally patent, and the antagonism is more pronounced,
more challenging than in the lectures on the Psalms. What
differentiates the Commentary from the works of his
scholastic predecessors, and even from those of Erasmus,
is its independent, original note. Luther attacks the
schoolmen in defiant, and at times passionate language ;
attacks even the theologians of his own school as well as
the Thomists and Scotists.[61] In his wrath he calls them
Sautheologen (hog theologians) in the drastic manner of
the time. His antagonism has become keener, more
impatient, more intolerant, and Aristotle, as the evil genius
of the scholastic theology, comes in for his full share of it.
Nor does he hesitate to differ from Lefèbre and Erasmus,
in spite of his respect for their humanist scholarship. As
against the schoolmen and even the humanists, his great
authority, next to Paul, is Augustine, whom he now prefers
as an exegete to Jerome, and with whose works he shows a
more extensive acquaintance than in his earlier lectures.
He draws largely on his exposition of Romans, his anti-
Pelagian writings, and the " De Spiritu et Litera." [62] But
the authority of even Augustine is not absolute and he
ventures on occasion to criticise him.[63] He has, too, a
predilection for the mystics—for Bernard, Hugo de St Victor,
Gerhard Zerbolt, whom he confuses with Gerhard Groot,
and for Tauler's sermons in the Vernacular.[64] The mystic
influence at this stage has become distinctive.

Not least he brings to bear on his task a remarkable
knowledge of the Scriptures. Throughout the Commentary
the Bible is the supreme authority. Christ and the Word
of Christ are the grand source and *summa* of theology,

[61] " Römervorlesung," ii. 110, 165.
[62] See Enders, i. 63, for his estimate of Augustine.
[63] " Vorlesung," ii. 336.
[64] *Ibid.*, ii. 145, 205, 312.

the touchstone of traditional doctrines and beliefs, though he may not always use the Word with historic discrimination. His office as doctor and professor of the Word laid on him the duty of expounding the Scriptures, and the Scriptures are for him both the absolute source of the knowledge of God and the norm of the religious life.   He begins his lectures on the assumption that the whole Bible, especially the prophets, is to be understood of Christ, though not according to the superficial sense of the letter.[65]   It is a revelation of the will and grace of God in Christ, no mere *summa* or system of theology, and is to be experimentally understood and applied.[66]

Hence the experimental note of the Commentary.   Like Paul, Luther is not a speculative but an experimental theologian, even if, like Paul, he works with ideas and terms derived from the speculative theology in which he had been trained.   If Paul reasons in terms of Phariseeism, Luther reasons in terms of the scholastic theology and is to a certain extent under the influence of its ideas.   But these are largely the modes of expressing the personal religious experience, the verities which have become the dynamic of a new spiritual life.   Whilst making use of conventional forms, he is substantially in antagonism to the conventional system.   As in the case of Paul, his task is to formulate his religious experience rather than a set of theological beliefs, and in doing so he is perforce led to take account of the scholastic teaching, as Paul in similar circumstances had to reckon with rabbinism in setting forth his conception of Christianity.   The effort is heavily laden with traditional matter, not always easily grasped or in itself particularly interesting.   It is regrettable that the demonstration of his religious convictions is so often of the nature of a detailed and rather tedious controversy with his scholastic opponents.   One could well dispense with these rather diffuse and subtle bouts of logic with the scholastics and their conceptions, which still condition his thought and are to us largely the theological lumber of the

[65] "Vorlesung," i. 4.   Hic magnus aperitur introitus in sacræ scripturæ intelligentiam, sc quod tota de Christo sit intelligenda.   *Cf.* 240.

[66] *Ibid.*, ii. 253.   Hæc omnia dicta, scripta, facta ut humilietur superba presumptio hominum et commendetur gratia Dei.

Middle Ages. But the experimental note that underlies it, or articulates itself, invests the Commentary with a perennial interest as a piece of self-revelation. There are passages in it which remind us of the Confessions of Augustine, with which he shows familiarity.[67] It is full of the human touch and has rightly been called " a great human document." As the revelation of a great religious personality, a pioneer religious thinker, it is a contribution to the religion of the time. Its originality consists in the distinctively personal sense in which, inspired by Paul, he apprehends God and the relation of the soul to Him. Making allowance for imperfect apprehension here and there, it may be called a rediscovery of Paul, in divergence from the traditional and the scholastic interpretation of him. This rediscovery is, indeed, already apparent in the lectures on the Psalms. But in the Commentary on Romans it is more fully developed and there is less of the old dependence on the scholastic system. Paul, and next to him Augustine, as his most authoritative interpreter, largely displace the schoolmen, though in adopting the new he is not always able to emancipate himself from the old. In creating something new it is, as he himself felt, difficult to throw off the old. " The smell of philosophy," he says, " is inherent in our breath." [68] As he tells us himself, he felt the need of a deeper insight into the Pauline teaching,[69] and the Commentary affords ample evidence of this progressive insight. " He was," he says in reference to these early studies, " like Augustine, one of those who advance in knowledge in writing and teaching, not one of those who take in at one intuition the whole spirit of Scripture." [70]

The Commentary is further interesting as an essay in religious psychology. It mirrors the experience of a soul in its quest for God and salvation and the attainment of what it seeks. Here also the standpoint is the experimental, not the philosophic or scientific one. He is repelled by the religious psychology, based on Aristotle, which he regards

[67] "Vorlesung," ii. III, 211, 257.
[68] Ibid., ii. 183. Olet philosophia in nostra anhelitu.
[69] "Documente," 17.   [70] Ibid., 18.

not only as erroneous, but as leading the soul away from God. He bases his on that of the Apostle—on the new knowledge of God and self, which he has attained through the Pauline-Augustinian teaching. He presupposes the darkened understanding, the sin-enslaved will, the impotent aspiration of the good without grace, the conflict of spirit and flesh. It is with these presuppositions that he dissects the spiritual life and envisages the soul and its faculties. It is not the psychic life in itself, but in relation to God and the divine plan of its redemption from sin that is the absorbing theme. The great problem, in this connection, is the problem of man and his sin in relation to God and His righteousness. It is in the light of this problem that he conceives of human nature. The whole gamut of the soul is gauged from this standpoint. It is not the normal but the abnormal state, from the religious point of view, that he seeks to diagnose. Mind, heart, and will are unsound, diseased, in need of healing, which God alone can effect. How the divine grace effects this in justification and regeneration through Christ is the psychological process which he depicts in his experimental fashion. There is much of himself in this process—so much that the Commentary might be described as an analysis of his own spiritual life.

In the course of it there are, in fact, many references, express or implied, to his own spiritual experience—his sense of sin, his past conflict with doubt and fear, his difficulties with the problem of predestination and the abstract subtleties of the scholastic teaching on free will and grace. Through these doubts, fears, and perplexities he has worked his way to certain definite convictions, and these are strongly, even passionately held. The dogmatic tone, the note of inflexible conviction is very characteristic, not only in the vehement contradiction and condemnation of scholasticism, but in the decided antitheses which condition his thought. He is very prone thus absolutely to work out his convictions to their logical conclusions from the premises with which he starts. We might call him, as the schoolmen termed Wessel, " the master of contradictions." He does not hesitate to face even the most extreme implications of his dogmatic presuppositions, as in his conception of the obligation to love above all a God who dooms the soul to damnation, however much it may wish to seek to be saved. These extreme feats of logic may only be incidental. But they reveal the impulsive temperament which is not easily amenable to the restraints of reason and is too prone to regard reason as an enemy of religion.

The personal touch appears also in the reforming note in the Commentary. Luther is no longer the self-centred monk, absorbed in his own spiritual well-being, though still the devotee of the monastic system. He is not solely the religious thinker, the theologian. He is in touch with life, actuality. His alert eye is directed beyond the cloister and the lecture room to the world around him. The Commentary reveals the man of character, the nascent personality, the reformer in the making. In this respect there is also a marked advance on the lectures on the Psalms. The antagonism to the old order is much more marked. His polemic is directed not only against the scholastic theology, but against the practical abuses rampant in the Church and society. The Commentary is, in fact, a Reform manifesto. He has discovered his mission as a Reformer, though he does not yet see whither this mission was to lead him. " In virtue of the office of teacher which I discharge by apostolic authority, it is mine to speak out against whatever I shall see to be amiss, yea even in the highest quarters." [71] The greatest value of the Scriptures lies in their application to actual life, which is to be measured and tested by them. Hence his striving to show their practical bearing on the existing order of things in the Church and the world.[72]

III. The Fact of Sin and its Effects

In working out the problem of salvation, Luther starts with the assumption of man's moral impotence through sin and his absolute dependence on God for salvation. He makes this clear at the outset. The purpose of the Apostle

[71] " Vorlesung," ii. 301.   [72] *Ibid.*, ii. 272, 301.

is, he holds, to destroy, root out, and demolish all wisdom and righteousness of the flesh, and to plant, establish, and magnify sin. Sin is the fundamental fact, and this fact and its implications are stressed in the strongest terms. Original sin is the basal conception of his religious anthropology. It manifests itself in concupiscence or the disposition to evil which is inherited from Adam and vitiates and dominates human nature. Concupiscence is no longer, as in the lectures on the Sentences, merely the weakness of human nature,[73] which remains as the punishment of original sin after its guilt has been taken away in baptism. It is itself sinful, the perpetuation in us of that mortal disease of the soul which is inherited from Adam, and not only manifests itself in the sensual tendency, but pervades the whole nature of man [74] and operates in human nature as long as life lasts. It involves guilt,[75] and the guilt is not, as in the traditional view, taken away in baptism, so that concupiscence only remains as a weakness of human nature in punishment of original sin. It is persistent and permanent and stands in constant need of remission and healing by the grace of God.

This, he contends, is what the Apostle means when he says, " Sin dwelleth in me." [76] To this conviction Luther was already veering in the lectures on the Psalms and it becomes the distinctive conception of the Commentary on the Romans. He still, indeed, in certain passages, has in his mind the milder view of concupiscence as only " the proneness to evil and the difficulty to the good." [77] He can still approve Augustine's view that concupiscence does not involve guilt unless the will consents to the evil thought or desire, and it thus passes into deed.[78] Practically, however, he has reached the conviction that it is in itself sin and that

[73] " Werke," ix. 74-76.
[74] " Vorlesung," ii. 110. Peccatum artaverunt usque ad minutissimum quendam motum animi.
[75] *Ibid.*, ii. 179. Concupiscentia sit ipsa infirmitas ad bonum quæ in se quidem rea est.
[76] *Ibid.*, ii. 176.
[77] *Ibid.*, ii. 107. Pronitas ad malum et difficultas ad bonum.
[78] *Ibid.*, ii. 179, 181.

man is the slave of this inherited tendency to evil, which vitiates his moral nature and renders him and all his works worthless in the sight of a perfectly righteous God.

In the characteristic passages in which he expresses this conviction there is no reservation or qualification in favour of even the relative goodness of human nature. Concupiscence is that "infirmity or wound of the whole man" from which he needs to be healed by the grace of God.[79] It enslaves the will which, in the moral and religious sense, is not free. The will is, indeed, free in regard to what is within its competence and dependent on it (*liberum naturaliter*). It is not free in respect of that which is beyond its capacity. Being held captive by sin, it cannot choose the good in the religious sense (*secundum deum*), for without grace it has no power for righteousness, but is necessarily under the power of sin. It is only made free by the reception of God's grace, which alone gives true freedom.[80] It is dominated by self-love (*se ipsum diligere*), and by reason of this engrained self-love it cannot, by its own power, so far repress itself as to seek to do solely and singly what God wills. For Luther, as for the mystics, from whom he borrows, it is this engrained love of self, this egoism that constitutes the state of sin. It leads reason to seek its own good, not the good for God's sake and that of others.[81] It makes man his own end and idol,[82] bends him to his own interest (*incurvatum in se*) in spiritual as well as material things.[83] By nature he cannot do otherwise than pursue this self-inflexion.[84] This bent to the self [85] is the deepest instinct of his nature, is irremediable without grace, and is not fully knowable.[86] It is the natural vice, the natural evil which can only be removed by extrinsic aid,

[79] "Vorlesung," ii. 180. Ipsa infirmitas velut vulnus totius hominis qui per gratiam ceptus est sanari.

[80] *Ibid.*, ii. 212.

[81] *Ibid.*, ii. 184.

[82] *Ibid.*, ii. 189.

[83] *Ibid.*, ii. 184.

[84] *Ibid.*, ii. 185. Nec potest aliter ex natura sua nisi sibi inflectere.

[85] Curvitas et pravitas et iniquitas, ii. 189.

[86] "Vorlesung," ii. 189.

not by his own natural powers.[87] This egoism, inherited and inveterate, affects his whole being and renders him incapable of rectitude or righteousness in the absolute sense which God requires, and which seeks what pleases Him and not self. No amount of legal observance can effect this, inasmuch as, in the words of the Apostle, "the law is weak through the flesh." "Both intellect and emotion in virtue of original sin are in a state of darkness and bondage, and until faith dawns on the soul and love (in the selfless sense) frees them, man is impotent to will or possess or work the good. Nay he can only work evil, even when he does what is good."[88]

With this conviction in his mind, he now attacks the Nominalist theology all along the line on this cardinal issue. The attack is waged not merely on dogmatic but on experimental grounds. He challenges the theory that sin, concupiscence, as far as guilt is concerned, is taken away in baptism, or even in the Sacrament of Penance, by the operation of sacramental grace in the twinkling of an eye, as darkness is taken away by light. In view of the persistence of sinful concupiscence, this is a mere hallucination, and he appeals to his own experience and the testimony of the fathers in disproof of this dogma. "Thus I, fool that I was (in reference to his experience of this problem), could not understand how I ought to repute myself a sinner and prefer myself to no one after I was contrite and confessed. For I thought that all sin had been removed and evacuated even intrinsically. But if past sin is to be called to mind (as they truly say, though not sufficiently) then, thought I, these sins have not been removed, though God has promised their remission to those who confess. Thus I fought with myself, not knowing that there is truly remission, but nevertheless not the removal of sin, but only the hope that it will be taken away and the grace of God given, which begins to take it away in the sense that it is not imputed as sin."[89]

[87] Ideo ex naturæ viribus non habet adjutorium, sed ab extrinseco aliquo potentiore opus habet auxilio, ii. 184.
[88] "Vorlesung," ii. 184.   [89] *Ibid.*, ii. 108-109.

For the same practical reason he challenges the Nominalist teaching on the will and its powers. In view of man's inveterate egoism, he denies absolutely the Nominalist assumption that the will can actually elicit the love of God above all, in virtue of its own natural powers, merely because the intellect postulates that it should do so. There is at most but a tiny movement of the will,[90] a mere wish to will, which is altogether insufficient to realise this supreme dictate of the intellect. Man's ingrained egoism precludes the pure love of God apart from any consideration of self, such as fear of punishment or hope of reward. In the face of the law with its high and inexorable imperative, this is pure presumption, and the true attitude is, therefore, humility and distrust of one's natural powers.[91] He now rejects even the idea of a synteresis, or remnant of the good will, which he had formerly professed, and pronounces it of no avail or value, since the whole man is full of concupiscence.[92] Similarly, he now denounces the Nominalist doctrine that to him that does what he can and cherishes a good intention, God gives grace, though in the earlier part of the Commentary he still speaks of preparing or disposing oneself for grace in as far as in one lies.[93] This he now regards as covert Pelagian error, and by this error almost the whole Church has been subverted. The Nominalists do not, indeed, openly profess or consciously teach Pelagianism. They are influenced by the assumption that unless a certain freedom is allowed to the will, man is shut up by God to the necessity of sin and his moral responsibility is, therefore, endangered.[94] Hence their distinction between the power to substantially fulfil the law and the inability to fulfil it according to the intention of the lawgiver, for which grace is necessary.[95] Luther denies the inference that man is compelled to sin, though he does not squarely face it. God permits the wicked to sin even in their good works, but they are not, therefore, compelled to sin. Belief

[90] Sed solum tenui motu velle, ii. 188.

[91] " Vorlesung," ii. 187-188.   [92] Ibid., ii. 111.

[93] Datur ei gratiam per sui præparationem ad eandam quantum in se est, ii. 38.

[94] " Vorlesung," ii. 322-323.   [95] Ibid., ii. 110.

in the power to do what one can, trust in one's good intentions only induces a false security in one's own works,
whereas the true attitude is that of distrust and fear.
" Wherefore those who do good works accomplish nothing,
but rather always reflect, Who knows if the grace of God
co-operates with me in these works ?   How can I be sure
that my good intention is of God ?   How can I know
that in doing what in me lies I can satisfy Him (*Deo
placeat*)? " [96]   The distinction between the substantial fulfilment of the precept to love God above all and its fulfilment
according to the intention of the lawgiver is mere sophistry.
The law cannot be fulfilled in any fashion without grace,
and his indignation at this metaphysical quibble boils
over in vituperative apostrophe.   " O fools, O hoggish
theologians, so, then, if one can fulfil the law by one's own
powers, grace is not necessary, except for doing something
complementary to the law imposed by God !   Who can
bear such sacrilegious reasonings in the face of the Apostle's
dictum that ' the law worketh wrath and is weak through
the flesh,' and absolutely cannot be fulfilled without
grace ? " [97]   The great test in this matter is not logic
but experience, and he ironically asks them to test their
theory in the light of experience.   " Prove what you say,
that you can love God above all, in virtue of your own
natural powers, without grace forsooth !   If you are without
concupiscence, then we shall believe you.   But your own
experience tells you that the disposition to sin is always in us
and only begins to be removed by grace, and this removal is not
accomplished and the perfect love of God attained except in
the case of believers who struggle and persevere to the end." [98]

His conception of concupiscence as sin and his sense of
its power in the human heart farther lead him to reject
utterly the scholastic view that original sin is merely the
deprivation or lack of original righteousness, which he
had assumed in the lectures on the Sentences, and that
righteousness being a mere quality of the will, original
sin is merely the absence of this quality in the mind and
will.   This metaphysical abstraction is wholly incommensur-

---

[96] " Vorlesung," ii. 323.   [97] *Ibid.*, ii. 110.   [98] *Ibid.*, ii. 110.

able with the terrible reality of sin. For this deprivation affects the whole nature of man. Sin is no mere negative quality. " According to the Apostle, on the contrary, it is not merely the deprivation of a quality in the will, not merely the deprivation of light in the intellect, of strength in the memory, but absolutely the deprivation of all rectitude, of the whole faculty of all the forces of body and soul, yea of the whole internal and external man. Much rather is it the proneness to evil, the nausea towards the good, the aversion of light and wisdom, the love of error and darkness, the fleeing from and abomination of good works, the actual inclination to evil. . . . It is that innate concupiscence which renders us disobedient to the command, Thou shalt not covet. . . . Thus, as the ancient fathers have rightly said, original sin is the *fomes*, the law of the flesh, the law of the members, the languor of our nature, the tyrant, the original disease. For man is like a sick person, struck by a mortal malady, and the malady deprives not merely one member, but all the members of health, resulting in the debility of all the senses and all the forces of the organism. More than this, it causes a nausea of all that is wholesome and a desire of all that is noxious. It is that many-headed hydra, that monster, so tenacious, with which we fight like Hercules in the Lerna of this life until death ; the Cerberus, the untamable barker, and Antheus who, though dashed to the earth, is, nevertheless, insuperable." [99] The nature and power of original sin, thus luridly described, he had found, he says, nowhere so well expressed as in Gerhard Groot (Gerhard Zerbolt he should have said), who was no rash philosopher but a sane theologian.

The passage is rhetorical, doctrinaire. There is not even a Rembrandtian ray of light to relieve the darkness of the picture. At the same time, it is not the mere visionary outburst of the doctrinaire. One feels in it the vibration of his own heart, the reflection of the sense of the power and heinousness of sin, which had tortured his sensitive conscience and cast its dark shadow over his imagination in the sombre days of his experience in the Erfurt monastery. It is the echo of the "De Profundis" of a soul to which the self had been the great obstacle in the quest of the divine life, and which had known what it means to strive after the ideal of the love of God above all and to fail in this striving. The passage has to be read in the light of the autobiographical passages, in which he tells of this striving and this failure in the face of the recurring conviction of sin and its power. It has to be read, too, in the light of the conception of God as absolute righteousness and of human nature and its moral incapacity, as measured by this ideal conception. For Luther diagnoses human nature not from the philosophical but from the religious standpoint. Man and his capacity and his works are surveyed in the light of the highest, the absolute good, God; the standpoint of Jesus Himself, when He asked, Why callest thou Me good? There is none good but God. From this standpoint, human righteousness may well clothe itself in sackcloth and ashes in the conviction that, in relation to God, it is as darkness to light. It is simply impossible for human nature to will and work the good according to this standard, which it must attain in order to enter into a worthy fellowship with God, the highest good. For this it must perforce depend, not on its own righteousness, but on the grace of a merciful God. Moreover, egoism is, in very deed, as Luther experienced and human history proves, a terrible, an evil thing. In its proneness to perversity, self-will, selfishness, it is, in truth, a disease, which affects the whole man and inflicts and has inflicted untold misery on humanity.

At the same time, even from the religious point of view, this rhetorical delineation of diseased human nature reflects the one-sided monastic and mystic view of the religious life. The monk is concerned with the task of attaining the perfection of the Christian life by the process of eliminating from his nature all that conflicts with his ideal. He is concerned with what he conceives to be the supreme love of God, and he regards the ordinary Christian life as an essentially lower state, incompatible with this pursuit. This assumption of a double standard of Christian morality is in itself questionable and certainly betokens a narrow and one-sided view of life. The service of God, even the highest

form of it, is not necessarily confined to the life of prescribed
regulation and formal, mechanical religious exercises. Such
an attitude of mind is certainly not conducive to a large
and objective view of human nature. It will perforce
exaggerate and distort what it sees both in itself and in
humanity. This was the atmosphere that Luther breathed
and this atmosphere is reflected in his view of life. It is
that of the monk to whom the minutiæ of the monastic life
are invested with an exaggerated moral and spiritual
significance and who is ever obsessed with the thought of
transgression. And the mystic, in emphasising the evil
of egoism, is equally apt to exaggerate and distort. To
him, to love God in the supreme sense is to hate self.[100]
In its extreme form mysticism strives after the complete
elimination of personality in the religious life and lands
itself in a nerveless quietism. The mystic forgets that
personality, the ego, is the supreme fact of man's nature
and that the expression of self in personality is not necessarily
an evidence of an evil nature. On the contrary, it is the
distinctive thing that separates him from the brute, and
Luther is giving away too much in representing it as
essentially evil and demanding the radical suppression of
self. As a person, man is rightly conscious of his high
estate in the order of things, and the development of
personality in the exercise of all its powers and potentialities
is not necessarily the evil thing that Luther, under the
mystic influence, tends in one-sided fashion to represent it.
To be a person, to develop, not to repress personality in
this higher sense, is the true ideal and at the same time
the condition of moral progress. To this end self-respect
must not be sacrificed to indiscriminate self-depreciation,
and as monk and mystic there is a lack of balance and
breadth in his delineation of human nature.

Unfortunately, too, he is already too prone to stress the
antithesis between reason and faith in the discussion of
problems of this kind, in which philosophy as well as
religion has something to say, and for the solution of which
calm reflection, to which he is not temperamentally given,

---

[100] " Vorlesung," ii. 219.

as well as fervent religious feeling, is indispensable. It is, in fact, a misfortune that in dealing with such themes he is too much under the influence of traditional dogma and belief and too inclined to prove the superiority of his own logic over that of his opponents in the schools. It is hardly by way of a controversy in the fashion of the schoolmen that the absolute truth in these questions is attainable.

Nor is his interpretation of Paul's teaching on this subject above question. He shares the traditional view of an originally sinless man and a fall into sin, which underlies all this reasoning, and we cannot reasonably expect him to anticipate the conclusions on this subject of modern historic criticism and anthropological science. But it is questionable whether he rightly apprehended Paul's doctrine of original sin. Paul holds Adam responsible for the entry of sin into the world and for the sinful state which his posterity inherited. But he does not say, as Augustine and Luther assumed, that all sinned in Adam, apart altogether from their own actual sin.[1] What he says is that, through the entry of sin into the world, all actually sin, whereas Luther, following Augustine, mistranslates the original Greek and holds that all sinned in or with Adam. He is thus from the outset under a misapprehension of Paul's teaching. Moreover, Paul does not assume that human nature is wholly evil in consequence of the fall, though he says that all are under sin and quotes the lurid language of the Psalmist in proof of the fact (Romans iii. 9 f.). He recognises, in truth, that the Gentiles do by nature the things of the law, and that, in virtue of the moral sense, " the law written in their hearts," conscience, they are capable of moral action and responsible for their actions (Romans ii. 14-16). Judged by the Pauline standard, the dogma of the complete moral impotence of human nature is thus an exaggeration, and Luther himself admits that the Gentiles did by nature the works of the law, whilst explaining the admission away in accordance with his theory.[2]

[1] " Vorlesung," i. 48.   In reference to Romans v. 12, Luther translates the Greek phrase " inasmuch as all have sinned," by *in quo, in whom* all have sinned, and adds, peccatores facti sunt, licet nihil operati sint.

[2] *Ibid.*, ii. 38.

IV. RIGHTEOUSNESS AND ITS ATTAINMENT

Given the fact of sin and its effects in vitiating human nature and rendering it (in the religious sense) impotent to do the good, the problem is, how can man attain to righteousness in the sight of an absolutely righteous God, and thereby secure salvation from sin and its guilt? In solving the problem, Luther assumes that the attainment of this righteousness is solely the work of God. Salvation, he holds with Augustine, depends entirely on His sovereign will and grace. By the fiat of His will He predestines and elects those whom He has decreed to save and effectively carries out His eternal purpose in the individual soul. With the Nominalists he conceives of God as the embodiment of omnipotent will. But he differs from them in denying that the human will has any part in the carrying out of this purpose. Salvation is not dependent on the human will, for even if it were possible for the will to attain to righteousness in the sight of God by its own efforts, this would make salvation dependent on human contingency and, therefore, doubtful. Dependence on the divine will, whose purpose nothing can impair or prevent, on the other hand, both eliminates the element of contingency and excludes the factor of our own righteousness. " Where, therefore," he asks in reference to Romans viii. 28, " is now our righteousness, where our good works, where the freedom of the will, the contingency of things? Thus to preach is to destroy the prudence of the flesh. If so far the Apostle has cut off its hands, feet, and tongue, here he silences it and utterly kills it. Because now he sees that in himself he is nothing, but his whole good is in God alone." [3] The divine decree is, however, no mere arbitrary act. For if the righteousness of God depends on His will, as he holds with the Nominalists, His will expresses the highest good.[4] The fact that God is God excludes the possibility of ascribing unrighteousness to Him.

[3] " Vorlesung," ii. 209.
[4] *Ibid.*, ii. 223. Et vere nulla est alia causa suæ justitia nec esse potest nisi voluntas ejus. . . . Deinde cum voluntas ejus sit summum bonum.

In order to understand aright the righteousness that justifies the sinner in God's sight we must, he contends, discard the philosophic or juristic conception of righteousness and apprehend it only in the religious sense.   The philosophers conceive it as the quality or attribute of man's action which lends it the character of righteousness.   Luther, viewing the problem from the religious standpoint, denies that man's action can be in itself righteous in God's sight. Man being by reason of sin unrighteous, he must first be made righteous before he can do righteous works. Morality in the ordinary sense of good works is of no avail, and it is only on condition that the person is made righteous that the quality of righteousness can be ascribed to these works.

This conception he reiterates in a number of characteristic passages in opposition to that of Aristotle and his followers in the schools, who conceive righteousness as a *habitus* of the soul. " The righteousness by which God justifies," he insists in commenting on Romans i. 17, " differs from that of man which is concerned with works.   According to Aristotle in the third book of the Ethics, righteousness follows and arises from man's acts.   According to God it precedes works and works arise from it.   For just as no one can do the works of a bishop or a priest unless he is first consecrated for this purpose, so no one can do righteous works unless he first become righteous." [5]   " Righteousness and unrighteousness," he says in the comment on Romans iv. 6-8, " are understood in Scripture very differently from what the philosophers and the jurists understand by these words. For these assert that it is a quality of the soul, etc. But the righteousness of Scripture depends more on the imputation of God than on the essence of the thing. For in the Scripture he has not righteousness who has only the quality of it ; yea, such an one is a sinner and altogether unrighteous, and only he is righteous whom God, on account of the confession of his unrighteousness and his imploring the divine righteousness, mercifully reputes and wills to esteem righteous." [6] Just as the fruit does not bear the tree (in reference to Romans viii. 7) but the tree the fruit,

---

[5] " Vorlesung," ii. 14.   [6] *Ibid.*, ii. 121.

so virtue does not flow from works and acts, as Aristotle teaches, but acts arise from virtue, as Christ teaches. And just as we must make the tree good, before it can produce good fruit, so the moral nature of man must be transformed before it can be righteous and bring forth righteousness.[7] " It is impossible," he further says in reference to Romans x. 10, " to attain to the righteousness (that justifies) by any works, or wisdom, or efforts of man. . . . Verily the acquisition of this righteousness is a new thing and contrary to or above righteousness, as taught by Aristotle, seeing that in the Aristotelian sense righteousness is begotten by acts habitually done. But righteousness in the ordinary sense [8] avails nothing in the sight of God, nay it is reprehensible (*reproba*)." Hence the fundamental fact that man must first be made righteous before he can be righteous in the religious sense, and that his own righteousness is of no avail for salvation.

Reverting to his own experience of the problem, he tells of the heart-searching misery that the philosophic conception of righteousness had cost him. In spite of all the reasonings of the jurists and the babbling about good intentions, he only found that " God laughs our righteousness to scorn." [9] From the religious point of view, philosophy is misleading and it is because of this that Paul condemns it. To Luther, speaking from his own religious experience, it is " the pursuit of vanity and perdition." [10] Aristotle's teaching is, indeed, useful and beneficial in some respects, if rightly understood.[11] But the theologians have allowed themselves to be deceived by his fallacious metaphysics.[12] They have been more subtle than scriptural and have based their noxious phantasies on the Aristotelian virtues and vices, on mere human tradition and the prudence of the flesh, not on the testimony of Scripture.[13] The Nominalists, indeed, discriminated between righteousness in the religious

---

[7] " Vorlesung," ii. 192.   [9] *Ibid.*, ii. 273.
[8] *Ibid.*, ii. 244.   Justitia politica.   [10] *Ibid.*, ii. 199-200.
[11] *Ibid.*, ii. 266.   Sic enim de rebus philosophatur Aristoteles et bene, sed non ita ipsum intelligunt.   [12] *Ibid.*, ii. 178.
[13] *Ibid.*, ii. 182-183 ; *cf.* 108 (theologi scholastici) autem ad modum Aristotelis, qui peccata et justitiam collocavit in opera.

sense and righteousness in the Aristotelian sense.   Luther, in fact, took the principle that the person must first be righteous in order to act righteously from the schools.[14] But they have, he contends, failed to interpret it in the true scriptural sense, and have, under Aristotle's influence, and in contrast to the ancient fathers, practically confused justifying righteousness with works.[15]   He appeals from them to the Gospel, in which is revealed the difference between human and divine righteousness, and how the sinner becomes righteous in God's sight.   The Gospel alone reveals the great secret.   " In human teachings " (in reference to Romans i. 17) " is revealed and taught the righteousness of man, *i.e.*, who is righteous, and how he is and becomes righteous in the sight of men.   But in the Gospel alone is revealed the righteousness of God, *i.e.*, who is, and how he is and becomes righteous in the presence of God, viz., by faith alone, by which the Word of God is revealed. . . . For the righteousness of God is the cause of salvation, not in the sense in which He is righteous in Himself, but in the sense in which we are justified, made righteous by Him, which comes through faith in the Gospel." [16]

This is the great thesis as far as the positive attainment of righteousness and salvation is concerned.   As in the lectures on the Psalms, man's attitude to God must be that of a condemned person, condemned by conscience and the law which he cannot fulfil, cannot in fact do otherwise than transgress.   He must come in humility, in self-despair (as in Tauler and the mystics), and absolutely eschew the sense of security in his own righteousness, which is the great enemy of this essential humility.   He must be content to be the recipient of God's gift of salvation, empty himself wholly of the prudence of the flesh, its pride, wisdom, self-security (*securitas*).   He must renounce the " justiciarians," who teach otherwise, subjecting himself, despairing of himself before God (*se desesperant*).[17]   He must rely on the power of God in the Gospel to save him and recognise

---

[14] Holl, " Aufsätze," i. 95-96.

[15] " Vorlesung," ii. 108-109, 178, 182-183.

[16] *Ibid.*, ii. 14.

[17] *Ibid.*, ii. 223-245.

his impotence to save himself by his own righteousness. The consciousness of unrighteousness is an indispensable condition of justification.

In working out his theory of justification Luther makes use of the Nominalist formula of "the acceptation" of the sinner by God, whilst transforming it in the light of Paul's doctrine of justification, as he understands it. As in the lectures on the Psalms, God "accepts" the sinner as righteous by way of the non-imputation of sin and the reputation of righteousness. This theory he now works out in greater detail in accordance with his fuller study of the Apostle's teaching. The non-imputation of sin and the reputation of righteousness are two aspects of the same thing.[18] Non-imputation is, however, distinctively the forgiveness of sin. It is not purely an arbitrary act, as in the Nominalist theology. It takes account of the moral condition of the sinner and the saving work and righteousness of Christ. God only forgives those who through His grace are conscious of and bewail their sin.[19] It takes account also of the satisfaction for sin made by Christ, though Luther does not stress this aspect of the subject in the main portion of the Commentary. The redemptive work of Christ is essential to the remission of sin. Man is, indeed, freely justified by the grace or mercy of God and not in virtue of any satisfaction or merit on his part. But this grace does not operate apart from the propitiatory death of Christ, by which He rendered satisfaction for the sinner and at the same time showed that remission is due, not to our righteousness, but to the righteousness of God. In the face of an accusing conscience and a troubled heart, we can only take comfort in the fact that "Christ has made satisfaction for us, that He has made His righteousness mine and my sin His."[20] "God," he says in reference to Romans

[18] "Vorlesung," ii. 119. Ergo idem est dicere, cui Deus reputat justitiam, et, cui Dominus non imputat peccatum, *i.e.*, injustitiam.

[19] *Ibid.*, ii. 118. Per non-imputationem Dei propter humilitatem et gemitum fidei pro ipso (peccato) ; *cf. ibid.*, ii. 119, quia omnes confitebuntur quod propter hoc peccatum (*fomes*, original sin) tibi sunt injusti in veritate ; ideo tu remittes, etc.

[20] *Ibid.*, ii. 44.

iii. 24-26, " does not freely give grace in the sense that He
exacts no satisfaction for sin. But He gave Christ as the
satisfier on our behalf in order that He might freely give
grace to those who thus themselves make satisfaction
through another . . . and that we, being unrighteous,
should seek our righteousness from God alone, who first
remits our sins on account of Christ's propitiatory
suffering." [21] More especially it takes account of the
righteousness which Christ, through His indwelling in the
justified soul, actively works in us, whereby the unrighteousness which still remains is covered.[22] Non-imputation is
thus not merely a judicial act. It has respect to the real
righteousness operated in us by Christ, as well as to the
righteousness by which He satisfies God in our stead. This
is, in fact, the characteristic element of it.

Non-imputation involves the other aspect of justification
—the reputing of righteousness to the sinner. This reputation is also conceived in no formal sense, for it also has an
ethical aspect. To repute righteous is also " to receive,"
" accept," " adopt." [23] God not only regards the sinner
as righteous. He receives, accepts him into fellowship
with Himself, makes capable of this fellowship one who,
before, was incapable of it, and He alone can create this
relation of fellowship. It is due solely to the exercise of
His mercy or grace in making him thus acceptable (*gratus*),
since his own righteousness is utterly incapable of achieving
it. " We are righteous extrinsically and not of ourselves,
or our works, but solely by the imputation of God. For this
reputation is not in ourselves nor in our power. And,
therefore, our righteousness is not in ourselves nor in our
power." [24] Whilst Luther makes use of the Nominalist
idea of " acceptation," he decisively repudiates the

---

[21] " Vorlesung," i. 33-34.

[22] *Ibid.*, ii. 123. Idcirco enim bene operando peccamus, nisi Deus per
Christum hoc imperfectum tegeret et non imputaret . . . quæ iniquitas
non invenitur in credentibus et gementibus, quia succurrit eis Christus
de plenitudine puritatis suæ et tegit eorum hoc imperfectum. *Cf.* ii. 113.
Tegitur, inquam, *per Christum in nobis habitantibus* . . . et tegitur
ipsius justitia.

[23] Accipere, suscipere, assumere, acceptare.   [24] " Vorlesung," ii. 104.

Nominalist view that God is pleased to accept our works and, therefore, reputes us righteous. In refutation of this view he adduces the explicit teaching of Paul in Romans iv. 6, that " God reckoneth righteousness apart from works," and reiterates his fundamental principle that the person must first be made righteous before it can do righteous works. " God does not accept the person on account of the works, but the works on account of the person." In other words, the person must first be righteous before the works can be accepted.[25] He rejects, too, the scholastic idea of meriting in any way this reputation. " The word ' repute,' " he insists, " expresses the sole, the gratuitous acceptance of God, and not any merit of works on the part of man." [26] Only the man who appears wicked (*impius*) in his own sight can be reputed righteous in God's sight.[27] " How," he asks, " can a man boast of his own merits and works, which are in no way pleasing to God because they are good and meritorious, but because God has decided from eternity that they shall be pleasing to Him. We, therefore, do well (*bene operamus*) only in giving thanks to Him that our works do not make us good, but our goodness, yea the goodness of God, makes us good and our works good. For they would not be good unless God reputed them such. They only are good or not in so far as He reputes, or does not repute them to be such. For our reputing or not reputing is nothing. He who understands this will always be fearful and await the reputation of God. And therefore he will know nothing of that pride and presumptuous contending of the ' justiciarians ' who are so sure of their good works, which are in truth abominable in God's sight and the contrary of pleasing to Him." [28]

He now repudiates even the relative merit of doing what in one lies (*meritum de congruo*), which the Nominalists assumed in the interest of man's moral responsibility. Man, he contends, may be free to do what he wills, to act

according to his good intention.[29]   But this does not make
his works acceptable to God.   To this end he can do nothing
of himself,[30] and the only possible attitude in the presence
of God is fear and the self-distrust, which implores the grace
of God and eschews the confidence that, if he does what he
can, he makes himself even relatively pleasing to God.
Luther, it must be remembered, in conceiving the relation
of fellowship into which God brings man by reputing him
righteous, always thinks of God as the absolute good, of
righteousness in the ideal sense.   His deliberate and
reiterated conviction is that, in virtue of the nature of God
as Absolute Good and of the imperfect nature of man,
this relation can only be brought into existence by the
merciful acceptation of God Himself.   So profound is this
conviction of the radical divergence between the two, so
deep his sense of human imperfection that he goes the
length of saying that, even in doing good, we sin, unless God
through Christ covers our imperfection and does not impute
it.   Our good works are, in fact, sins in the judgment of an
infinitely perfect God.[31]   From this point of view he rejects
the traditional distinction between venial and mortal sins,
since sin, as the fruit of this imperfection, cannot be otherwise than mortal in God's sight.[32]

At the same time he hardly faces the question of man's
moral responsibility, or that of the moral quality of man's
works apart from this acceptation.   He still thinks of the
problem in terms of the Nominalist conception of the
acceptance of God as solely an act of the divine will, whilst
emphasising the ethical nature of the relation between God
and the soul, which it creates.   He is hampered by the
scholastic train of thought.   One could wish that he had
discarded the scholastic apparatus of this theory of non-
imputation and reputation, and, recognising man's dependence

[29] " Vorlesung," ii. 223.   Non quidem coguntur ad peccatum, sed
faciunt quæ volunt et secundum bonam intentionem.

[30] *Ibid.*, ii. 223.   Homo ex se nihil potest facere.

[31] *Ibid.*, ii. 123.   Stultus itaque nimis est qui ex operibus suis sese
justum putat habendum, cum si judicio Dei offerantur, peccata sint et
inveniantur.

[32] *Ibid.*, ii. 123.

on God for salvation and eschewing the dogmatic explanation of the divine method, simply ascribed it to the exercise of the grace of a merciful God in reckoning righteousness to the sinner, as Paul more simply does. Nor does he free himself from the influence of the old terminology in writing of this subject. He still speaks, for instance, of " preparing oneself for receiving God's grace," of " meriting grace and justification," of " disposing oneself by works for the grace of justification," of " self-discipline as necessary for the giving of grace." [33] The language in which the theory is expressed is not at times strictly consistent with the theory itself. But the context shows that, if he sometimes uses the old phraseology, he has discarded the old idea of actively preparing for or meriting the acceptance of God, the exercise of the divine grace in reputing man righteous. It is the Pauline conception of grace, not that of the schoolmen that he has laid hold of. " Not," he is careful to add in reference to the phrase ' meriting grace,' " that grace is given to them by reason of such merit, since in this case it would not be grace. . . . Both Jews and Gentiles are under sin, however much they do the good. All and each are sinners and need the grace of God." [34] " None of the saints," he adds, in speaking of preparation for justification, " esteems and confesses himself righteous, but always seeks and awaits that he may be justified." [35]

V. FAITH AND THE ASSURANCE OF SALVATION

The attainment of righteousness is possible only for those who believe in Christ. For the unbeliever Christ's redemptive work is an act of judgment, not of redemption, since it shows forth the condemnation of sin and condemns those who do not in faith accept its benefit.[36] To faith, therefore, Luther assigns a superlative part in the salvation

[33] " Vorlesung," i. 42 ; ii. 84, 91, 93, 95.
[34] *Ibid.*, ii. 42.
[35] *Ibid.*, ii. 95.
[36] *Ibid.*, i. 34. Potius in tribunal et judicium mutatur.

of the soul. It is a *sine qua non* for the effective realisation of God's saving purpose, since remission is only given to those who believe in Christ. Simply stated, faith is for him the conviction in the mind of the truth of God's word and promise in the Gospel. He rejects the scholastic distinction between incomplete and complete faith.[37] To believe is to be absolutely convinced that what God has revealed and promised in Christ, or the Gospel, is true, and that He will implement this revelation and promise.[38] It means, farther, to maintain this conviction in the face of every predilection or prejudice to the contrary, and thus to justify the ways of God in His dealings with man.[39] We must implicitly believe what God reveals and promises in the Gospel, even if this involves, as it must do, disbelieving all our cherished convictions about ourselves and our works. He even goes the length of saying that we cannot believe God to be true, good, wise, and righteous unless we believe ourselves to be mendacious, foolish, unrighteous, and evil in His sight.[40] We must absolutely subject our understanding (*nostrum sensum*) to the Word of God, speaking in the Gospel, in all that concerns our salvation.[41] An indispensable condition and feature of faith is, therefore, humility and obedience— humble distrust of self and all its powers and works, readiness to subject oneself to God's word and will. Hence the reiterated emphasis on the humility and obedience of faith, which leads us to seek salvation outside ourselves and our works in the grace and mercy of God.[42] By this humility and obedience alone can we attain to the true knowledge of God and the true knowledge of self.[43] Such knowledge, begotten of faith, is impossible to the proud of heart, who presumptuously rely on their wisdom and

---

[37] Fides informis and fides formata.

[38] " Vorlesung," ii. 64. Igitur Deus justificatur in sermonibus, *i.e.*, dum creditur ei in evangelio de impletione promissi ut verax et justus habeatur. Sermones enim isti sunt verbum evangelii in quibus justificatur, dum ei creditur quod vera in illis dicat.

[39] *Ibid.*, ii. 62 f.

[40] *Ibid.*, ii. 57.

[41] *Ibid.*, ii. 89-90.   [42] *Ibid.*, ii. 112.   [43] *Ibid.*, ii. 67.

righteousness, and nullify God's word and promise in the
Gospel by their proud incredulity and rebellion.[44]

From this point of view, Luther conceives of faith as an
act of the intellect. It denotes the true understanding or
perception of the divine plan of salvation. It is the
apprehension of God in Christ, in submission to the divine
authority. Luther is still under the influence of the scholastic
conception of faith as an intellectual act, as a new knowledge
perception of the will of God. He thinks in terms of the
Occamist view of the knowledge of God as based solely
on an authoritative revelation which the mind apprehends
in faith. But if faith is the right apprehension of what is
revealed in the Gospel, it is not determined by the understanding itself. It is the gift of God.[45] The mind is purely
receptive of the Gospel.[46] God lays hold of, captivates the
intellect in bringing it to the knowledge of Christ.[47] In
begetting faith He transforms the mind and leads it to the
knowledge of His will.[48] From the intellectual point of
view, faith is, in short, a divinely inspired intuition of
what the mind is otherwise incapable of perceiving.[49] It
is an experience operated by the Spirit of God.[50]

Moreover, this experience is of a moral and spiritual as
well as an intellectual character. It affects the will as well
as the intellect, the affections as well as the mental faculties.
In his definition of faith Luther thus does not merely borrow
from the abstract reasonings of the schools. He speaks
from his own experience of it as both illuminating the mind
with a new conception of God and His saving purpose, and
as suffusing the heart and the will with the love of God.
" Faith," he says, " is life and the living word abbreviated "

[44] " Vorlesung," ii. 64, per superbam incredulitatem et rebellionem.

[45] *Ibid.*, i. 107, fidem donat ; *cf.* ii. 66, donum ipsuis ejus.

[46] *Ibid.*, ii. 206. Ad primam gratiam sicut et ad gloriam semper nos
habemus passive, sicut mulier ad conceptum.

[47] *Ibid.*, ii. 234.

[48] *Ibid.*, ii. 270. Fides enim ipsa transformat sensum et ducit ad
agnitionem voluntatis dei.

[49] *Ibid.*, ii. 269, super omnem sensum ; ii. 270, contra omnem sensum
et consilium nostrum veniat.

[50] *Ibid.*, ii. 269, sola autem experientia cognosci possit.

—the quintessence of the Gospel apprehended by the mind and appropriated as the dynamic of the will.[51] It begets " a passion, a throbbing for God (*affectus et requisitus Dei*), and this is the love of God itself, which impels us to will what the intellect had impelled us to understand." [52] " Therefore unless faith illumines and love frees, no man is able to will, or possess, or work anything good." [53] It may operate through the intellect.   But it is only as it penetrates into the interior darkness of the soul (*in medias tenebras interioris*) and produces this experience of God that we can have any real knowledge of Him as He has revealed Himself in the Gospel.   Even so, this knowledge is not of the nature of a definite apprehension of what He is, since in Himself He is transcendental, incomprehensible, inexperimental.   It is only attainable through the emotions, through love.[54]   This aspect of faith reveals the mystic rather than the scholastic influence on Luther's thought.

Faith, being the conviction of the truth of God's word and promise in the Gospel, involves farther the assurance that what He has promised, undertaken, He will perform. It is reliance, confidence, trust (*fiducia* [55]) in the fulfilment as well as the conviction of truth.   To believe is also, necessarily, to confide (*confidere*), and this confidence finds its expression in hope (*spes*),[56] not merely in the vague sense of the possible or probable realisation of what we seek or desire, but of the definite assurance that what we seek or desire will be realised.   The believer is assured that God will maintain him in faith and so direct and sustain him that he will ultimately attain salvation.   Here again Luther owed something to the schoolmen.   But here also his conception of the assurance of salvation differs from the Nominalist view of *fiducia*, which was based on the confidence that God will ultimately accept the works of the

---

[51] " Vorlesung," ii. 234.   Fides est vita et vivum verbum abbreviatum.
[52] *Ibid.*, ii. 76.   [54] *Ibid.*, ii. 138.
[53] *Ibid.*, ii. 184.   [55] *Ibid.*, ii. 115.
[56] *Ibid.*, ii. 114-115.   Quæ omnia in nobis non nisi per fidem et spem in ipsum (Christum).

believer as meritorious in His sight and grant him salvation accordingly.   Luther, on the other hand, bases it solely on faith in God's gracious promise of salvation, begetting the confident hope that He will bring to pass what we have not merited and cannot merit in any sense.   An indispensable condition of its realisation is self-distrust, not self-confidence (*securitas*).   Such security is totally false, and against this security he emphasises the element of self-distrust, which is ever a cardinal feature in the life of the believer.   For hope, assurance does not exclude all fear, anxiety about our salvation.   So emphatic is his testimony in certain character-istic passages, in which he denounces the false security of those who confide in their works, regarded as merits, that he almost seems at times to undermine the hope that springs from faith.   Because we are sinners, always under the power of concupiscence, we are ever under the necessity of seeking, recurring to the mercy and grace of God.   Thus the life of the believer is one of constant humility, penitence for sin, absolute dependence on God's grace in not imputing sin.   Fear, anxiety because of innate sinfulness is, therefore, the indispensable mark of the believer's life, in contrast to the false security of " the hypocrites," as he calls those who cherish the false confidence in themselves and their works.   " Therefore," he says, " this very security is the mother of hypocrites and the cause of hypocrisy.   For thus God leaves us in sin, in concupiscence, that He may keep us in the fear of Himself and in humility, so that we may always recur to His grace, always be fearful lest we sin, praying always that He may not impute it to us and may not permit it to rule over us.   Yea, we sin in the very fact that we do not fear, since the evil in us is, by itself, sin, because thereby we do not fulfil the obligation to love God above all.   Herein alone, however, it is not imputed in that we bewail it, imploring His mercy, praying that it may be taken away by His grace, and thus confessing ourselves to be sinners and esteeming ourselves sinners in beseeching, repenting, deploring, and weeping." [57]

But given this indispensable humility and self-distrust,

<hr>

[57] " Vorlesung," ii. 116.

the believer may, on the other hand, assuredly hope that
God will ultimately implement His promise of salvation in
the Gospel. This promise is, indeed, the guarantee of its
realisation, since God must be true even if all men are liars.
On this ground this assurance must maintain itself even
in the face of the grim problem of predestination. " Those
who fear and tremble about their election have the best
token (*signum*) of it. . . . For in despairing of themselves
the Word of God which produces this fear does its own
work. . . . Wherefore if anyone fears and is greatly tried
concerning his election, let him give thanks to God for such
fear, let him rejoice that he fears, since he knows assuredly
(*scit fiducia*) that God cannot lie who says, ' the sacrifice
of God is a broken spirit, and a broken and contrite heart
Thou wilt not despise.' " [58] From this point of view predestination and election are now to Luther " the sweetest
of words," though " to the prudence of the flesh they are
bitter and hard above all," [59] and in view of his own
experience he warns his hearers to beware of the Nominalist
speculations on this subject, if they would not fall into an
abyss of horror and desperation, and exhorts them first to
cleanse their vision by meditation on the wounds of Christ.[60]
Moreover, to build on the sure foundation of Christ, on God's
grace, and not on our own works, is to have peace of conscience
and assurance of heart.[61] Above all, such trust is involved
in the filial relation to God into which faith brings the
believer, who is made conscious of his sonship by the Spirit
of God. Here the intellectual aspect of faith is completely
merged in the emotional. In its most intense form, assurance
has its root in the heart, not the intellect. In this consciousness of sonship we ought not to fear God or anything that
He wills and loves. In this conformity of love we become
" sons of God and fashioned unto God." [62] Luther's faith
is prepared to submit even to damnation, if such be the will
of God. To will what God wills even in this extreme case

[58] " Vorlesung," ii. 214.

[59] *Ibid.*, ii. 208.

[60] *Ibid.*, ii. 209-210, 226.

[61] *Ibid.*, i. 110. Requiem conscientiæ et fiduciam cordis.

[62] *Ibid.*, ii. 197. Deiformes homines et filii Dei.

is not to endure evil,[63] and the believer who attains to the highest form of love will even joyfully and freely desire to be eternally damned, if God so wills, in order that His will may fully be done. But it is impossible for those who so absolutely conform to the divine will to remain in hell, because they would not be without God, and where God is there is no hell.[64] This is the faith of the religious virtuoso, and Luther here unmistakably reflects the influence of Tauler and the mystics. The doctrine was not unknown even to the Nominalists in their abstract tendency to stress the divine will, and herein Luther also shows the scholastic proneness to reason out a theory to its extreme logical conclusions, without asking whether the premises are really tenable, or whether the theory is anything but a feat of logic.

The assurance of salvation in virtue of the truth of God's word and promise in the Gospel and of the consciousness of sonship is thus a cardinal feature of Luther's theory of justification by faith. It distinguishes this theory from that of the Nominalists, which makes justification dependent on the will of God in accepting or not accepting man's works, regarded as merits, and therefore makes his final salvation problematic. On the other hand, he speaks at times as if this assurance is not equivalent to certainty. He makes, for instance, a distinction between " believing in Christ " and " believing in all that Christ stands for, or is." [65] " Although we are certain that we believe in Christ, we are nevertheless not certain that we believe in all His words. And because of this to believe in Him is uncertain." [66] In view of this uncertain faith, he even says that " we can never know whether we are justified, whether we believe." [67] " No one," he says again, " knows by experience that he is justified." [68] Again, " No one knows the reputation of

---

[63] " Vorlesung," ii. 223.

[64] Ibid., ii. 217-218 ; cf. 215.

[65] Ibid., ii. 87. Credere in Christum and Credere in omnia quæ Christi sunt.

[66] Ibid., ii. 89.

[67] Ibid., ii. 89. Nunquam scire possumus an justificati simus, an credamus.

[68] Ibid., i. 54. Nemo enim experitur se esse justificatum.

God, but ought only to ask and hope for it." [69] "As God and His counsel are unknown to us, so is our righteousness, which wholly depends on Him and His counsel." [70]

How explain this inconsistency? There seems in these utterances to be in him a remnant of the old scholastic dubiety on the subject. Luther has not yet caught the absolutely confident tone of Paul in the triumphant conclusion of the 8th chapter of Romans, "There is, therefore, now no condemnation to those that are in Christ Jesus," etc. A certain inconsistency there is in his teaching on this point. This inconsistency is, in part, due, it seems to me, to the fact that in such passages he regards the subject from the side of the sinner who distrusts himself and is the humble suppliant for God's grace and mercy. Humility and fear are here the uppermost emotions. It is partly due also to the emphatic repudiation of the self-security of those who presume on their works for acceptance with God. Moreover, salvation being entirely the work of God and in the ultimate resort traceable to His will and decree, there must always be an element of mystery in it, a lack of absolute knowledge, on man's part, of the divine will and action. Though he has overcome his former doubts about election and holds that it is certain that the elect are saved, it is nevertheless an inscrutable mystery, and without a special revelation, as in the case of Paul, no one can be certain of his election. [71] For Luther, justification is not the act of one moment in the consciousness of the believer, though the believer is constantly conscious of the exercise of the divine mercy and grace towards him. It is a lifelong process of remission by a gracious God, because the believer is always subject to sin and, therefore, in need of being justified as long as he is in this life. From this point of view there is, therefore, a certain element of uncertainty or suspense in his experience of it. Luther, it must also be remembered, has not yet said his last word on the subject of justification in the Commentary on Romans, although the doctrine in its essentials is already there.

[69] "Vorlesung," ii. 104. Cujus reputationem nemo novit, sed solum postulare et operare debet.
[70] *Ibid.*, ii. 124.   [71] *Ibid.*, i. 81.

At the same time, the assurance of salvation is the conclusion to be drawn from the general and fundamental principle that God is both true and able to bring to pass His will and purpose, in spite of the mystery that enshrouds them and the constant need of justification on the part of the believer. His work must finally prevail, even if complete knowledge of it is impossible, and the believer may never presume so far as to forget his absolute dependence on Him. His attitude must always be that of seeking, awaiting the realisation of God's saving word and promise in the Gospel. As long as sin lasts, that is, as long as life lasts, God's work with the believer is not fully realised. In view of its incompleteness, we can never absolutely know that we are finally justified and saved, whilst we may assuredly confide that God's grace will accomplish what we ourselves cannot do or merit.[72]

VI. The Moral Regeneration of the Believer

Justification involves for Luther far more than the formal reputation of righteousness. As God is Himself absolute righteousness, so His purpose in justification is the moral regeneration of the sinner. The reputation of righteousness is but the beginning, the condition of this process of moral regeneration. God thereby seeks to change and does change the heart of man from evil to good, begets the new will to righteousness in begetting the faith that saves him from his own unrighteousness. Justification is not really a

[72] The theologians are divided in opinion as to the question of the attainment by Luther of the certainty of salvation. Loofs (" Dogmen-Geschichte," 707) holds that he had not yet attained to this conviction in the Lectures on Romans. This is also the conclusion of Braun (" Koncupiszenz," 60 f.). Ficker thinks that he is still hesitating between two opinions. " Certainty is there, and yet it is not there " (Introduction to " Lectures on Romans," 77). Seeberg holds that he has already decided the question in the affirmative (" Dogmen-Geschichte," iv. 107), and Holl agrees with him (" Aufsätze," i. 91 f.). Holl points out that the question of the certainty of salvation is not the same as that of the certainty of predestination and election, as to which he had certainly not yet made up his mind, and that Loofs confuses the second with the first question.

question of formal but of real righteousness in the sinner, wrought in him by God, and God alone, through Christ. It is a process of healing the disease of sin from which the sinner suffers, effecting his moral restoration, and Luther's favourite illustration of it is the action of the Good Samaritan in taking compassion on, caring for, and healing the wounded wayfarer.[73] Christ is the Good Samaritan who heals wounded, sin-stricken humanity, through whom the grace and mercy of God operate in the cure of the disease of sin.[74] As the Great Physician, God in Christ has reached down in His infinite goodness to draw the sinner to Himself,[75] to heal, to restore him to that moral and spiritual state in which alone he can enter into fellowship with Him. In justification the process of healing, restoring, means, therefore, more than merely to repute the sin-stricken sufferer righteous. It means also to render him righteous.[76] God's righteousness, in the scholastic phraseology which he uses, is active as well as passive. " He endues man with righteousness when He justifies the wicked." [77] " The resurrection of Christ is not only the seal (sacramentum) of our righteousness ; it also affects it in us." [78] On the part of God, to whom time is non-existent, justification, in the double sense of reputing and making righteous, is one and the same thing. It is an instantaneous operation of His power and grace, the effect of His eternal fiat, to which will and act are one. For Him the beginning includes the end. Reputing and making righteous are simultaneous in His sight.[79] " Just as," says Holl, " the great sculptor already sees in the block of marble the finished

---

[73] " Vorlesung," ii. 108, 111.

[74] *Ibid.*, ii. 108 f. ; *cf.* ii. 94 and 332.

[75] *Ibid.*, ii. 296. Deus convertit quos convertit per intuitum suæ bonitatis, *i.e.*, per amorem et benignitatem.

[76] Not merely reputare justum, but facere or efficere justum. *Ibid.*, ii. 65, 98.

[77] Justitia Dei qua induit hominem, cum justificat impium. *Ibid.*, i. 32.

[78] Resurrectio ejus non tantum est sacramentum justitiæ nostræ, sed etiam efficit eam in nobis. *Ibid.*, ii. 129-130.

[79] *Ibid.*, ii. 141. Licet jam coram Deo essemus in prædestinatione justi. Quia in prædestinatione Dei omnia facta jam sunt quæ in nobis futura sunt.

statue, so God already sees in the sinner whom He justifies the righteous person whom He will fashion." [80] On the part of man it is a process in time, prospective as well as actual, and begins from the moment that faith consciously begins to operate in the mind and heart of the believer. It is actual only in the sense that God thereby begins in him a process of moral healing, regeneration. It is prospective in the sense that He will finally and surely bring it to completion. " God begins in order that He may complete." [81] " It is with the believer as with the sick man who believes the physician promising him most certain restoration to health, and who, obeying his precept in the hope of this promised restoration, abstains from those things which the physician prohibits, lest he hinder his restoration and aggravate the disease, until the physician fulfils his promise. Is the sick man then sound ? Yea he is at the same time sick and sound. He is sick in fact ; he is sound by the certain promise of the physician whom he believes, who reputes him sound because he is certain that he will heal him, because he has begun to heal him and does not impute to him a sickness unto death. In the same way Christ takes the half-dead man, His sick one into His hostel (*stabulum*) for the purpose of curing him, and begins to heal him, promising him the most perfect restoration to eternal life, and not imputing sin unto death, but meanwhile prohibiting him to do whatever may impede his restoration and increase sin and concupiscence. Is he, therefore, perfectly righteous ? By no means. But he is at the same time sinner and righteous, a sinner in fact, but righteous in virtue of the imputation and certain promise of God that He will free him from sin until he is perfectly whole. And thereby he is perfectly whole in hope, though in deed a sinner, having yet the beginning of righteousness, so that he seeks it more amply, knowing himself to be unrighteous." [82]

From this point of view, he is not yet justified (*justus*), but to be justified (*justificandus*), and, therefore, Luther

[80] " Aufsätze," i. 104.
[81] " Vorlesung," ii. 94. Non enim justificavit nos, *i.e.*, perfecit et absolvit justos et justitiam, sed incepit ut perficiat.
[82] *Ibid.*, ii. 107-108.

can speak of stages in the process of justification—of being so far justified, of always being justified, of the progress of justification, of preparing for complete justification.[83] In this sense he frequently uses the phrase, " always a sinner, yet always righteous ; always penitent, yet always being justified." [84] From this point of view, too, he can even say that it is indispensable for justification to fulfil the law by works. " No one is reputed righteous except him who by his works fulfils the law." [85] " Only the doers of the law will be justified in the sight of God." [86] At first sight these utterances are startling and perplexing. They appear to be contradictory of his fundamental principle of justification by faith alone. The law, he has reiterated with Paul, condemns, because it cannot be fulfilled. The belief in work righteousness by way of the law is the fatal error of the justiciary theologians ; the irreligious expression of human pride and self-security, begetting " hypocrisy," and leading to delusion and damnation. None the less, only the doer of the law will be justified ! Is not this a remnant of the scholastic leaven working unawares at the back of Luther's mind and practically nullifying his whole doctrine of justification ? By no means. For Luther is careful to add that " no one fulfils the law except him who believes in Christ," and that " the doers of the law who will be justified are those alone who have grace to overcome the evil will in them." [87] The law, as the expression of the will of a perfectly good God, condemns, indeed, and cannot be fulfilled by the sinner, because of the power of sin, concupiscence within him, which renders him and all his efforts unacceptable to God. But in virtue of the non-imputation of sin and the reputation of righteousness, by which God reckons him righteous in His sight, and the power of His grace

---

[83] " Vorlesung," i. 45, adhuc semper justificamur ; ii. 15, ut qui justus est, justificatur adhuc. ne quis statim arbitratur se apprehendisse et ita desinat proficere ; ii. 91, ut justificentur magis ac magis . . . sed per ea ad justificationem se parant ; ii. 95, ad sequentem profectum justificationis.

[84] *Ibid.*, ii. 267.

[85] *Ibid.*, i. 20. Nullus autem reputatur justus nisi qui legem opere implet.

[86] *Ibid.*, i. 20.   [87] *Ibid.*, i. 20.

operating in his mind and heart by faith, God Himself fulfils in him the law, spiritually regenerating, morally healing him. " The law was, in fact, given that grace might be sought, and grace was given that the law might be fulfilled." [88] There is an infusion of grace [89] which both renders him acceptable to God and gradually works in him, prepares him for that complete justification in the life to come, when his nature will be fully renewed and the process of becoming righteous will be complete. Nay, Christ Himself takes possession of him, lives in him, produces His own righteousness in him. For Luther has grasped the Pauline conception of possession by the Spirit, or by Christ.[90]

Only, this process of justification is not equivalent to the scholastic conception of infused righteousness or grace. Luther will know nothing of the formula of " faith formed by love," in the scholastic sense, as the principle of justification. Here he also diverges from the Augustinian conception of it as the result of faith and love, which the scholastics expressed by this formula, though he retains Augustine's idea of it as a process of healing. He angrily denounces that " accursed phrase, formed by love," as used by the scholastic doctors.[91] Against this conception he contends that justification requires not the works of the law, but a living faith, which operates its own works.[92] Faith being God's gift, the works of faith are His, not ours, and, therefore, these works are good if we do not confide in them but in the grace that makes them effective.[93] Nor does he speak of an infusion of grace in the sacramental

[88] " Vorlesung " ii. 93. Lex ergo data est ut gratia quereretur. Gratia data est ut lex impleretur ; cf. ii. 99. Extra fidem nullus hoc facit, i.e., opere legem implere. He quotes Augustine's famous saying, Lex operum dicit, fac quod jubeo ; lex fidei autem, da quod jubes. Ibid.

[89] Ibid., ii. 218, gratiæ infusio.

[90] Ibid., ii. 157. Sicut enim radius solis est æternus, quia sol æternus, ita vita spiritualis est æterna, quia Christus æternus est, qui est vita nostra, qui per fidem in nos per radium gratiæ suæ influat et manet ; cf. i. 66. Deus in Christo regenerat hominem generatum sanatque vitiatum a reatu statim, ab infirmitate paulatim.

[91] Ibid., ii. 167. Maledictum vocabulum illud " formatum charitate."

[92] Ibid., ii. 86.　　　　　　　　　　　　[93] Ibid., ii. 91.

sense. God acts directly with the individual, not through the sacramental medium of the Church, in giving the grace that reputes righteous and makes righteous. In either case the notion of merit is excluded. Justification is, from beginning to end, wholly, exclusively the work of God, on whom the sinner is absolutely dependent.[94] In this respect Luther also differs from the later view of Melanchthon, who in effect represented faith as the ground of justification and thus imparted to it something of the character of a merit, instead of simply regarding it as the instrument in effecting God's purpose of reputing and rendering the soul righteous.[95] Luther's doctrine of justification as a process of moral regeneration has often been misunderstood and misrepresented. Roman Catholic writers like Denifle, for instance, can see in it nothing but the moral bankruptcy of its author and the moral atrophy of human nature. " Of the driving out of sin," says Denifle, "there can be no question in this system." [96] Grisar is more discriminating and admits that his doctrine did involve the struggle with sin and was intended to effect the moral regeneration of the sinner.[97] At the same time, for Grisar, his view of justification by non-imputation is something exterior and mechanical, in contrast to the Roman Catholic conception of it as an interior organic process, showing itself in works of penance and purification from sin by contrition. The inference, it is to be feared, betrays a rather exterior and mechanical knowledge of what Luther actually taught. Anglican critics like Mr Mozeley also speak without due knowledge in

[94] "Vorlesung," ii. 124.   Quid ergo merita sanctorum adeo predicantur? Respondeo quod non sunt eorum merita, sed Christi in eis propter quem Deus eorum opera acceptat quæ alioquin non acceptaret.

[95] See Holl, " Aufsätze," i. 107. Melanchthon hat die Luthersche Rechtfertigungs-lehre verdorben, indem er die Lehre von der göttlichen Alleinwirksamkeit abschwächte. Er hält diese Lehre wohl aufrecht bei der schilderung der Entstehung des Glaubeus ; aber er vermag nicht ebenso wie Luther das ganze neue Leben als ein zusammen hängendes Gotteswerk, als das ziel auf das Gott mit der Rechtfertigung hinstrebt zu begreifen. Bricht man aber dies Stück aus, so wird Alles bei Luther schief.

[96] " Luther und Lutherthum," ii. 465.

[97] " Luther," i. 96, 112 f.

describing the doctrine as Antinomian. Luther does not, as
Mr Mozeley contends, deny the applicability of the law
in the case of the justified person.[98] He is bound to fulfil the
law as the expression of the divine nature and will. Only,
he does this by the divine power or grace operating in him
and rendering his works acceptable to God. The critic has
overlooked the fact that for Luther there are two functions
or aspects of the law—the law as testifying to sin and
condemning the sinner, and the law as the expression of
God's nature and will, which, by the power of His grace,
the sinner is enabled to fulfil. Nor is salvation merely a
matter of imputed righteousness.[99] The imputation of
Christ's righteousness is at the same time a real moral
conversion to God and the beginning of a process of growth
in righteousness. Mr Mozeley's knowledge of Luther's
thought is rather superficial. It may be said by way of
excuse that he wrote before the discovery of the Commentary
on Romans, and, therefore, without the aid of this inestimable
key to a knowledge of his early development. The same
excuse cannot be adduced on behalf of Mr Pullain,[100] who
gives a still more one-sided and superficial version of Luther's
doctrine of justification.

Such critics fail to realise what his conception of sin
and justification implies. It is conditioned by his lofty
conception of God, and he will not admit that, from the
religious point of view, anything short of the perfect good
can avail in the sight of a perfectly righteous God. Even
if we question his view of human nature as inherently
corrupt, we must logically admit that, if there is to be a
feasible relation between God and man, God Himself must
lift man up to the capacity of this fellowship. But, while
he thus magnifies human sin and impotence from this point
of view, he also magnifies righteousness, and he certainly
does not regard the doctrine of justification as a mere
refuge from moral bankruptcy. Justification has undoubtedly for its object the real and effective moral

[98] " Essays, Historical and Theological," 342 (1878).
[99] *Ibid.*, 339, 350.
[100] " Religion Since the Reformation " (1923).

transformation and elevation of sinful human nature. In developing this doctrine he is no more Antinomian than Paul. In rediscovering Paul he gave to the modern Church the magnificent dynamic of the spiritual life, which consists in faith expressing itself in love, in the evangelical sense, and in the mystic indwelling of Christ in the soul. Buried with Christ in baptism, rising with Him to new life, whereby He becomes incarnate in us anew, is characteristic of the teaching of Luther as of Paul.[1] Already in the Commentary he enunciates the great principle of his later work on "Christian Liberty," that the Christian, whilst lord of all, in virtue of justification by faith, is also the servant of all and subject to all in ardent self-discipline and service for others. In this respect the altruistic note of the Commentary is unmistakable. The quietistic note is, indeed, very marked in the emphasis on the receptivity of the soul in the hands of God. But equally emphatic is the insistence on the necessity of self-discipline and service by the grace of God in active obedience in doing what He wills and thereby overcoming all.[2] If he emphasises the nullity of the works of the law for justification, he only does so in contrast to the works by which God realises His righteousness in us and which are an essential of the process of justification.[3] Justification is not a mere covering of sin. It is a conversion from death to life, from sin to holiness. " The justified person, whose sins are covered, is already converted and pious, for he worships God and seeks Him in fear and hope." [4] The Christian life is a warfare against sin and the devil on behalf of God and righteousness. We are called, not to ease and self-security, but to the warfare with self and sin. " Those who have been baptized or absolved from sin in the Sacrament of Penance, forthwith esteeming themselves without sin, become secure in their acquired righteousness and fold their hands in restful calm, being unconscious of the sin which with groans and tears, lamentation and labour they should overcome and purge out. But sin remains in the spiritual man for the exercise of grace,

---

[1] " Vorlesung," ii. 129.
[2] *Ibid.*, ii. 297-298.
[3] *Ibid.*, ii. 99-100.
[4] *Ibid.*, ii. 113.

for the humbling of pride, and the repression of presumption.
. . . For we are not called to ease, but to labour against
the passions. Sin is alone not imputed to those who manfully
fight against their own vices, invoking the grace of God.
Therefore let not him who comes to confession think that
he casts off his burden in order that he may live in ease,
but let him know that, having cast it off, he takes upon
himself the warfare of God, and subjects himself to another
burden for God against the devil and his own internal
vices." [5] In this warfare God energises the will and so
strengthens it that it joyously and freely seeks to attain the
highest good, not relaxing its efforts because of the hardness
and irksomeness of the struggle, but persevering in its
pursuit. " For this, I say, we must insistently pray, learn,
work, chastise ourselves until the old leaven is eradicated
in the will and the new is formed. For grace will not be
given without this self-husbandry." [6] Good works are not,
therefore, to be reprobated in as far as they are good and
holy, as if they were to be neglected, but only as to the
meaning and estimation of them for the attainment of
righteousness in God's sight. [7] On the contrary, the
operation of God's grace through faith brings out the
highest moral capacity of the soul, develops the highest
moral life in fellowship with God, the object of which is the
liberation of the soul from the power of sin. " We groan
to God for liberation ; yea we long for the close of life itself
in order to attain the state of perfect righteousness. [8] . . .
Meanwhile believing His promise that He will liberate us,
we persevere that sin may not rule over us." [9] Of this
liberty we have already a foretaste in love, which enables
us to serve God joyously, freely as sons, and not as slaves
who serve from fear or reward and therefore reluctantly
and with a mercenary will. [10]

Justification thus means for Luther the acquisition of
real as well as reputed righteousness. It is the work of

[5] " Vorlesung," ii. 178-179.
[6] *Ibid.*, ii. 93.   Sine ista agricultura sui ipsius.
[7] *Ibid.*, ii. 71.   [9] *Ibid.*, ii. 106.
[8] *Ibid.*, ii. 95.   [10] *Ibid.*, ii. 139.

God from beginning to end and only the operation of God's mercy and grace makes it possible. It is the divine method of achieving the regeneration of the believer, and it assuredly realises God's purpose, of which it is alike the vindication and the triumph.

CHAPTER VII

LUTHER AND THE MYSTICS (1515-1517)

I. THE THEOLOGIA GERMANICA OR GERMAN THEOLOGY

" IF," wrote Luther to Spalatin in December 1516, " you take delight in pure and solid theology in the German language—a theology very similar to that of the ancients— get the Sermons of John Tauler, of the Order of Preachers, of whose teaching I send you herewith an epitome. For I have not found in Latin or German a more wholesome theology, or one more consonant with the Gospel. Taste, therefore, and see how sweet is the Lord, where formerly you have seen how bitter is whatever is of ourselves." [1] The epitome mentioned in this letter was a fragment of the mystic teaching current among the Friends of God in the fourteenth century. This fragment he published in 1516 under the title of " Ein Geistlich Edles Buchlein " (A Spiritual Noble Booklet), with a preface in which he points out that the style and contents are similar to those of Tauler's Sermons. [2] In a subsequent letter he informs him that nothing so valuable in theology had hitherto come under his notice and that not even the most erudite Erasmus could have composed such a treasure. [3] He was so fascinated by its teaching that in 1518 he published the whole work from a manuscript which had meanwhile come into his hands, under the title of " Ein Deutsch Theologia," with a new preface, in which he reminds the reader that St Paul

[1] Enders, " Briefwechsel," i. 75 ; cf. 90. Luther seems in this letter to regard Tauler as the author. This is, of course, an inaccurate impression.
[2] " Werke," i. 153 ; Mandel, " Theologia Deutsch," Introduction, 1-2 (1908).
[3] Enders, i. 90.

had despised the art and wisdom of men, and warns him against being repelled by the crude style of the work, which is all the richer because of its simplicity and divine wisdom. Next to the Bible and St Augustine, he had never come across any book in which he had learned more about God, Christ, man, and all things. It is for him a striking testimony that his own theology, which has aroused so many opponents as if it were something unheard of, is not new, but old. " Let who so will read this little book and then say whether our theology is new or old. I thank God that I thus hear and find my God in the German tongue as I, and they along with me, have not hitherto found either in the Latin, Greek, or Hebrew tongue." [4]

Who the author was is unknown. In the preface to the manuscript of 1497, on which Pfeiffer based his edition,[5] the author is said to have been " a priest and warden of the house of the Teutonic Order at Frankfurt." Certain it is that he was a member of the brotherhood of the Friends of God, the widespread mystic association which flourished in Western Germany in the fourteenth century, and of which Tauler, Nicolas of Basle, Henry of Nordlingen, Rulman Merswin, Suso, Margaret and Christina Ebner were the leaders.

Luther's appreciation of this product of German mysticism has been shared by many since his day, though it has found some notable critics in Calvin, Beza, and others. In the original German, and in French, Dutch, English, and Latin translations it has had a wide circulation in innumerable editions, and has continued to exercise considerable influence on religious thought. In the letter prefaced to Miss Winkworth's English translation in 1854, Baron Bunsen calls it " a golden book." In the preface to this version Kingsley refers to it as " this noble little book." Dean Inge considers it superior to " The Imitation of Christ," [6] and Rufus Jones describes it as " the literary gem of the religious movement " represented by the Friends

---

[4] "Werke," i. 378-379.
[5] "Theologia Deutsch " (1851-52).
[6] "Christian Mysticism," 181.

of God.[7]   What strikes one at once is the contrast, in content, style, and spirit, to the conventional scholasticism. It discards the scholastic method of logical discussion and demonstration of doctrine. Religion is for the author, as for the circle of which he was a member, a thing of the heart, not of the intellect. It is based, not on reason, but on intuition, on the inner light, as directed by the teaching of the New Testament, especially the mystic utterances of Christ in the Fourth Gospel, and of Paul. Dionysius, Boethius, and Tauler are the only writers he quotes by name, outside the new Testament. For him the intricate scholastic theology is non-existent, and for the subtle reasonings of the scholastics he substitutes the experience of God in the individual soul in its aspiration after the divine life. Luther had already, as we have noted, sought enlightenment and peace in his troubled quest for God in the speculative mysticism of Bonaventura, only to be repelled by his abstract reasonings on the union by contemplation of the soul with God. The author of the German Theology starts, indeed, with a speculative conception of God as Perfect Being, which he takes from Meister Eckhart, the speculative genius of the Friends, and which goes back, through Scotus Erigena, to the Neo-Platonic philosophy of Plotinus. The book is a combination of Neo-Platonism, as reflected in the writings of Eckhart, from whom he directly borrows, with the teaching of the New Testament, especially the mystic element in Paul and the Fourth Gospel. It is in this respect a characteristic product of mediæval mysticism. To this underlying speculative conception, God in Himself is a pure abstraction, who cannot be concretely conceived, is in fact the negation of anything that man can predicate of himself, such as consciousness, reason, will, or even personality. The divine, thus abstractly conceived, cannot be known or expressed, because we cannot ascribe to it any faculty or quality in ourselves, and to rise to it, to attain to union with it, we must seek to get beyond self, repress self and all that pertains to it. This speculative element, which he asserts and reiterates in the characteristic mystic style, is certainly not the feature that attracted Luther, for the God of Luther is no pure abstraction of this kind, but a concrete, personal being, the perfect embodiment of man's rational and moral nature. But the object of the writer is not to develop a mystic philosophy in the style of Meister Eckhart. He has, in fact, no faith in reason as a means of finding God, who is above reason and all that reason can postulate, and is to be known only as He reveals Himself in the soul, in intuition, the inner light, experience, and especially in the incarnation in Christ, in whom the divine perfectly dwelt. God's immanence in the soul and the world is the characteristic conception, in contrast to the scholastic conception of Him as transcendental. But the speculative element is subordinate to the practical problem how He may be thus found, and in what the divine life engendered in the soul by Christ consists, and how it is to be attained.

In working out this theme he has certainly grasped certain distinctive points of the Pauline and Johannine teaching, which he enforces in practical fashion and in striking contrast to the scholastic, dialectic method. It was this feature of the work that appealed so powerfully to Luther. In his train of thought and religious experience there is, in truth, not a little that is akin to that of Luther. There is a keen sense of sin and its evil effects, of the impotence of human nature by reason of sin to attain the divine life apart from God, of the complete dependence of the soul on God for salvation, of the innate disposition to seek the good of self instead of the good for its own sake, of the necessity of self-distrust, self-effacement in the relation of man to God. For him, as for Luther, sin is self-will in disobedience to the will of God, the egoism of the creature over against the Creator, which led Adam, and with him humanity, astray in the pursuit of his own good in place of the perfect good, which is God. This egoism is the fatal aberration from which God alone can restore man.[8] In order to be restored he must begin by realising that he can do nothing by himself to effect this restoration. " In this restoration and recovery I can, may, and shall do nothing,

[8] Ch. 3, 4, 14, 34 (Mandel's edition).

but simply yield myself, so that God alone may do and work all things in me, and I suffer Him and all His works and His divine will." [9]   For the mystic, as for Luther, there is a spiritual crisis in which the soul thus becomes conscious of sin, guilt, unworthiness, and in which it tastes of hell. This is what is involved in true repentance for sin, which God works in it.   The soul must first, like that of Christ, descend into hell before it can ascend into heaven.   But God does not leave it in this hell, though this experience may often recur.   He lays hold of man, brings him to Himself so that he desires nothing, regards nothing but the eternal good and becomes a partaker of the mystic joy, bliss, and peace of heaven.[10]   This heavenly peace does not, indeed, imply absence of tribulation, for true peace does not consist in external things, but in peace of heart.   As with Christ, the Cross, suffering is the inevitable experience of the mystic Christian.

The restoration of man to God is effected in the incarnation of Christ.   For the mystic Christian, as for Athanasius, God assumed human nature in Christ in order that man might become divine.   By no other way could his self-will in disobedience to God be remedied.[11]   Hence the surpassing significance of the life and death of Christ. By His life of perfect obedience to the will of God, that which died in man by Adam's disobedience has again become alive in Christ.   Through him the death of self-will, the old man, disobedience to God, has been accomplished, and the new man, the life of perfect obedience, has become a reality and has been made possible for his followers.   Christ's human nature was so utterly bereft of self that it became the very " house and habitation of God." [12]   Thus through Him His followers may be restored from sin and its evil effects and become partakers of the divine life in Him.[13] In proof of this mystic teaching he appeals, not to the fathers or the scholastic theologians, but to the words of Christ and Paul, the exclusive authorities for his soteriological teaching.   " Therefore St Paul exhorts to put off

---

[9] Ch. 3 ; cf. 4 and 5.   [10] Ch. 11 and 35.
[11] Ch. 3.   [12] Ch. 13.   [13] Ch. 13 and 14.

the old man with all his works and put on the new man
which, after God, is created and formed (in Christ) and His
followers. Behold where the old man dies and the new
is born, there takes place the second birth of which Christ
spoke, Except a man be born again he cannot enter the
Kingdom of God. Likewise St Paul says, As in Adam all
die, even so in Christ shall all be made alive. . . . Whence
it followeth that all Adam's children are dead before God.
But he who is with Christ in true obedience is with God
and lives. As already said, sin consists in the turning away
of the creature from the Creator. For he who is in disobedience is in sin, and sin can never be atoned or remedied
but by a returning to God, and this is brought to pass by
humble obedience. For as long as a man is in disobedience,
his sin can never be atoned ; do whatever he will, it avails
him nothing. . . . But when a man comes into obedience,
all is remedied, atoned, forgiven." [14] Man's obedience
can, indeed, never be so perfect as that of Christ, because he
cannot be sinless, perfectly selfless. But it is possible to
every one by God's grace to approach so near to this perfect
obedience that he may be said to be divine and a partaker
of the divine nature.

At the same time, he may not presume that he is without
sin or regard the good in him as his own doing, since goodness belongs to God alone. He may only credit himself
with what he does amiss. Nor does the death of self in
him mean indifference to or irresponsibility for the evil
in him.[15] It means the fashioning of his life after that
of Christ. Christ's life is the best and noblest that ever
has been lived, and this highest life he must live as long as
he is in the body, though it involves the Cross and is bitter
to human nature.[16] Moreover, he must put on the life of
Christ, the new man, from love and not for the sake of
reward.[17] Without this pure, selfless love, however great
his knowledge, he cannot become a partaker of the divine
nature. " In such a man must all thought of self, all self-
seeking, self-love and all that pertains to self be lost and
surrendered to God, to whom the self belongs, except in so

[14] Ch. 14.   [15] Ch. 15.   [16] Ch. 14 and 18.   [17] Ch. 36 and 40.

far as personality requires its exercise. And whatever comes to pass in a God-like, deified man, whether in doing or in suffering, it is done in this light and in this love, from the same, through the same, unto the same again. There is in his soul a content and a restfulness in not desiring or seeking to know more or less, to have, to live, to die, to be or not to be or anything of this sort—these are all one and alike to him, and he complaineth of nothing, but only of sin." [18] " Briefly, where this true light is, there is the true and right life which God values and loves. And if it is not the life of Christ in its perfection, it is framed and formed after him, and Christ's life is loved, and all that pertains to probity, order, and virtue, and all self, I, mine, and such like is lost and nothing is purposed or sought than the good for its own sake and as good." [19]   The Friend of Christ will seek only to become the instrument of the will of God, of whom Paul says, " For as many as are led by the Spirit of God they are the sons of God and are not under the law, but under grace." [20]   He will submit with complete patience and resignation to all the crosses that befall him, without desire of redress, or deliverance, or resistance, or revenge, in accordance with the example of Christ.[21]   In this respect he is a thorough-going quietist. Nor will he substitute licence for liberty, like the Brethren of the Free Spirit, who follow the false light of nature and are misled by spiritual pride, are without conscience or sense of sin, practise a lawless freedom, and regard all restraints, laws, and regulations as " weak and beggarly elements." [22] Though he is not under the law, but under grace, and external regulations are not necessary for the perfect, and though salvation does not depend on them, he will submit to the laws and precepts and sacraments of the Church, knowing that laws and ordinances are necessary for the multitude, and that Christ thus submitted Himself. This too is necessary to that complete union with God in Christ, wherein our will is one with the eternal will, yea is swallowed up and lost therein.[23]

[18] Ch. 41.   [20] Ch. 19 and 20.   [22] Ch. 23, 29, 37, 39.
[19] Ch. 38.   [21] Ch. 21.   [23] Ch. 25 and 27.

So far he has said nothing about the significance of faith in the restoration of man to God, and it is only towards the conclusion of the book that he touches on faith as a fundamental element in the experience of the mystic Christian. Faith in Christ, he says, must precede knowledge, and this faith is not identical with mere belief in the articles of the creed, which is common to all professing Christians, whether they be sinful or saved, wicked or good. It is the inward experience of the words of Christ. " He that believeth not shall be damned," and without this experimental faith one can have no true knowledge of these things. In what it consists he does specifically tell us, for his concern is rather with the divine life in the soul through Christ, and what this life involves, than with the theological interpretation of it.

This is the main content of the message of this naïve fourteenth-century mystic which impressed Luther so powerfully. It was the experimental, evangelical element in his thought, rather than the speculative element underlying it, that arrested him. For both, sin is self-will, egoism ; salvation from sin the work of God alone. It is not attainable by human goodness or any act of the will apart from that of God. It is made possible only by God in Christ, and the life acceptable to God, the true, divine life, is attainable in no other way. At the same time, this mystic redemption is not for Luther the whole Gospel, and he did not attain to his characteristic principle of justification by faith along the channel of mediæval mysticism. His enthusiastic appreciation was evidently influenced by the fact that he found so much in it akin to his own thought in its revulsion from the scholastic theology, and tending to justify and support his antagonism to this theology. He found in it, in fact, an evidence that his theology was, in some respects at least, old, not new, and he was inclined to make the most of this evidence as against his opponents. In this mood he was prone to find a fuller reflection of his teaching in any work that strongly moved him than the facts really warranted. The mystic strain in him responded enthusiastically to this discovery, and he undoubtedly assimilated some ideas from this mystic source. But the source of his mysticism was mainly the New Testament itself, and this little book appealed to him just because in it the mystic element in Paul and the Fourth Gospel was so characteristically assimilated.

On the other hand, what strikes the reader of it, fresh from the perusal of the Commentary on Romans, is the absence of the Pauline doctrine of justification by faith, which to Luther was the kernel of the Gospel. The author seems to have no interest in or aptitude for this cardinal element of the Pauline teaching. He has no ear for the Pauline reasoning on the law and grace, faith and works, though believing in Christ is to him an inward experience, and not a mere intellectual apprehension. This is all the more singular inasmuch as he frequently quotes Paul in support of his mystic Gospel. He certainly had no grasp of this side of his doctrine of salvation. Equally striking is the quietistic note, which ill accords with the virile evangelical spirit of the Apostle, who so characteristically combined his mystic conception of the indwelling Christ with a consuming missionary zeal. The monotonous emphasis of the writer on self-effacement to the extent of the annihilation of the will suggests too much the negative life, though he is at times superior to his theory and has some room, in his culture of the divine life in the individual soul, for the active Christian spirit of service for others. He sometimes means, too, by self-repression only the repression of the evil in self—the dying to self in order truly to live. " I would fain," he finely says, " be to the Eternal Goodness what his own hand is to a man." [24] Nevertheless he was in spirit and outlook a passivist rather than a reformer, and Luther would never have learned from him the secret of militant service in the warfare against the evils rampant in the Church and the world.

II. LUTHER AND TAULER

Tauler, whose sermons Luther appraised so highly, was also a disciple of Eckhart. The speculative background of these sermons is derived from the same mystic

[24] Ch. 10.

source. But they were not addressed exclusively to the
select circle of the Friends of God, to which he also belonged,
but mainly to the congregations that crowded to hear the
popular preacher at Strassburg and Cologne. Though a
member of the Dominican Order, his vocation as popular
preacher brought him into close contact with the people,
and whilst the speculative mysticism of Eckhart forms
the philosophic kernel of his message, he strove to make
it intelligible to the ordinary Christian in the interest of
practical Christianity. Many of his sermons are, in fact,
powerful appeals to the heart and conscience of his hearers
in the style of the impassioned evangelist. Even when
he seems to forget the limited capacity of the ordinary man
for such mystic speculation and discants on the mystic way
of salvation in the manner of Meister Eckhart, the practical
note is seldom altogether absent. Along with the speculative
tendency he has an alert eye for the concrete side of religion.
He is the preacher of a living piety, an exalted Christian
ethic which has its root in the dependence of the soul
on God and its model in the life of Christ. His preaching
is Christocentric. His central theme is the incarnation of
Christ, His revelation of God as the divine Word or Logos,
His perfect life as the God-man, His suffering and death,
His indwelling in the believer, and the surpassing significance
of His person, His teaching, His work in the regeneration of
the soul. His sermons begin with the nativity and he never
gets far away from the thought of the eternal, the historic,
the crucified, and the exalted Christ and what He means
for the divine life, which the soul has lost and to which
it is restored through Him. In this respect, the biblical,
evangelical note of his preaching is much more marked
than in the German Theology. The Bible is the great source
from which he draws his inspiration and his message, and
though he quotes freely from the fathers and the schoolmen,
especially from Augustine, St Gregory, Anselm, and Aquinas,
as well as from the mystics—the pseudo-Dionysius, Hugo
of St Victor, St Bernard, Eckhart—his paramount authority
is the prophets and the New Testament, especially the
mystical and practical teaching of the Gospels and the
Apostles.

Unfortunately his predilection for the allegoric method of interpretation, which he shares with his age, enables him to exercise his ingenuity at will in defiance of the historic sense of the Scriptures, and greatly lessens the force of his message for the modern reader. Equally questionable is the ingrained tendency to read the Gospel in the light of the Neo-Platonist mystic speculation, to make Jesus and Paul the exponents of mediæval mystic theology. With this is mingled the mediæval ecclesiastical conception of Christianity. For Tauler, though in some respects an opponent of the current theology and ecclesiasticism, is a devout and obedient son of the mediæval Church. The evangelical note does not, therefore, always ring true to the teaching of Jesus and Paul. At the same time there is so much in his train of thought akin to that of Luther that it is not difficult to understand why these sermons made such an appeal to his mind and heart.

The great problem is the attainment of the divine life in God, which is necessarily conditioned in man by the limits of his creaturely existence, and has farther been impaired by the corrupting influence of sin. There is a divine element in the soul, and for Tauler, as for Eckhart, this divine element is what he calls its " inner ground," its highest being or essence, which is higher than the rational and sensuous element in it, and in which the image of God consists. In virtue of this divine element, man was originally, and may become again, a partaker of the divine nature, one with God. He may attain to deification, and in this divine state he will not only be freed from the sensuous side of his nature. He will rise above the limits of reason, which can only conceive and know God in terms of the finite, and will become conscious of Him (*erkennen*) as He is in Himself—the inconceivable, incomprehensible entity, of whom reason can predicate nothing that really corresponds to what He is. This, simply stated, is the thesis which recurs again and again in his sermons in as far as they deal with the problem of the attainment of the divine life from the speculative-mystic standpoint.

But this abstract side of the problem, which leads dangerously near to pantheism, is for the initiated or more advanced Friend of God, and it was certainly not this aspect of his mystic teaching that appealed to Luther. Tauler himself, in fact, warns his hearers against losing themselves in this abstruse train of thought, though he constantly harps on it in his sermons. No teacher, he says, should entangle himself in these abstruse questions, but should confine himself to what he has experienced. What impressed Luther was just the experimental treatment of the problem in the light of the teaching of Scripture, rather than of mystic speculation. If Tauler, on the intellectual side, was obsessed by the ideas of Meister Eckhart and works them into his sermons, his main interest as a preacher lies in experimental religion, and his great theme is the incarnation, life, suffering, and death of Christ in their bearing on the regeneration, the spiritual and moral uplift of the individual soul. Hence the biblical, practical, evangelical note which overtones the speculative one in most of them.

With Augustine he regards human nature as totally corrupted by original sin, which, as in the German Theology, consists in self-will. He pictures this corrupting effect of sin as luridly as Luther himself. Sin has enslaved the will and poisoned man's nature; it has alienated him from God and doomed him to eternal death and damnation—the spiritual misery of hopeless estrangement from God as well as the bodily pains of hell. " Thereby," we read in Sermon 1, " he lost all the grace and all the powers and virtues that should lead him into the likeness and fellowship of God and the holy angels, and poisoned his originally pure and holy nature, inflicting deadly wounds on himself. Thus his understanding has become quite darkened, his will completely perverse and wicked, his natural appetite and desire wholly shameful, and his zeal and indignation against evil utterly weak and powerless. He is under the dominion of the world, the flesh, and the devil, and wholly impotent without God's grace to do the good. He is, indeed, capable of self-determination. In his fallen state he retains, in the inward ground of the soul, something of the divine image in spite of its defacement by sin. As a sculptor is said to have exclaimed on seeing a rude block of marble, ' What a God-like beauty thou hidest,' so God looks on man, in whom

His own image is hidden." But it is only in virtue of the divine grace, operating in the inward ground of the soul, that he can turn to God and free himself from the bonds of sin. Conversion, regeneration is wholly the work of God. It is God that seeks man rather than man that seeks God,[25] and in this experience the soul is purely receptive, cannot even co-operate with God. It cannot take place except through self-humiliation, self-negation, springing from true self-knowledge and repentance, and the sense of absolute dependence on God's grace and mercy. Moreover, true repentance is not that which springs from the fear of hell and the mere desire to escape its consequences in the interest of self. This is mere self-seeking, the love of the creature, not of God. Repentance considers God, not self. It is the fruit of the consciousness that sin is an offence against Him, and only such repentance is acceptable to Him and experiences His grace in forgiveness.[26] It is in this selfless spirit that man must repress his own will in order that God may work His will in him.[27] "The Spirit," he says, in the Sermon on Pentecost, "must prepare a place for himself in the heart and must conceive himself in man. This he does in two ways. In the first place, he makes empty and free of self; in the second place, he fills what he has made empty. . . . Where God is to enter in and dwell in the soul, the creature and all that belongs to it must go out. . . . It must be quit and free of self-will, self-love, self-esteem." [28] Nor may anyone take credit to himself for this self-repression, for it cannot be accomplished without God's grace, and he may not attribute the work of God's grace, even a hairsbreadth of it, to himself or his works, but always regard himself as an unworthy sinner.[29]

Not only is the experience of conversion, regeneration wrought solely by God's grace. It is not possible without

<hr />

[25] Tauler's "Predigten," edited by Kuntze and Biesenthal, in modern German, i. Ser. 3 (1841).
[26] Ser. 42 (K. and B., ii.).
[27] Ser. 7 and 12 (K. and B., i.).
[28] Ser. 22 (K. and B., ii.) ; Vetter, "Die Predigten Taulers aus der Engelberger und der Freiburger Handschrift," Ser. 60 c. (1910).
[29] Ser. 39 (K. and B., i.) ; cf. ibid., 41.

the incarnation, life, suffering, and death of Christ.   By becoming man and living the divine-human life, Christ made it possible for man to become through grace like God.   From this point of view he emphasises the superlative importance of Christ's incarnation and example as the God-man. Through the God-man the image of God is restored in human nature and, in and through Him, the believer becomes a child, a son of God, and attains the true knowledge (*Erkenntnis*) of God and fellowship, union with Him.[30]

This is regeneration considered from the more intellectual point of view.   But it has another aspect—that of deliverance, salvation from sin and its guilt and power, and in this aspect the suffering and death of Christ are strongly emphasised.   Christ is the Saviour who, in His unspeakable grace and mercy, seeks the sinner and receives him who comes to Him with a broken spirit.   By His death He has saved us from sin and its guilt and the power of the devil, and rendered it possible for God in His grace to forgive sin.[31]   He took our sins on Himself and made satisfaction to God.   " Our sins were ascribed to Him, and His works to us.   For Christ has not otherwise made satisfaction for our sins than if He had Himself committed them, and what He has merited by His works, that we do not otherwise receive and enjoy than if we had merited it ourselves." [32] By His atoning death He has made possible for fallen man restoration, reconciliation.   " This is the day," we read in the Sermon on Pentecost, " in which the precious and dear treasure, which was lost in Paradise through sin and disobedience, was restored.   Thereby the whole human race fell into eternal death and lost the Holy Spirit, the Comforter, with all His gifts and consolations, and all men fell under the eternal wrath of God and under the bonds of death. These bonds Christ broke asunder when on Good Friday He allowed Himself to be seized and bound, and died on the Cross.   Through His death He made peace and reconciliation between man and His Heavenly Father.   To-day this

---

[30] Ser. 2, 3, 8, 9, 10 (K. and B., i.).
[31] Ser. 4 (K. and B., i.).
[32] Ser. 11 (K. and B., i.).

reconciliation is confirmed, and the noble, precious treasure which was lost is restored, viz., the Holy Spirit." [33] Even where, as in Sermon 40,[34] Christ's death is set forth as an evidence of the infinite love, mercy, and obedience of the Son of God, its significance as an atonement for and a reconciliation of the sinner with God, is reflected. The evangelical note is also clearly discernible in the interpretation of the healing of the sick man in the pool of Bethesda.[35] No one can be healed from sin, as the infirm man was healed by the stirring of the water, except through the blood of Christ, and without this healing all will be eternally lost in soul and body. " But when thus the Holy Spirit moves the heart, then the sick man, *i.e.*, the outward man with all his powers and outward senses, is immersed in the true pool, which is the crucified Jesus Christ, and washes himself in His sacred and precious blood, and becomes in his inmost nature truly healed from all sickness of soul, as it is written, ' All who touched the Lord were made whole.' "

In the presence of the Cross the sinner realises the heinousness of sin. Like the soldier who was crucified along with Christ, he is conscious that " no pain is so great that it would suffice for the punishment of his sins according to the divine justice." But it also arouses within him a firm faith in the unspeakable grace and mercy of God in Christ and the sure hope of eternal life, which rests not on his own works or merits, but on this firm faith, manifesting itself in love.[36] At the root of this faith and hope is the conviction of sin and impotence, the true humility and sense of unworthiness in God's sight. " A man," he says, " must take the lowest place as a miserable sinner among his fellow-men, realising that through himself he has nothing, can do nothing, will nothing that is acceptable to God, and that all of good in him he owes to the grace and mercy of God." It is only as we set all our hope and trust in God's mercy, crying with the publican, God be merciful to me a

---

[33] Ser. 22 (K. and B., ii.) ; Vetter, Ser. 60 c.
[34] (K. and B., i.).
[35] Ser. 22 (K. and B., i.).   [36] Ser. 28 (K. and B., i.).

sinner, that we can build the Christian life on its true foundation.[37]

Faith is thus for Tauler not exclusively the intellectual conviction that leads to the true knowledge or consciousness of God, as in the more speculative aspect of his teaching. It involves trust in God's word and promise of forgiveness. This promise we must accept in the firm faith that He will fulfil it. " Nothing," he says, " is so certain as the word and promise of God, for has not the Lord said, ' Heaven and earth shall pass away, but my word abides for ever.' " [38] Faith in this sense is equivalent to the confidence in the certainty of forgiveness, which brings peace and rest to the troubled conscience and casts out fear at the thought of God's justice or righteousness. To this faith, God's mercy is not incompatible with His righteousness, for as the Father of His children His righteousness even demands the exercise of His mercy. It is in this faith that the believer receives and offers the body and blood of Christ in the sacrament, which shows forth His sufferings and death for sin. " The conscience of the believing soul, which receives the sacred body and blood of Christ and offers them to the Heavenly Father on the altar of the heart, is washed and cleansed from all the stains of sin, as is said in the Book of Revelation, ' They have washed their robes and made them white in the blood of the Lamb.' This is that lovely pledge whereby our souls are saved from all the bonds of sin." [39]

The emphasis in such passages on faith, trust in God's word and promise, in humble dependence on His grace and mercy in Christ, constitutes the most evangelical note in these sermons. In keeping with it is the reiterated stress on inwardness in religion, on the direct relation and contact of the soul with God, on the futility of external works apart from the inner disposition. Whilst he reverences the teaching, sacraments, ordinances, and usages of the Church, the main thing in religion is the inner voice of God speaking in the soul, the operation of His spirit in the heart of the

---

[37] Ser. 29 (K. and B., i.) ; *cf*. Ser. 9 (K. and B., ii.).
[38] Ser. 42 (K. and B., ii.).   [39] Ser. 43 (K. and B., ii.).

believer, the inner light and the inner life as the really essential things. Christ, as the eternal Logos or Word of God, is the grand revelation which brings the soul to the true knowledge and understanding of God, inspiring it with a heartfelt love of Him, and bringing it into union with Him. This revelation is not, however, confined to the written word, for the Logos, through the Holy Spirit, speaks in the believing soul, which, through this inner light, is directly taught of God.[40] The immanence of God in the soul, the inner light is the great source and nurse of the spiritual life.[41] Religion is for Tauler in this respect markedly subjective. He does not, indeed, ignore the supreme value of the written word. He exhorts his hearers to make diligent use of it as the norm of the religious life. But it is by no means the only medium by which God speaks to the soul, and it is in " its inner ground," in the recess of its highest being that His secret word makes itself known.[42]

Hence the marked opposition in these sermons to the current externalism in religion. If he does not proclaim the Pauline antithesis of faith and works, he systematically distinguishes between outward and inward religion and persistently denounces the formalism of his time, which confounds religiosity with religion. Works in the ecclesiastical sense, he insists, are of no spiritual value in themselves. True holiness does not consist in outward works.[43] In speaking of the birth of God in the soul, he ignores the ecclesiastical side of religion. Salvation is not attainable by works, but only by yielding ourselves to the working of God in us. The principle of seeking salvation by good works is false, for we must not rely on our works or gifts, on the saints or the angels, but on God alone, and consider nothing in all our works but His glory. " Man shall empty himself of all reliance on any creature in heaven or earth, and rest himself on no one but God alone." [44] Good works are to be done not for any reward, but purely and solely in obedience to God's will and from the pure love of Him.[45]

[40] Ser. 8 (K. and B., i.).   [41] Ser. 17 (K. and B., i.).
[42] Ser. 36 (K. and B., i.); cf. Ser. 16 (K. and B., ii.); Vetter, Ser. 19.
[43] Ser. 9 (K. and B., i.).   [44] Ser. 26 (K. and B., i.).
[45] Ser. 21 (K. and B., i.); cf. 28 (K. and B., i.).

God, he says, with Augustine, crowns not our works, but His own.[46] Though outward ordinances and forms have their uses, they are only figures and shadows, with which alone God is not content.[47] To trust in our own works and esteem ourselves highly in virtue of them is mere self-deception and false confidence.[48] Penitential works, self-discipline in obedience to the ecclesiastical regulation of the Christian life, are serviceable. But only if they are done from the pure love of God, and not with the thought of reward.[49] There is, in fact, no merit or reward in such, since it is God who by His grace works in us.[50]

He equates the schoolmen and the zealots for external religion of his own day with the Scribes and Pharisees, from whom Jesus departed into the coasts of Tyre and Sidon. The former seek to comprehend religion by reason and concern themselves with subtle and profitless speculations, and are utterly barren in experimental religion. The latter lay all the stress on the performance of ordinances, usages, customs in order to augment their self-righteousness. They condemn the Friends of God who devote themselves to the religion of the spirit. They know nothing of spiritual experience in the search for God, in the conflict of the higher with the lower nature, in which Jesus, departing from the Scribes and Pharisees, comes to the lowly soul.[51] The ordinances of the Church, the rule of the monastic life are of value only if they are observed in the right spirit. Otherwise we are no better than the Jews with their ceremonial law, their religious formalism.[52] We must banish all thought of self or our own good, of merit and reward, all self-complacency, all trust in our own worthiness by reason of them. Whilst we owe God everything, God owes us nothing in return for our works, and what He does, He does purely out of grace.[53]

The Kingdom of God is within you, he insists, and he who would find Him must seek Him, not in external things,

---

[46] Ser. 15 (K. and B., i.).
[47] Ser. 23 (K. and B., i.).
[48] Ser. 29 (K. and B., i.).
[49] Ser. 30 (K. and B., i.).
[50] Ser. 31 (K. and B., i.).
[51] Ser. 32 (K. and B., i.).
[52] Ser. 35 (K. and B., i.).
[53] Ser. 38 (K. and B., i.) ; *cf.* Ser. 1, 2, 3, 9 (K. and B., ii.).

but in the depth of his own soul and conscience.[54]   Hence the recurring emphasis on the inner disposition rather than on the outward form or act.   " The churches," he tells the people of Cologne, in a sermon in which he again denounces the religion of the Scribes and Pharisees, "do not make you holy, but pious, God-fearing people make the churches holy." [55]   The sacraments are signs of spiritual truth, and not the outward symbol, but the inner meaning and effect, spiritual discernment is the great thing.[56]

Mysticism like this, with its emphasis on the religion of the spirit in direct contact with God, is the great antidote to religious externalism and ecclesiasticism.   It is really incompatible with the religion of ecclesiastical authority and ritual.   At the same time, Tauler does not on principle reject either.   Nor does he preach against good works done in the right spirit.   His sermons are, in truth, mainly concerned with enforcing the moral side of the Gospel, the cultivation of the virtues by the repression of the lower self and their exemplification in the life of active welldoing. The true Friends of God do not neglect good works, only they do not build on them.[57]   In opposition to the Brethren of the Free Spirit, he insists on the obligation of the moral law and rebukes their tendency to despise the laws and ordinances of the Church, to refuse obedience to the Pope, the bishops, and the clergy, and give themselves up to licentious living on the ground that they are above the law. No one is holy or can become holy without good works. No one can be united with God in sheer emptiness of self, without heartfelt love, nor rise to Him as long as he does not experience Him in his heart.   Every one must be a fellow-worker with God in love in order that the divine working in him may not be hindered.[58]

Tauler is a Reformer as well as a mystic preacher.   He repeatedly declaims against the moral declension of the Church and the world.   He denounces the degenerate condition of the clergy, high and low, secular and regular.   The

---

[54] Ser. 36 (K. and B., ii.).
[55] Ser. 61 (K. and B., ii.).
[56] Ser. 12 (K. and B., ii.).

[57] Ser. 9 (K. and B., ii.).
[58] Ser. 31 (K. and B., i.).

Church is for him really the community of the Friends of God, who, whilst reverencing the actual Church and its teaching and participating in its ordinances, live the true spiritual life in direct inner fellowship with God. The Friend of God is essentially an alien in both the Church and the world and can only attain the divine life by withdrawal into himself, in the solitude of his own soul. In this connection he cites the dreary saying of Seneca, " I never come among men but I return home less of a man than before." [59] But while he insists on self-negation in extreme terms at times, he is not really a quietist. He would fain reform both the Church and the world and he stresses the practical Christian life in active love of God and our neighbour. Though prone to speculate in mystic fashion over the heads of his hearers, he can bring religion into common life. Emptiness of self does not mean a nerveless Christianity and contemplation is not identical with ignorance. All service, however lowly, may be made the service of God. " One can spin ; another make shoes ; some have skill in external business, which bring them much gain and for which others are unfit. These are all gifts which come from the Spirit of God. If I were not a priest and belonged to some craft, I should esteem it a great privilege that I knew how to make shoes, and should strive to do it better than anyone else and gladly earn my bread with my own hands. There is no work so small, no art so mean but it all comes from God and is His special gift. Thus let each do for the benefit of his neighbour what his neighbour cannot do for himself and return from love gift for gift. And know that whoever does not serve his neighbour with the gift that God has given him lays up a great reckoning against himself in the day of judgment." [60]

The evangelical train of thought in these sermons is thus much more definite than in the German Theology. There is in them, in addition, the fire and force of individual conviction and a living religious experience. Luther had more justification than in the case of the German Theology in

[59] Ser. 9 (K. and B., i.).
[60] Ser. 47 (K. and B., ii.) ; cf. Ser. 57 (K. and B., ii.) ; Vetter, Ser. 42.

regarding them as an anticipation of his own evangelical teaching, and his thought was to a certain extent undoubtedly influenced by them. The reader will easily recognise, in this very condensed summary of his teaching, the resemblance of certain leading ideas of the Sermons to those of the Commentary on Romans. Both, for instance, emphasise self-negation in the quest for God, the absolute submission of the will to the divine will, the elimination of the thought of merit and reward in the service of God, the dependence of the soul for salvation on the exercise of God's mercy and grace, its purely receptive attitude in the experience of His grace and mercy, humility as the indispensable condition of this reception, the experience of salvation as a present reality and not merely as a thing of hope. Both seem to draw on a common fund of thought which is traceable, in its various aspects, through the works of Gerson, Tauler, Eckhart, Bernard, and other mediæval mystics back to Scotus Erigena, Dionysius, Augustine, and even Plotinus, and farther back to Paul and the Fourth Gospel. For Luther, like Tauler before him, drew from this age-long heritage of mystic speculation and aspiration, as well as directly from Tauler's Sermons and the German Theology. Even so, his notes on these sermons [61] and his publication of the German Theology show his special interest in these two writers and, on his own testimony, he derived from them a very real inspiration. In addition to this evidence and that of the letters to Spalatin, quoted at the beginning of this chapter, he acknowledges his appreciation of Tauler in the Commentary on Romans, in one of his early sermons [62] and in one of his early controversial writings. " Although," he says in the last-mentioned work, " John Tauler is ignored and held in contempt in the theological schools, I have found in him more solid and true theology than is to be, or can be found in all the scholastic doctors of the universities." [63] Moreover, Tauler's sermons had for Luther a practical value which rendered his appreciation of them all the more cordial. In view of his long spiritual conflict in the quest for a gracious God, the ever-recurring emphasis

[61] " Werke," ix. 95 f.   [62] *Ibid.*, i. 137.   [63] *Ibid.*, i. 557.

on the Cross, suffering as the normal experience of the soul in its ascent to the higher life, seems to have appealed to him with special force.[64] From the psychological point of view, Tauler undoubtedly did him a real service in showing him that the troubled way he had gone in search of peace of conscience, deliverance from the sense of sin and condemnation, was the God-appointed way.

On the other hand, it is questionable whether he did not read into these sermons more of his own apprehension of the Gospel than they really contained, and whether in making use of these mystic ideas and terms he did not impart to them a different significance from that of Tauler.[65] In spite of the evangelical note in the sermons, Tauler was only relatively a forerunner of Luther, and Preger goes too far in ascribing to him the clear and unequivocal assertion of the Lutheran principle of justification by faith.[66] Making due allowance for the evangelical element, what strikes one in these sermons is just the absence of any definite statement of the Pauline doctrine of faith and works. Tauler contrasts the law and the Gospel.[67] But the contrast is not worked out in the Pauline fashion. He is not, like Paul and Luther, obsessed by the thought of God's righteousness and how to attain righteousness in His sight. The thought of God's righteousness only occurs incidentally and the sinner is not arraigned at the bar of a righteous God and shown how he may be justified by the non-imputation of sin and the reputation of righteousness, apprehended through faith in the mercy of God in Christ. He quotes Paul incessantly. But the specific Pauline scheme of justification by faith and not by works is not unfolded and enforced in these sermons. It may be assumed, and some of the elements of it are undoubtedly there—man's impotence by reason of sin, his dependence on God's grace for the good, the satisfaction and reconciliation made by Christ,

[64] See his notes on the Sermons, ix. 102. Deus non agat in nobis nisi pruis nos et nostra destruat, *i.e.*, per crucem et passiones.

[65] On this latter point see Boehmer, " Luther im Lichte der neueren Forschung," 65 f.

[66] " Deutsche Mystik," iii. 194.

[67] Ser. 50 (K. and B., ii.) ; Vetter, Ser. 73.

for instance. But the doctrine of justification as developed in the Epistle to the Romans and the distinctive significance of this doctrine, as Luther grasped and worked it out in his Commentary, are lacking. The idea is rather absorption in God by faith, than justification by faith. From these Sermons he would hardly have been led back to the real Paul, and it is certain that he came to this doctrine independently of Tauler or the German Theology. Moreover, in spite of his insistence on the futility of works and the impossibility of meriting salvation thereby, Tauler has not quite emancipated himself from the mediæval idea of merit and reward accruing from works. He speaks of making satisfaction for sin in the Sacrament of Penance and even for others by good works.[68] Outward works, he says, have no merit unless wrought in love, and he can speak of winning eternal life by such works.[69] Again, the emphasis in Tauler is on the inner Word as the highest norm for the mystic Christian, whereas Luther's grand criterion of truth is God's word and promise in the Scriptures. Whilst both depreciate reason and exalt faith in the apprehension of truth, with Tauler the inward vision of God is superior to the mere acceptance of an external revelation.

Nor does he profess to proclaim a new Gospel in antagonism to the received teachers of the Church, though he has no liking for the subtle syllogising of the schoolmen. He believes himself to be and, in essentials, he actually is in accord with traditional belief and usage. He is a disciple of the great scholastic theologians as well as the fathers, and he frequently appeals to Aquinas and other schoolmen whom Luther disliked and denounced. He is not, like Luther, a predestinarian, but a universalist, and believes in man's responsibility for both his sin and his salvation.[70] Nor is he, as a Reformer, the forerunner of Luther. He criticises the rampant abuses of the Church of his day. But he has no constructive scheme of reform and shows no power of initiation in grappling with the problem of the removal

---

[68] Ser. 50 (K. and B., ii.) ; Vetter, Ser. 73.
[69] Ser. 1 (K. and B., ii.).
[70] Ser. 17 (K. and B., ii.) ; Vetter, Ser. 20.

of these evils. The Friends of God are too contemplative and self-centred to undertake or achieve such a task.

Luther, it is evident, was mistaken in assuming that " his theology," as he was beginning to describe his evangelical views in opposition to the schoolmen, was a replica of that of Tauler. The mistake is quite explicable in view of his belief that what he himself taught was in accord with what the Church believed and proclaimed. Like Tauler he, too, at this stage was a pious and devoted monk, conscientious in his observance of the rule of his Order and the usages of the Church, unconscious of any radical divergence in doctrine or practice from use and wont, still an ardent believer in the virtue of obedience to ecclesiastical authority and in the heinous sin of heresy.[71]

[71] The best edition of the German Theology is that of Mandel in " Quellenschriften zur Geschichte des Protestantismus " (1908). The other edition used is that of Pfeiffer in the original German with translation into modern German and based on the 1497 MS. (3rd edition, 1875). There is a translation into English by Miss Winkworth (1854, new issue, 1924). There is difference of opinion on the question of the authenticity of a number of Tauler's sermons. For a succinct account of this question see the introduction to A. W. Hutton's translation into English of the Thirty-Six Sermons for Festivals under the title of " The Inner Way " (2nd edition, 1909). Kuntze und Biesenthal, " Tauler's Predigten," 2 vols., modern German version (1841). Vetter has published them in the original fourteenth-century German (1910) from the Engelberg, Freiburg, and Strassburg MSS. Miss Winkworth also translated twenty-five of the Sermons (1857). Of modern works in English on mysticism, Inge, " Christian Mysticism " (1899), and Rufus Jones, " Studies in Christian Mysticism " (1909), are the more recent. The standard work in German is that by Preger, " Geschichte der Deutschen Mystik," Theil iii. (1893). On Tauler, in particular, the article by Cohrs in " Herzog-Hauck Realencyclopädie " (1907); Jundt, " Les Amis de Dieu " (1878).

CHAPTER VIII

LUTHER AND THE HUMANISTS (1509-1517)

I. THE HUMANIST MOVEMENT

LUTHER was fortunate in his age. He appeared, it may be said, in the fullness of the time—a time when powerful forces were at work quickening the mind and soul of his generation, transforming its intellectual life and broadening its outlook. The term Renaissance which is applied to this age is no misnomer. In the late fifteenth and early sixteenth centuries there was taking place a rebirth of mind and soul which was manifesting itself in literature, art, theology, education, science, political thought, exploration, and invention. This rebirth was inspired by the study of the ancient classic literature, to which the term Humanism is applied, in contrast and in opposition to mediæval scholasticism, with its predilection for the dialectic, abstract method in the pursuit of the higher knowledge. In the narrower meaning of the term, humanism denotes the revival of the study of the classic literature of antiquity. In this sense, it was more particularly a literary and educational movement, concerned with scholarship, with the acquisition of a knowledge of the classic languages and literature, and the application of these as the chief instrument of education. But humanism, in the wider sense, came to denote more than mere scholarship or the substitution of one kind of knowledge or intellectual training for another. It concerned itself with human life and thought as a whole. As against the mediæval attitude, it stood for a more human culture, a more independent spirit, a wider outlook on life. It claimed, especially, for the individual the right of free self-development against the limitations, the bonds imposed by corporate ecclesiastical authority in Church and State.

It championed the free application of reason in the pursuit of truth, in opposition to the dogmatic spirit dominant in the mediæval Church and university. It sought to apply the critical-historic method to the study of doctrine and institutions. It not only evinced a larger appreciation of the literature and thought of classic antiquity. It contributed a powerful impulse to the independent study of the Scriptures in the original languages, the works of the fathers, and the early history of Christianity, and thus showed the way back to the sources (*ad Fontes*), in reaction from the accretion of tradition which the mediæval Church had incorporated.

This humanist movement took its rise in Italy in the fourteenth century with Petrarch and Boccacio, who represented the revulsion, in its early form, from the dominant scholastic culture, and drew their inspiration from the ancient classics, from Nature, and the unsophisticated emotions and aspirations of mind and soul. As a literary movement, it derived a great impulse from the Greek scholars who migrated to Italy before and after the capture of Constantinople by the Turks in the middle of the fifteenth century. As the result of their teaching, or their inspiration, there appeared in the second half of the century a brilliant group of Italian scholars, who devoted themselves to the study of the literature and the interpretation of the thought of ancient Greece. Among them were Poggio, the translator of Diodorus Siculus and Xenophon, and a great searcher for Latin MSS. ; Filelfo, who went to Constantinople to study Greek ; Lorenzo Valla, the translator of Thucydides and the keen critic of ecclesiastical tradition ; Ficino, the great exponent of Plato and St Paul ; Pico della Mirandola, who knew not only Greek and even the Kabbala, but claimed to know everything ; Politian, the greatest scholar of them all, and Bembo, who, cardinal though he was, was so enthusiastic a votary of the pagan writers that he would not read St Paul or his breviary for fear of spoiling his style.

The chief centres of this new culture were Florence, Rome, Naples, Venice, Ferrara, where the movement was organised in academies or literary associations, and found generous patrons among Italian rulers like Cosimo and Lorenzo di Medici at Florence, Popes Nicolas V., Sixtus IV., Julius II., and Leo X. at Rome, Alfonso of Naples, the Duke of Ferrara, Frederick of Urbino, the Sforza at Milan. Their patronage enabled collectors to ransack the libraries all over Europe for MSS. of the ancient classics, whilst the printing press multiplied the editions of these MSS. and contributed to the diffusion of the knowledge of them.[1]

This humanist movement could not fail to have far-reaching effects on the fabric of mediæval civilisation. Its individualism, its critical spirit, its innovating and emancipating tendency were the harbingers of an inevitable transformation of the old order in culture and religion, and might even eventuate in a revolution of this order. As usually happens, the new movement, in its more developed form, embodied a moderate and an extreme tendency. One section, of whom Ficino and Mirandola were the most distinguished representatives, and to whom the description Christian humanists has been applied, was not hostile to the Church or anti-Christian in thought and life. Among others of less fame were Leonardo Bruni, Traversari, Manetti, Vittorino da Feltre. Ficino combined the study of the Epistles of St Paul with that of the Platonic and Neo-Platonic philosophy. Towards the close of his life he lectured to large audiences at Florence on the Epistle to the Romans and formed the plan of writing a Commentary on the Epistles, which was frustrated by his death.[2] It was to him that the revival of interest in the Pauline theology was due ; from him that Lefèbre, Colet, and, above all, Erasmus took their inspiration.[3] As head of the Platonic Academy at Florence, he carried, indeed, his enthusiasm for the

[1] Burckhardt, " The Civilisation of the Period of the Renaissance in Italy," i. 311-320. English translation by Middlemore (1878). Symmonds, " The Renaissance in Italy," ii. 496-500 ; Voigt, " Die Wiederbelebung des Klassischen Alterthums," i. 444 (1859) ; Guiraud, " L'Église Romaine et les origines de la Renaissance " (4th edition, 1909) ; Pastor, " History of the Popes," i. ; Gregorovius, " History of Rome in the Middle Ages," vi.-viii.

[2] Corsi, " Marsilii Ficini Vita," quoted by Denifle, " Die Abend-ländische Schriftauslegung bis Luther," 280 (1905).

[3] Troeltsch, " Kultur der Gegenwart," i. 4.

Platonic philosophy to the verge of worship, and inaugurated the cult of the master, before whose image a lamp was kept burning, and whose birthday was celebrated as a high festival.[4] But in thus extravagantly honouring Plato, he was not actuated by the striving to substitute his teaching for that of Christ, but rather to reconcile Platonism and Christianity, in which he was a firm believer. His pupil Mirandola, besides being an ardent student of Greek philosophy, added a knowledge of Jewish theosophy. His immense hybrid knowledge exposed him to a charge of heresy, and whilst in his speculations on the Godhead and his interpretation of Genesis under this twofold influence, he professed that he was only adducing additional arguments for the truth of Christianity, it is doubtful whether he really held the orthodox doctrine of the Trinity. At all events, he was compelled for a time to seek refuge in France in order to escape the heresy hunt of his orthodox opponents.[5] But there can be no doubt about his profoundly religious spirit and his ardent personal piety, which was due, in the first place, to the preaching of Savonarola, and which led him to burn the amatory poems of his unconverted days and to sell a part of his patrimony for the benefit of the poor. He had some thoughts of entering the Dominican Order and at his own desire was buried in the Dominican habit. In his letters to his nephew he inculcates the pursuit of practical piety in self-denial and love of God. He exhorts him to persevere in the true Christian life in the midst of the allurements and the vanity of court life and the ridicule of his fellow-courtiers, and commends to him the practice of daily prayer and the devotional reading of the Scriptures. In these " there lieth a certain heavenly strength, quick and effectual, which with a marvellous power transformeth and changeth the readers' minds, if they be clean and lowly intreated." [6] With this deep personal piety he combined a keen interest in the practical reform of the Church in the spirit of Savonarola.

[4] Creighton, " History of the Papacy," iv. 163-164.

[5] Rigg, Introduction to the " Life of Pico," by his nephew, translated along with some of his letters by Sir Thomas More, 26 (1890).

[6] Rigg, 37.

In contrast to the Christian humanists, many of the votaries of the new culture in Italy lost their Christian faith in their enthusiasm for pagan antiquity, or ceased to take it very seriously. To this section, which has been described, with some reason, as that of the Pagan humanists, belonged men like Filelfo, Poggio, Valla, Pomponius Laetus, and Pomponazzi. They were freethinkers in religion, though they might not always avow their scepticism. Some of them, in fact, held office in the Curia as apostolic secretaries and thus devoted their Latin style to the composition of the papal Bulls and other official documents. They were only too eager to sue for the patronage of the popes, to earn emolument and preferment in the papal service, as well as in that of the secular princes, who appreciated their power as publicists, and conciliated their goodwill by their patronage. Some of them like Pomponius and his fellow-humanists of the Roman Academy even affected an artificial revival of the old paganism. At Florence the Greek Gemistos Plethon even proposed to found a new universal religion out of ancient Greek thought and polytheism, and wrote a book in support of his project, which the Greek patriarch, Gennadios, consigned to the flames after his death. Nevertheless, he was celebrated among his adherents in Italy, whither his body was brought from Greece after his death, as " the prince of the philosophers of his time." [7] Pomponazzi carried his scepticism the length of attacking in his book " De Immortalitate " (1516) the doctrine of the immortality of the soul, though he sought to save himself from the consequences of the charge of heresy by professing to leave the decision as to the validity of the doctrine, on the ground of revelation, to the decision of the Apostolic See. [8]

Of the critical-historic tendency the most distinguished representative was Lorenzo Valla. Valla, following in the wake of Dante and Marsiglio of Padua a century earlier, and of Roger Bacon at a still earlier time, was the pioneer

[7] Creighton, iv. 41 f.
[8] See A. N. Douglas's " Philosophy and Psychology of Pomponazzi," edited by C. Douglas and R. P. Hardie (1910).

of historic criticism in the age of the Renaissance. He not only attacked the scholastic method, the scholastic theology, and the monastic conception of the religious life. He exposed on historic grounds the falsity of the so-called Donation of Constantine, and in so doing denounced in no measured terms the temporal power of the popes.[9] He attacked the assumption that the Apostles' Creed was composed by the Twelve Apostles, disputed the authenticity of the letter of King Abgar to Christ, given by Eusebius, and the writings ascribed to Dionysius the Areopagite, questioned the correctness of the text of the Vulgate and pleaded that it should be compared with the original Greek.[10] All this was in accordance with a legitimate application of the historic method. None the less he shared the mercenary, opportunist spirit of too many of these free-thinking humanists by retracting his opinions in his eagerness to secure a post in the papal service, which he at last obtained from the tolerant Nicolas V.[11]

Unfortunately these freethinkers were not conspicuous as moralists. If personality was a feature of the Renaissance age, it was too frequently of the unregulated or ill-regulated type. Their main interest was literary or artistic, and they showed and gave rein to the egotism and opportunism too often characteristic of this temperament. They were not only lacking in independence and strength of character, writing merely for fame or pensions, prostrating their pens to celebrate the so-called virtues and exaggerate the petty achievements of the patrons who bought their services. They represent a revulsion from Christian morality, as well as ecclesiastical dogmatism and the one-sided monastic conception of the Christian life. In their enthusiasm for individual freedom, they ignored the restraint of the moral law, mistaking license for liberty and elevating it into a

[9] Döllinger, " Fables Respecting the Popes in the Middle Ages," 175, English translation by Plummer ; Pastor, " History of the Popes," i. 18-20 ; Creighton, " History of the Papacy," iii. 171.

[10] Sandys, " History of Classical Scholarship," i. 571 (1908), and the " Revival of Learning," Harvard Lectures, 1905 ; Voigt, " Wieder-belebung," i. 461-476.

[11] Pastor, i. 22.

principle of conduct, glorifying the life of sense, self-gratification in accordance with Nature. The reform of culture did not necessarily mean the regeneration of the individual. They attacked clerical immorality and were themselves the worst examples of an ill-regulated sensuality. The naturalist conception of life, in reaction from the mediæval ascetic conception of it, brought out in too many of these Italian humanists the worst side of individuality. Poggio, Filelfo, Beccadelli, for instance, disgraced themselves by producing some of the most obscene rubbish ever printed.[12] In the demoralised state of the Church and society in the fifteenth and early sixteenth centuries, this excessive license was only too much in keeping with the spirit of the age. There was not much to be expected in the way of a moral renewal in the Rome of the pre-Reformation popes, or in the Florence of a Lorenzo di Medici, in which religious convention was coupled with a deplorable degeneration of morals. Savonarola, who attempted such a practical reformation, was burned, and the higher type of humanist, like Ficino and Pico, who took morality and religion seriously, made no impression as far as the practical reformation of Church and society in Italy was concerned. It was not this aspect of the movement that commended it to its papal and princely patrons, who valued it on its intellectual and literary side, as the ornament of a refined civilisation, rather than as the instrument of an effective reform of the corruption permeating this civilisation. The appreciation of the Medici Pope Leo X. is characteristic of the dominant frame of mind. " We have been accustomed," wrote Leo in the brief conferring the papal privilege on Beroaldo's edition of the Annals of Tacitus, " even from our early years to think that nothing more excellent and more useful has been given by the Creator to mankind, if we except only the knowledge and the true worship of Himself, than these studies, which not only lead to the ornament and guidance of human life, but are applicable and useful to every particular situation—in adversity consolatory, in prosperity pleasing

---

[12] Beccadelli's " Hermaphroditus " ; Filelfo's " De Iocis et Seriis " ; Poggio's " Facetiæ."

and honourable, insomuch that without them we should be deprived of all the grace of life and all the polish of social intercourse." There was, indeed, in Italian humanism more than the grace of life and the polish of social intercourse, which Pope Leo valued as its highest achievement. There were in it far more potent factors in its critical method and spirit, its individualism in thought and aspirations, the impulse it might give to the study of the sources of Christianity, the isolated demand for reform. It was not, however, in Italy, but in the lands north of the Alps that these factors were to come powerfully into operation, with effects undreamt of by complacent and superficial patrons of the type of a Leo X.

II. REUCHLIN AND ERASMUS

Germany, like other northern lands, derived its humanism from Italy through scholars like Agricola and Reuchlin, who had been pupils of Italian humanists.[13] Wessel Gansfort may also be reckoned among its pioneers in Germany.[14] It was at first largely a literary and educational movement and shows, in this respect, the same features as in Italy—its appreciation of the ancient classic literature and its antagonism to the scholastic method. As in Italy, too, it enjoyed the patronage of a number of the secular and ecclesiastical rulers, notably the Emperor Maximilian, the Elector of Saxony, the Archbishop Elector of Maintz, the Count of Würtemberg. Here, too, it found a focus in some of the cities. Humanist circles were formed at Augsburg by Peutinger, at Nürnberg by Pirkheimer, at Strassburg by Wimpheling and Sebastian Brant. Another group owned Mutianus Rufus, the humanist canon of Gotha, as its head, and included Hermann von dem Busch, Ulrich von Hutten, Crotus Rubianus, Eobanus Hessus, Peter Eberbach, George Spalatin, and John Lang. The more

---

[13] Geiger, " Renaissance und Humanismus in Italien und Deutschland," 334 (1882).

[14] Miller and Scudder, " Wessel Gansfort," i. 80 f.

pugnative of the earlier classicists, like Conrad Celtes, the wandering scholar, who finally settled as professor of poetry and rhetoric at Vienna in 1497, and Heinrich Bebel, who in the same year became professor at Tübingen, strove to gain a footing for the movement in the universities. During the 150 years from the middle of the fourteenth century to the beginning of the sixteenth, no less than seventeen universities had been founded in Germany, among the most recent being Wittenberg in 1502 and Frankfort in 1506.[15] They were dominated by the scholastic method and the scholastic philosophy and theology, and, with some exceptions, were not minded to welcome the new culture. In the face of conservative opposition, the humanist attack seemed a forlorn hope. To the votaries of use and wont in education and knowledge, it was obnoxious as a pagan invasion, in spite of the fact that philosophy and theology had long been dominated by the Aristotelian dialectic and philosophy. There was some ground for this attitude in as far as German humanism reflected the lax, freethinking spirit of the Italian movement. Conrad Celtes and Heinrich Bebel were a German reflection of the naturalist school of a Poggio, whose " Facetiæ " Bebel imitated in a work of his own with this title. Mutian, though a moralist and professedly orthodox, speculated very freely on religion in private, and Ulrich von Hutten was certainly no paragon of self-control.

But license of thought or conduct was not generally a characteristic of the movement in Germany. Its early precursor, Agricola, had been educated in the school of the Brethren of the Common Life at Deventer which, under Hegius, favoured classical study within strictly Christian lines. Wimpheling had been trained in a similar atmosphere in one of the offshoots of Deventer at Schlettstadt in Alsace, and also represents the more conservative type of humanist. Reuchlin, like Agricola, brought back from Italy the more serious spirit of Italian humanism, as represented by

---

[15] Hartfelder, " Der Zustand der Deutschen Hochschulen am Ende des Mittelalters, Hist. Zeitschrift " (1890) ; Bezold, " Geschichte der Deutschen Reformation," 201-202.

Mirandola, and combined allegiance to the faith with the critical spirit as applied to the sources of Christianity, particularly the Hebrew scriptures, and with a striving to bring about thereby a renovation of Christianity. He was first and foremost a philological and critical scholar, and though a jurist by profession and a layman, produced a number of works, among them a combined Hebrew grammar and lexicon, in which he did not hesitate to point out, after the method of a Valla, the errors of the Vulgate translation of the Old Testament. Though no active polemic, he became, in spite of himself, the hero of a violent controversy over the question of the confiscation and destruction of all anti-Christian Jewish books, including the Talmud. The question was started by a fanatical converted Jew, named Pfefferkorn, who was abetted by the Inquisitor-General, Hochstraten and the Dominicans of Cologne. In a written opinion Reuchlin protested against the intolerant proposal on the ground of the value of the Talmud and other Jewish writings for the study of Christianity, and emphasised its injustice as well as its futility. This judgment roused against him the bitter animosity of the Anti-Semites, who accused him of heresy and inaugurated a lengthy controversy which concerned not merely the particular question at issue, but developed into a battle royal between the humanists and the votaries of the old culture. It called forth the famous "Epistolæ Obscurorum Virorum," mainly written by Crotus Rubianus, whose nimble but coarse ridicule set the laugh against the pedantry, stupidity, casuistry, and antiquated ideas of the opponents of the new culture, as these appeared in the eyes of the less moderate and more contemptuous of its votaries.

Reuchlin, though unwillingly inveigled in this far-reaching polemic, was more a critical scholar than a moralist. Erasmus was both, and though a cosmopolitan, he became the master spirit of the German humanists. He represents in its most potent form the combination of the critical scholar and the practical reformer, though by nature he was unfitted to be the active leader of a militant reformation. In this double capacity he represents the humanist movement at its best, as it developed in the lands north of the Alps. Like Agricola, he owed his initiation into the classics to the school at Deventer. But he was largely self-taught and amassed his supreme knowledge of Latin and Greek literature and formulated the results of it in the course of a wandering career, which carried him to France, England, Italy, the Netherlands, and finally to Basle. His chief contributions to learning were his critical editions of the Greek New Testament and the Fathers. In these works, as well as in his lighter and didactic writings, his aim was largely practical. With him humanism was not merely a means of self-culture. Its object was, directly or indirectly, a reforming one. His critical edition of the New Testament bears also, characteristically, the subsidiary title of " Novum Instrumentum." He set himself, in opposition to scholasticism, to provide and diffuse a sound and critical knowledge of the New Testament and the early Christian writings, to bring the Church and the schools back to the sources of the Christian religion, which were for him the real norm of Christian teaching and life. In historical criticism, as applied to the Scriptures, he follows the method of Valla, whose work as a critical scholar he appraises highly, and whose Annotations on the New Testament he republished in 1505.[16] In these writings are to be found the true theology as against its later scholastic development. With the exception of Aquinas, he had no interest in the scholastic theologians, unless to criticise and satirise their dialectic hairsplitting and their contentiousness over abstruse and profitless problems. The great fact of Christianity is Christ, and the great requisite in religion is a living faith in Him. In the introduction to the edition of the New Testament, published early in 1516, he advocates the Bible for the common people. Like W. Tyndale, he wished that the peasant following the plough should be familiar with its contents, though he did not, like him, translate it into the vernacular for this purpose. " I long that the husbandman should sing portions of them to himself as he follows the plough, that the weaver should hum them to the tune of his shuttle, and that the traveller should beguile

---

[16] See Nichols, " Epistles of Erasmus," i. 70-73, 379-386 (1901).

with their stories the tedium of his journey." [17]   The
independent, critical attitude comes out strongly in the
Latin paraphrases of the various books of the New
Testament. He denies, for instance, that the saying about
the rock in Matthew xvi. 18 applies exclusively to the Pope,
and maintains that Christ is the only teacher that has been
appointed by God Himself.[18] Though no freethinker, and
apprehensive of the progress of unbelief, he handles the
Scriptures in the light of history, admitting that they are
coloured by the historic circumstances in which they were
written and by the personality of their authors. In this
respect the historic sense is beginning to assert itself, if he
still clings to the allegoric method of interpretation.
Mr Murray thinks that, like Lefèbre, he even, in the
paraphrases, anticipated the Lutheran doctrine of justification by faith. He does, indeed, say that " when Christ
forgives sins, he speaks neither of our satisfactions nor our
works. . . . It suffices to come to the feet of Jesus." [19]
But this does not prove that he held the doctrine in the
Lutheran evangelical sense, and Luther himself, as will be
seen, certainly did not think so. The fact is that he did not
go beyond the traditional view of justification by faith joined
with love. Moreover, he does not share Luther's conception of the complete impotence of the will. Man can desire
the good, though he is dependent on grace for its
attainment. The will is so far free that it can accept or
reject grace, though all the good we do is the work of God.[20]
The man who so believed could not be in agreement with
Luther's developed doctrine of justification, of which the
complete impotence of the will for good is a cardinal
condition.

On the other hand, he is at one with Luther's early
attitude of respect for and submission to the authority of
the Church, the teaching of which he is prepared to accept
as binding, whilst not subscribing to the later scholastic
interpretation of it, subjecting even the New Testament
as well as the ancient fathers to criticism, and protesting

[17] Murray, " Erasmus and Luther," 21.
[18] *Ibid.*, 23.   [19] *Ibid.*, 25-26.   [20] *Ibid.*, 28.

against the use of force in the maintenance of creed. The
Church never goes wrong in whatever pertains to salvation.
The Pope, as the successor of Peter, is invested with supreme
power over the Church, though he may sometimes abuse
this power to establish unjust laws. He recognises the
legitimate power of General Councils and the hierarchy.
In this respect he is not an advocate of the thoroughgoing
individualism of the Renaissance. Even so, his critical
scholarship in directing the minds of his many followers to
the sources of Christianity as the fountain of true theology,
and in bringing the light of critical knowledge to bear on the
abuses and assumptions in both doctrine and usage, which
had overlaid and obscured it, was a contribution of the
utmost potential value to the Reformation.

Erasmus was a moralist and a publicist as well as a
critical scholar, and in this capacity he also prepared the
way for Luther and the Reformation. In the " Enchiridion
Militis Christiani " (usually translated " Handbook of the
Christian Soldier," but also rendered " The Christian
Soldier's Dagger," 1505), the " Praise of Folly " (" Encomium
Moriæ," 1509), and other works of a practical character,
he sought to educate opinion in favour of a practical
reformation. " The Enchiridion," he tells Colet, " was not
composed for the mere display of genius or eloquence,
but only for the purpose of correcting the common error
of those who make religion consist of ceremonies and in
almost more than Jewish observances, while they are
singularly careless of the things that belong to piety." [21]
The same purpose inspired the " Praise of Folly." " As
nothing," he writes in the dedication to Thomas More,
in whose house he composed it, shortly after his second
arrival in England in 1509, " is more trifling than to treat
serious questions frivolously, so nothing is more amusing
than to treat trifles in such a way as to show yourself
anything but a trifler. We have praised folly not quite
foolishly." [22] In both of these works, but especially in the
latter, he attacks, with a boldness astounding in one who

[21] Nichols, i. 376 ; Allen, " Opus Epistolarum Erasmi," i. 403 (1906).
[22] Nichols, ii. 3.

was by nature not remarkable for courage or militant conviction, the formalism, the superstition, and the hypocrisy of
churchmen. The audacity of the attack shows the serious-
ness of the abuses against which it is directed, and Erasmus
must have felt fairly sure both of his case and of the sympathy
and approval of powerful partisans in Church and State,
before running the risk of the censure of the Church. In
" The Praise of Folly " the attack takes the form of a
stinging satire on the society of his time. In cap and bells
Folly mounts the rostrum and addresses all sorts and
conditions of people. Her votaries are to be found among
those who pride themselves on their wisdom as well as
those who live according to their passions. They include
the Pope himself (Julius II.), cardinals, bishops, monks,
scholastic theologians and philosophers, grammarians.
Especially scathing is the indictment of the Pope and the
dignitaries of the Church, and here Folly assumes a serious
tone. It is a daring anticipation, without the coarseness, of
the " Epistolæ Obscurorum Virorum," and far more caustic
and outspoken than anything Luther uttered in his early
sermons and his Lectures on Romans.

III. Luther's Early Attitude

As a reformer Erasmus seemed, in fact, the precursor
of Luther, and though such a forecast was not destined to be
fulfilled, it is nevertheless evident that the humanist movement, as represented by a Valla, a Ficino, a Mirandola, a
Reuchlin, an Erasmus, was a real, nay an indispensable
preparation for the Reformation. Without this preparation
the work of Luther would hardly have been possible. It was
by no means an accident that the Reformation was contemporary with the Renaissance. Here was a movement
which, in its insistence on a Biblical theology in opposition
to scholasticism, its appeal to the sources of Christianity
as the real norm of faith, its application of the critical
method to the study both of theology and ecclesiastical
history, its new conception of life, its keen sense of
individual liberty, its insistent demand for a reformation of
religion, anticipated much that Luther ultimately stood for,

and materially aided him in the attempt to realise it. Luther at first, in fact, found in the humanists ardent allies and defenders, and their alliance contributed not a little to encourage and strengthen him in the conflict with corporate authority, into which he was gradually drawn. It was, in particular, in the study of the Pauline Epistles, which Ficino, Mirandola, Lefèbre, Erasmus, and Colet had brought into vogue, that he found the way to an effective reformation which they desiderated, but were powerless to achieve. Moreover, whilst the more conservative type of humanist, including Erasmus himself, ultimately hesitated and halted in their adhesion to the militant reform movement, it was in the school of Erasmus that many of the leaders and adherents of the evangelical Reformation were trained. Zwingli, Capito, Melanchthon, Calvin, Tyndale, Patrick Hamilton, and many others had been Erasmians before they became evangelical reformers. True, the new culture could not by itself have achieved the work of Luther. Erasmus was too optimistic in his belief that all that was needed was the leavening, the pervasion of men's minds by a new knowledge, an enlightened reason. Far more than this was needed to purify the Church and bring about the return to the faith and the institutions of a purer age, which he and other reforming humanists desiderated. Personality, character, combined with the dynamic of an overmastering religious conviction, could alone suffice for even the practical reformation, not to speak of the far-reaching religious transformation which Luther effected. This dynamic Luther discovered in the overmastering power of personal faith, operating in both heart and mind. But whilst only this could make him sufficient for his mission, humanism did contribute to make this mission possible.

Though Luther had humanist sympathies, he was never a professed humanist and did not come to his distinctive religious views by the humanist approach. As a student at Erfurt, he had read a number of the Latin classics and had learned and appreciated their wisdom and practical guidance.[23] He tells us in a passage of his " Table Talk "

[23] Melanchthon, " Vita," 157.

that he had read Ovid and Virgil. Melanchthon adds
Cicero, Livy, and others.[24] He had attended the humanist
lectures of Emser.[25] He tells in another passage of his
" Table Talk " that after resolving to become a monk he
had returned all his books to the booksellers except Plautus
and Virgil, which he took with him into the monastery.[26]
He would certainly not have done so unless he had had a
more than conventional interest in the classic writers. He
was a leading member of the student circle to which Crotus
Rubianus belonged, as this humanist long afterwards
reminded him,[27] and John Lang tells us that, as Luther's
fellow-monk at Erfurt, he had owed not a little to his help
in his study of " good letters." [28] At the university his
main interest was, however, in the scholastic philosophy,
and according to Rubianus it was as " a philosopher " that
he distinguished himself in the intimate circle of his fellow-
students,[29] whilst in the Erfurt monastery he devoted
himself mainly to the study of the scholastic theology. In
his notes on Augustine and the Sentences and in his early
lectures on the Psalms, as well as those on the Epistle to
the Romans, he was, indeed, already availing himself of the
critical results of the new learning, and shows a knowledge
of the works of Reuchlin, Mirandola, Valla, Lefèbre, and
ultimately Erasmus.[30] But his knowledge of Greek was
rather scanty, and he does not seem to have seriously concerned himself with its study before the lectures on Romans.
Whilst ready, even in his early theological studies, to make
use of the scholarship of Mirandola and Reuchlin, he threw
himself into the controversy on behalf of his Order against
the humanist Wimpheling with all the zeal of a confirmed
adherent of the old system.[31] His interest in this scholarship
is that of the scholastic theologian, not of the humanist

---

[24] Melanchthon, " Vita," 157.   [26] " Tischreden," i. 44.
[25] Scheel, " Luther," i. 231.   [27] Enders, ii. 208, 391.
[28] *Ibid.*, i. 36. Is Doctor Martinus est, quocum Erphurdii perquam
familiariter vixi, nec parum auxilii bonis in literis olim mihi attulit.
[29] *Ibid.*, ii. 391.
[30] See, for instance, " Werke," ix., 27 (Mirandola), 32, 63, 67
(Reuchlin) ; iv. 183 (Valla's Annotations), etc.
[31] " Werke," ix. 12.

At the same time, if not a perfervid humanist like John Lang, Peter Eberbach or Petrejus, and George Burkhard or Spalatinus, his intercourse with them tended to foster the receptive mind and a readiness to make increased use of the critical method. Besides the evidence of the lectures on the Psalms and the Epistle to the Romans, his early correspondence with Spalatin and others, from 1514 onwards, shows that, while his main interest is the purely religious one, he has advanced so far as to take the side of Reuchlin against his obscurantist opponents. All three friends belonged to the humanist circle of Mutian. Lang, who had studied at Erfurt University and had been his fellow-monk in the Erfurt monastery, had, like him, removed to Wittenberg, where he graduated as Biblical Bachelor in 1515, and was closely associated with him in the theological instruction of the Wittenberg monastery before becoming, in the following year, prior at Erfurt. Through Lang he had become acquainted with Peter Eberbach as early as 1510, if not earlier.[32] Whether his friendship with Spalatin began during his student days at Erfurt is uncertain. At all events he was at Wittenberg as tutor to two nephews of the Elector from 1511-13, when he became the Elector's chaplain and private secretary, and henceforth Luther found in him a warm and influential supporter. In a letter to Lang about the end of 1513, Spalatin already refers to his intimacy with their common friend, and wishes to know whether Luther has read Reuchlin's defence of Hebrew literature against its obscurantist opponents in the University of Cologne.[33] Luther in reply, early in 1514, warmly espouses Reuchlin's cause and vigorously condemns the Cologne theologians, who snuff heresy in a mere judicial opinion on a question of this kind. If this sort of inquisition is allowed to go on, not even the most orthodox will be safe from these zealots, who would be far better employed in trying to reform rampant ecclesiastical abuses than in wasting their energy in such foolish and profitless bickerings.[34] In a subsequent letter in August of the same year he gives energetic expression to his indignation at

---

[32] Oergel, " Vom jungen Luther," 116-117.
[33] Enders, i. 12.   [34] *Ibid*., i. 15.

the scurrilous philippic of Ortwin, one of the Cologne theologians, against Reuchlin. He himself indulges in the drastic controversial style only too usual in the literary and theological quarrels of the age. Ortwin he had hitherto regarded as an ass. He has now shown himself to be a dog, yea a wolf and a crocodile, who vainly gives himself the majestic airs of the lion. He would be disposed to ridicule the whole business if it were not so harmful to religion, and rejoices that the disputants have remitted it to the judgment of the Holy See, in whose wisdom he hopes for a speedy and equitable settlement.[35] In the following year (1515) Reuchlin's opponents were pilloried in the " Epistolæ Obscurorum Virorum." Whilst approving of the object of the anonymous author, he did not share the humanist appreciation of the rather irreverent spirit of this and other facetious effusions at the expense of the opponents of the new culture. The subject appeared to him too serious for such coarse ridicule, which, he said, smelt too much of the chamber-pot.[36]

He had no taste for the cynicism, the flippancy, the naturalism of the laxer type of humanist, or for the speculative freethinking of a Mutianus. The monk and the theologian outweighed in Luther the humanist. In spite of the tendency to break loose from the scholastic bonds, he was too conservative in theology to appreciate independent speculation or look at religion in the broad human sense. For him there were certain dogmatic assumptions (original sin, the impotence of the will, etc.) which he regarded as fundamental. In 1516 he appears, indeed, in correspondence with the liberal-minded Canon of Gotha, to whom Lang had spoken about him. But he neglected to pay him a visit when at Gotha in this year on an inspection tour, as District Vicar of his Order, and the letter is merely a polite note excusing himself for this neglect on the ground of lack of time. Had he been as ardent a humanist as Lang or Spalatin, he would doubtless not have missed the opportunity to make his personal acquaintance.

Nor was he prepared to enrol himself unreservedly as a

follower of Erasmus. He appreciated his learning and shared to the full his strictures on the scholastic theology and his demand for a practical reformation. He speaks of him as "our Erasmus."[37] He was conscious of his own defects as a classical scholar and declared himself to be "a barbarian" compared with him or Mutian.[38] But he was convinced that his own interpretation of Paul's teaching was superior to his, and was not prepared to take his theology from him. In particular, he was not satisfied with his views on original sin and justification, as expressed in his annotations on the Epistle to the Romans. Erasmus, he objects, wrongly limits the righteousness of the law, of which the Apostle speaks, to the works of the ceremonial law. Unlike him, he has learned to prefer Augustine to Jerome as an interpreter of Scripture, and in October 1516 he begs Spalatin to make known to him what he regards as the true teaching of Paul on faith and works.[39] " I have read our Erasmus " (*Erasmum nostrum*), he writes to Lang in 1517, "and from day to day my estimation of him decreases. I am, indeed, pleased that he refutes, not less stoutly than learnedly, both the monks and the priests, and condemns their inveterate and lethargic ignorance. But I fear that he does not sufficiently promote Christ and the grace of God, in which he is more ignorant than Lefèbre. The human prevails in him more than the divine. Although I am unwilling to judge him, I nevertheless venture to do so in order to forewarn you not to read or accept his writings without discrimination. For we live in dangerous times, and it seems to me that a man is not necessarily a truly wise Christian because he knows Greek and Hebrew, since even St Jerome, who knew five languages, is not equal to Augustine, who knew but one, although it may seem far otherwise to Erasmus. But the judgment of one, who attributes something to free will, is very different from that of one who knows nothing but grace. Nevertheless, I carefully conceal this judgment, lest I should seem to

---

[37] Enders, i. 88.   [38] *Ibid.*, i. 35.   Martinus inquam barbarus.
    [39] *Ibid.*, i. 63-64.   This Spalatin did in a letter to Erasmus without naming Luther. *Ibid.*, i. 65-66.   Amicus mihi scribit, etc.   Erasmus seems not to have entered on the subject.

encourage his opponents. Perhaps the Lord will grant him understanding in His own time." [40] In both letters he deplores the same lack of insight in Lefèbre as an exegete, whilst recognising his spirituality and sincerity.

A common bond between him and the humanists was the polemic against the scholastic theologians. In this respect Luther and the humanists were firm allies. The motive of this polemic was, in his case, religious and theological rather than intellectual or rational, and Erasmus and his followers might not be prepared to accept his characteristic doctrine of justification, based, as it was, on the denial of the natural powers of the will and the reason and the depreciation of reason in the sphere of religion. Even so, in drawing his theology from the early sources of Christianity, he might well appear to the humanists as a true Erasmian. They saw in him, in fact, a brilliant protagonist of the enlightened Christianity for which Erasmus, by his critical labours, was preparing the way. For this reason alone he was already exciting a growing interest in humanist circles. His reputation was no longer confined to those who, like Lang and Spalatin, had been closely associated with him as student or as monk. He gained the friendship of Christopher Scheurl, a former professor of canon law and doctor of the University of Wittenberg, and subsequently senator of his native Nürnberg, who, as his correspondence shows, became a warm admirer and won for him a number of friends in the Nürnberg humanist circle. Scheurl and his friends, Wencelaus Link and Hieronymus Ebner, were ardent adherents of Staupitz and the Augustinian theology, and Luther cordially responded to his offer of friendship. At this period even John Eck, professor at Ingolstadt and his future antagonist as the champion of the scholastic theology and the papal power, was eager to enter into correspondence with him, and at Scheurl's request Luther wrote him a letter and exchanged works with him.[41]

[40] Enders, i. 88.

[41] *Ibid.*, i. 79-84, 92-96, 110-112. Eckiüs noster, he terms him at this period.

CHAPTER IX

THE REFORMER IN THE MAKING (1514-1516)

I. LUTHER AS DISTRICT VICAR

LUTHER'S activity was not limited to his chair as Professor of Holy Writ. As sub-prior he took his share in the administration of the Wittenberg monastery under the prior, Link, and with Lang as assistant, was responsible for the theological instruction of the younger members. It was also part of his duty to preach in the monastery chapel, and these early sermons gained him such a reputation that he was invited by the Town Council to become preacher in the parish church.[1] At a meeting of his Order at Gotha in May 1515 he was elected District Vicar of the Augustinian monasteries in Meissen and Thuringia—ten in number, to which the newly-founded house at Eisleben was erelong added. This office involved an annual visitation, besides a heavy correspondence in connection with the administration and discipline of these institutions. He took his office very seriously and his letters show that he was both alert and zealous in the discharge of its duties. He showed himself a strict disciplinarian, whilst ready to treat the erring with discriminating consideration and anxious to reclaim them by patience and kindness. He is, in fact, already, as District Vicar, the strenuous practical reformer. He has a keen eye for the minutiæ of administration as well as the maintenance of discipline. For instance, he admonishes Lang, who had become prior at Erfurt in 1516, to keep a strict account of the provisions consumed in the students' hostel, and impresses on him the necessity of a careful control of

[1] A number of these sermons have survived and are printed in the Weimar edition of his works, i. 20 f.

such expenditure.[2]   He gives injunctions about the dress of the novices.[3]   He insists on the strict observance of the Rule of the Order,[4] and directs Lang to send those guilty of disobedience to Sangershausen to be punished.[5]   He writes to the prior of the Augustinian monastery at Maintz (which was outside his jurisdiction) to send him a monk who had left the monastery at Dresden, which belonged to his district, whilst assuring him that he will deal considerately with this erring brother.[6]   He deposes the prior of Neustadt on account of the dissension among the inmates, and directs them to elect a new one.[7]   On the other hand, he exhorts the provost of Leitzkau to have patience with his degenerate monks rather than cause contention and quarrels, which only make things worse.[8]   He concerns himself with the Elector's mania for collecting relics for the castle church at Wittenberg and informs Spalatin, his chaplain, of the efforts of Staupitz in the region of the lower Rhine to add to the collection.[9]

So great is the number of applicants for admission to the Wittenberg monastery, under his auspices, that he is at his wits' end to know how to provide accommodation for them.[10]   To add to his anxieties, the pest has broken out at Wittenberg, and has already claimed its victims.   If it spreads, he will disperse the Brethren, but for himself he is determined to remain at his post as long as his duty requires.   " I hope," he writes to Lang, who had advised flight, " the world will not collapse even if brother Martin goes under.   Not that I do not fear death.   I am no Apostle Paul, but only a lecturer on Paul.   But I trust that the Lord will deliver me from my fear." [11]   The anxiety told heavily on his spirits.   " My life," he writes to the Provost of Leitzkau towards the end of 1516, " approximates day by day to a hell.   Daily I become more and more miserable." [12] The pressure of work was becoming unbearable.   " I

---

[2] Enders, i. 37-38.
[3] *Ibid.*, i. 56-57.
[4] *Ibid.*, i. 43-44 ; *cf.* 98-99.
[5] *Ibid.*, i. 45.
[6] *Ibid.*, i. 33.
[7] *Ibid.*, i. 53.

[8] *Ibid.*, i. 77-78.
[9] *Ibid.*, i. 73.
[10] *Ibid.*, i. 54-57, 67.
[11] *Ibid.*, i. 67-68.
[12] *Ibid.*, i. 76.

should need two scribes," he wrote to Lang about the same time. " I do almost nothing day by day but write letters, and I know not whether in writing I do not repeat the same things. I am conventual haranguer and reader at table. I am sought daily as parish preacher. I am director of studies, district vicar, *i.e.*, eleven times prior (in reference to the eleven monasteries which he supervised). I am collector of the revenue of the fishery at Leitzkau. I conduct the negotiations about the church of Herzberg in Torgau. I lecture on Paul, I edit the Psalms, and, as I have said, I spend the greater part of my time in writing letters. Rarely do I find sufficient time to perform my canonical devotions and celebrate Mass on account of my troubles with the flesh, the world, and the devil. See what a lazy fellow I am." [13]

No wonder that he had not sufficient time for his canonical devotions and got into the habit of shutting himself up in his cell at the week-end and repeating the prescribed prayers for the whole week seven times over until, he tells us, " his head swam so that he could not sleep a wink for nights-on-end." [14]

The contrast between the Luther of the Erfurt monastery and the Luther of this early Wittenberg activity is very striking. He is no longer the introspective recluse, the self-centred devotee. He has been transformed into the busy teacher and man of affairs, who is in close touch with actual life and is beginning to concern himself with the practical problem of the betterment of the Church and society. He is evidently not going to remain the protagonist of a mere anti-scholastic movement within the schools. His new teaching was the fruit of his religious experience, and, with this dynamic behind it, could not fail to make its influence felt on current religious life. The aggressive, reforming note already finds expression in his lectures, his sermons, his official letters as District Vicar. Grisar ascribes this tendency to criticise the evils of his time to presumptuous and contentious arrogance.[15] Making allowance for his gift of drastic utterance and a dogmatic temperament,

---

[13] Enders, i. 66-67.   [14] " Documente," 42.   [15] " Luther," i. 78 f.

Grisar's interpretation of his aggressive attitude shows a lack of insight into religious psychology. The denunciation of abuses and the demand for their reform is the fruit of an impelling religious experience, not of an overweening tendency to criticise and innovate. With the new illumination which had come to him from Paul, it was impossible for him to hide his light under a bushel.

II. CONDITION OF THE GERMAN CHURCH AND THE DEMAND FOR REFORM

Moreover, there was much in the condition of the Church in Germany, as elsewhere, in the early sixteenth century, to challenge the aggressive activity of the evangelical reformer. Luther was, in fact, only following in the wake of the many would-be reformers of the previous two centuries, who had denounced and vainly striven to rectify the rampant religious declension of their time. The root of this declension lay in the corruption and worldliness of the Roman curia, of which he had learned something from personal observation during his recent visit to Rome. There can be no doubt that in criticising in drastic fashion the rampant abuses in the Church, for which the curia was largely responsible, he was giving expression to a widespread revulsion in Germany, on national, material, and moral grounds, from the secularised Papacy of an Alexander VI. and a Julius II. The Papacy was a political power, as well as an ecclesiastical institution, and under these popes it was dominated by the Machiavellian statecraft of the time in its scramble for aggrandisement, of which Italy was the arena and the victim. The moral and spiritual interest of Christendom seemed little more than a hollow pretence on the part of a profligate like Alexander VI., or a scheming politician like Julius II. Even as an ecclesiastical institution the Papacy, under such auspices, appeared in the light of a mere agency for the financial exploitation of Christendom for the benefit of a corrupt and alien régime. Hence the widespread estrangement from this institution on material or national grounds, which found expression in the recurring outcry against the oppressive papal taxation, the trafficking in benefices, under the name of Provisions, for the benefit of the curial officials and other hirelings, the abuse of pluralities and the tenure of benefices *in commendam* without even the obligation to perform by deputy the duties of the office conferred, the vexatious and costly practice of appeals to Rome, the mercenary indulgence traffic in support of the nepotism and the political schemes of the popes, the misuse of ecclesiastical penalties, of excommunication and interdict in the service of this corrupt system. The evil effects of this corrupt alien régime were inevitably reflected in the internal condition of the German Church—in the secular spirit of the greater part of the hierarchy, the ignorance, inefficiency of the lower clergy, the widespread declension of the monastic orders, both male and female.[16] Apart from these abuses, the clergy were widely unpopular on account of the immunity of the Church lands and the industrial undertakings of the monks from State and municipal taxation.

Alongside the widespread declension of the Church there was, however, and had long been, a movement in favour of reform within the Church as well as among sects like the Waldensians and the Hussites, which this declension had driven into active antagonism to it. Prelates like Cardinal Cusanus, preachers like Geiler of Kaiserberg and John of Wesel, theologians with evangelical sympathies like Wessel Gansfort, the Observantine sections of the Franciscan and Augustinian Orders, reforming associations like the Brethren of the Common Life, the numerous brotherhoods of a religious and philanthropic character, translations of the Bible into the vernacular—of which no less than fourteen editions appeared before Luther's advent, in spite of the opposition of the hierarchy—facts like these indicate an earnest striving to stem the tide of religious declension. The Reformation was, in fact, only the more drastic culmina-

---

[16] For details see von Bezold, " Geschichte der Deutschen Reformation," 75 f. (1890) ; *cf.* Grisar, i. 45 f. ; Pastor, " History of the Popes," vii. 290 f. ; Jansen, " History of the German People " ii. 297 ; von Below, " Ursachen der Reformation," 21 f. ; Müller, " Kirchen Geschichte," ii. 189 f. (1902).

tion of this reform movement, and without the preparation of this movement, this culmination would hardly have been possible. There were, indeed, other contributory influences of a political, social, economic, and intellectual nature working towards the great disruption of the Church, which Luther ultimately operated. But the Reformation, as an ethical and spiritual movement, could only succeed in as far as it could appeal to the aspiration after a more ideal form of the religious life, which, in spite of the degeneration of the Church, was finding expression in various ways within it. There was, in fact, a religious revival of a kind in the period immediately preceding the Reformation. This revival took the form of an enhanced devotion to external observances —of a mania for pilgrimages, an intensified worship of the saints, especially of St Anna, the mother of the Virgin, a superstitious reverence of relics, of which the collection of the Elector Frederick at Wittenberg is an example, and a widespread popular eagerness to take advantage of the device of indulgences. This religiosity, though to a certain extent the expression of genuine piety, was, however, too crude, too steeped in the current formalism and superstition to be in itself an effective Reformation. It rather aggravated than vitalised this formalism and invited the criticism of the more spiritually-minded reformers, like John of Wesel and Wessel Gansfort, who anticipated Luther in the attack on indulgences and other gross notions and practices of the time.[17] Luther recognised in Wessel, in particular, his forerunner as a reformer both of doctrine and practice. " If I had read Wessel sooner," he said later, though not with sufficient discrimination, " my enemies would have presumed to say that I had borrowed everything from him. So great is the agreement between our minds." [18]

Luther already realised his mission as a practical reformer at least. " It is my duty," he told his students, " to declare whatever I see to be amiss even in the highest ranks." [19] His attitude was still, like so many of his

---

[17] See Ullmann, " Reformers Before the Reformation," English translation (1855), and Miller and Scudder, " Wessel Gansfort " (1917).

[18] See his preface to Wessel's " Farrago Rerum Theologicarum " (1522); Ullmann, ii. 579.   [19] " Vorlesung," ii. 301.

reforming predecessors, that of a reformer within the Church. He respects its authority and its institutions and denounces the heretics who err in preferring their own opinions to its authoritative teaching. His standpoint in the Commentary on Romans and his early sermons is identical, in this respect, with that of the lectures on the Psalms.[20] As against the heretics he adduces the authority of the Church in its Roman form as the embodiment and guardian of the truth.[21] The Church and its prelates possess a monopoly of truth. Their voice is the voice of Christ Himself, and those who despise their teaching and follow their own understanding are no real believers in Christ.[22] Extremists like the Beghards, who would sweep away the whole fabric of ecclesiastical institutions and usages, are false apostles of liberty. Against such he dogmatically defends the papal power. Without such a single head the unity of the Church would be at the mercy of every opinionative schismatic, and there would be as many heads and churches as there are heretics. Hence the power of loosing and binding was given to one man in order to preserve the unity of the Church.[23] He is still an ardent believer in the monastic life freely adopted for the love of God,[24] and ascribes to the life in accordance with the evangelical counsels a higher value than to that in accordance with the precepts of the Gospel.[25] It is, indeed, an error to regard the monastic life as essential to salvation, and he warns against the exaggerated and perverse notion of its efficacy. Only if the monastic vow is freely taken, from the pure love of God, can one be a good monk. In this sense he commends the religious life to those who would take up the Cross and follow Christ, and he thinks that the present time is an opportune one, compared with 200 years ago, inasmuch as to become a true monk nowadays is to become the butt of the hatred and contempt of the world.[26]

[20] For the Psalms, see " Werke," iii. 292, 334 ; iv. 345.

[21] " Vorlesung," ii. 249. Sic ergo authoritas Ecclesiæ instituta, ut nunc adhuc Romana tenet ecclesia.

[22] *Ibid.*, ii. 96.　　[23] " Werke," i. 69.　　[24] " Vorlesung," ii. 316-317.

[25] *Ibid.*, i. 58. Superius docuit (apostolus) quod perfecte faciunt qui omnino continent, divitias contemnunt, honores fugiunt, et in consiliis evangelicis ambulant.　　　　　　　　　　[26] *Ibid.*, ii. 318.

He respects the usages which the Church has imposed from ancient times, and which are to be observed in a spirit of obedience to ecclesiastical authority, though in themselves they are not absolutely necessary or immutable.[27]   He accepts the sacramental system of the Church, whilst criticising and virtually nullifying it by his insistence on justification by faith alone, and on the direct relation of the soul to God implied in this doctrine.

III. Reforming Note of Early Lectures and Sermons

Whilst thus maintaining the authority of the Church and defending its institutions against the heretics, Luther realises the urgent need for a drastic reformation of the actual Church.   His early sermons and his Commentary on Romans show a marked advance, in this respect, on the lectures on the Psalms.   The critical note is more in evidence and the criticism is more comprehensive.   Whilst the standpoint is still that of the reformer within the Church, who, like other contemporary reformers, is concerned with the reformation of practical abuses, it is evident that he also views the problem of reform in the light of his personal apprehension and experience of the Gospel. Nor does he confine his criticism to the monastic life in which he was more immediately interested, both as monk and as District Vicar of his Order.   One of his earliest extant sermons deals, indeed, with this specific theme. This sermon was delivered at a chapter of the Order at Gotha in May 1515.   It is an outspoken harangue on the vice of detraction, which, it seems, was all too common among the monks.[28]   Though it is not in the best of taste, judged by the modern standard, it apparently did not shock his hearers, who deemed him the right man to be entrusted with the office of District Vicar of the Order, and the coarseness of style is exceptional in his pulpit oratory.   In another of these early sermons which he wrote about the same time for the

[27] " Vorlesung," ii. 317.
[28] " Werke," i. 44 ; Köstlin, " Luther," i. 125-126, 129.

Provost of Leitzkau, and which the Provost delivered before a provincial synod, he shows a wider outlook as well as a more dignified treatment of his theme. He deplores the miserable state of religion and the prevalence of superstition and vice among the people. This, he contends, is due to the lack of the true preaching of the Word. For this state of things he blames the clergy, who are more intent on temporal things than on the ministry of the Word and the cure of souls. Without the preaching of the pure Gospel, all reforming statutes will be in vain and the synod will merely expose itself to the merited contempt of the world. Moreover, it is far more important that the clergy should reform themselves than that they should pass decrees about ceremonies and church festivals.[29]

He is already on the warpath against the abuse of indulgences, to which he devotes a couple of sermons. Although the practice, being based on the merit of Christ and the saints, is to be accepted with all reverence, it has become a most disgraceful ministry of avarice. The commissaries and their agents, who promote the traffic, strive rather to fill their money bags than to save souls. They urge the people to give and do not trouble to instruct them in the true meaning of the practice, but leave them under the delusion that, in return for their money, they are freed from penance and satisfaction and have full remission of all their sins. The result is that the foolish crowd go away with the notion that they may sin with impunity. The Pope has no power to absolve from the pains of purgatory. He can only intercede for the souls of the departed and can only dispense from penalties imposed by himself. How rash, therefore, to preach that souls can be redeemed by this mercenary device. It would better become the Pope to concede gratis what it is within his power to give. In any case plenary remission should only be given to those who are truly contrite and confessed. He has grave doubts about the whole subject and concludes that it is not safe to rely on this expedient, since even in the case of intercession for the dead, which the Pope and the

[29] " Werke," i. 10 f.

Church may exercise, the fate of the soul lies in the hands of God. At the same time, he does not reject the practice, in spite of its abuse, whilst warning against a false reliance on it to the neglect of the true spiritual life, which seeks God for the love of Him and out of hatred of self.[30] True contrition craves not indulgence from, or the remission of penalties, but seeks rather their exaction. It is not a mere " gallow repentance," which does not hate sin, but only fears the punishment of it. Herein lie the peril and the perversity of this indulgence preaching, which can only magnify the efficacy of this expedient to deliver from the pains and penalties of sin, at the cost of minimising true contrition.[31] " There is thus apparent very little fruit of indulgences except the greater security and liberty in sinning. For unless people feared the punishment of sins, nobody would care to look at them, if offered for nothing. They ought rather to be exhorted to love punishment and embrace the Cross. Would that I lied in saying that indulgences are perhaps most fitly so named, because to indulge is to permit, and means permission to sin with impunity and the license to evade the Cross of Christ. Alas! the dangers of the time. O slumbering priests, O darkness worse than Egyptian ! How secure we are in the midst of all these our worst evils." [32]

In most of the sermons delivered in the parish church the evangelical note is unmistakable. Luther's main object is to preach Christ and the Cross as the only means of salvation, the true wisdom in contrast to the wisdom of the flesh, though it may seem foolishness to many of the theologians and the priests.[33] Under the wings of Christ alone can the sinner find a refuge from his sins, not in his own righteousness.[34] He evidently regards himself as the prophet of the true Gospel, which consists in the absolute distrust of one's own righteousness and the unconditional submission, in faith, of the heart and the will to God in Christ. Hence the recurring polemic in these sermons against the

---

[30] " Werke," i. 65 f.   [31] *Ibid.*, i. 98-99.   [32] *Ibid.*, i. 141.

[33] *Ibid.*, i. 52. Unum prædica, sapientiam crucis. *Ibid.*, i. 31. Ego semper prædico de Christo, Gallina nostra.

[34] *Ibid.*, i. 31. Nos nostris justitiis prorsus salvari non possumus.

preachers of salvation by the conventional method of work righteousness. He already realises that he is swimming against the tide of religious convention, and he evidently has his opponents as well as his admirers. He is by no means abashed by such opposition, for so it has always been. The true prophet, he boldly reminds his critics, has always been persecuted by the votaries of conventional religion and has only found a hearing from the publicans and sinners.[35]

In this connection he denounces not only the heretics, but those who pride themselves in their own works—their prayers, fasts, and vigils.[36] Such devotees of an outward righteousness are the false prophets of a mechanical religion, who make a parade of outward works like the heretics and the schismatics. Their much fasting, praying, zealotry, preaching, watching, and poor garments are but the wool under which is concealed the ravening wolf. Works must proceed from the inner, hidden man, and those who do them make little of their outward form, but rather seek to bring forth the fruits of humility, meekness, charity, and patience. " There is not a greater pest in the Church than these false prophets who are ever crying up their mechanical works, whilst they are crassly ignorant of what is really good and evil. They are the enemies of the Cross, i.e., of what is truly good in the sight of God." [37] Through them the devil is everywhere busy setting snares to entangle souls not only in what is evil, but even under the guise of good works. They are evidently doing their utmost to undermine the influence of the preacher by their secret machinations. " I make mention of these things," he says, " because these subtle intriguers and invisible transgressors of the command-

---

[35] " Werke," i. 31. Prophetæ, sapientes, scribæ, dum mittuntur ad justos, sanctos, pios, non recipiuntur ab ipsis, sed occiduntur, recipiuntur autem ab injustis et peccatoribus, publicanis et meretricibus, quoniam hi cupiunt doceri.

[36] Ibid., i. 36. Ideo in his maxime pereunt Hæretici et superbi, dum ea pertinaciter diligunt quasi ideo Deum diligant, quia hæc diligunt. Cf. ibid., i. 38. These are good if done in the true fear of God, and not with a view to placate God and escape damnation.

[37] Ibid., i. 61-62.

ment of God are secretly shooting their arrows against those who are right of heart." [38] These are the Pharisees of the present time who, in their self-righteousness, have established an idol in their hearts.[39]

He would not, however, be understood as condemning good works, but only the superstitious principle underlying them—the confidence and self-complacency which has its root in human pride.[40] In the early stage of the religious life, indeed, it behoves us to exercise ourselves in good works—in fasting, watching, praying, works of mercy, service, obedience. But we must beware of the spiritual dangers involved in these outward exercises, and not, like the Pharisees, "the proud saints," permanently stick fast at this stage and never get beyond it.[41] "Those," on the other hand, "who are led by the Spirit of God, after they have exercised themselves in this outward discipline of the internal man, come to regard this discipline as a mere beginning, and do not trouble themselves much about such things. Rather, they offer themselves to God for whatever works He may call them, and are led by God through many sufferings and tribulations, knowing not whither they are led, but committing themselves to Him alone, and not attaching themselves to any outward works." [42]

Along with this insistence on the nullity of works for salvation, he emphasises, with equal insistence, faith, trust in God in Christ as the only means of righteousness before God. The righteousness which justifies in God's sight does not consist in works, but in the imputed righteousness which is appropriated by faith, trust, hope in His mercy. This faith excludes all idea of merits and works, and this Gospel he will proclaim, however much he may scandalise " the justiciarians (*justitiarii*), who worship the idol of their own merits." [43] Christ came to heal the sick, not the whole. The defect of " these proud and incorrigible

[38] "Werke," i. 62.   [39] *Ibid.*, i. 64.
[40] *Ibid.*, i. 70. Non prohibentur justitiæ fieri et bona opera, sed debent sine superstitione fieri, *i.e.*, humiliter non in ea confidendo aut ea amando, reputando præ amore Dei et spei in illum.
[41] *Ibid.*, i. 71.   [42] *Ibid.*, i. 73.   [43] *Ibid.*, i. 81 and 84.

justiciarians " is that they do not realise that they are sick and do not really wish to be healed of the disease of sin. " True faith," he says with a reminiscence of his own spiritual conflict, "is not attained by speculation and by one's own efforts, but only by a living experience (*sed per viam practicam*). God in manifold ways frustrates mere human prudence and subdues the understanding of a man till he despairs of himself and his own understanding, and learns by experience that he cannot direct himself and must willingly give up the reins to God. Then he is prepared to be led by the Word alone, having discovered that he can effect nothing by his own works and his own counsels." [44] All through these sermons he is obsessed by the Pauline teaching on faith *versus* works—so much so that he twists his text at times in order to make it the vehicle of this supreme verity. In this respect they are an echo of the Commentary on Romans, and may be described as a public manifesto of the doctrine of justification by faith alone, in protest against the current preaching, which is concerned almost wholly with the inculcation of works and contains almost nothing about faith and inner righteousness, from which all good works must proceed.[45] Their most distinctive notes are, in fact, the futility of works and the dependence of man on God, in simple trust, for salvation. Not that he is to despise good works and take his ease. For if the righteousness of faith is given without works, it is also given in order to works.[46]

The critical, reforming note is equally audible in the lectures on Romans. He does not hesitate to arraign the Pope, the curia, the hierarchy, the clergy both secular and regular. The thought of the Papacy and the curia under Julius II. revolts him, and there is evidently a reminiscence of his own impressions of Rome in the scathing denunciation

---

[44] "Werke," i. 87-88 ; *cf.* 43, in which he speaks of the despair with which the current doctrine had filled him.

[45] *Ibid.*, i. 118.

[46] *Ibid.*, i. 119. Luther's early sermons from 1514-17 are in vol. i. of the Weimar edition. They were first published by Löscher in " Reformations Acta und Documenta " (1720-29). Most of them are also given in Walch's " Luthers Sämmtliche Schriften," xii. and xix., translated into German.

of the corruption and vileness, the luxury, the pomp, the
avarice, ambition, and sacrilege that reign in the Holy
City.[47] Modern Rome has reverted to the ancient manners
described in Romans xiii. 13, and has infected almost the
whole world by its example. It stands in need once more
of the admonition of the Apostle.[48] At Rome they are
busy enough in giving dispensations, which mean giving
an occasion to the flesh.[49] The Pope and the priesthood
seduce the people from the true worship of God.[50] They
have brought back into the Church Jewish superstition,
the old Mosaic servitude. Owing to the neglect of the
true preaching of the Word, the people have come to believe
that they cannot be saved without the observance of manifold
ceremonies. He would, therefore, drastically diminish these
excessive observances. These increase daily, and the more
they increase, the more faith and love decrease, and avarice,
pride, vain glory are nurtured.[51] He would allow a large
measure of individual liberty in this matter. If the mere
fear of hell were eliminated from all this externalism, and
only the love of God were the motive in religion, he thinks
that almost all the churches and altars would be deserted
in the course of a single year.[52] The clergy are more intent
on their temporal advantage than on the performance of
their spiritual functions. They are very eager to maintain
the liberties, rights, authority, and powers of the Church,
to make use of excommunication in their defence, to
fulminate their thunders against those who infringe them,
as heretics and enemies of God and the Church, whilst
they themselves may most fitly be so described. " You
may possess the whole catalogue of the vices, but you are,
nevertheless, a very pious Christian, if you uphold the
liberties and rights of the Church." [53]

He compares the Church of his own time with that of

[47] " Vorlesung," ii. 301-302.   [48] Ibid., ii. 310.
[49] Ibid., ii. 319. Verumtamen Apostolus monet Galatas ne hanc
libertatem dent in occasionem carnis, ut nunc faciunt Romæ ubi nihil
eorum amplius curant quæ dicta sunt ; omnia sunt devorata per dispensa-
tiones. Libertate ista potiuntur perfectissime.
[50] Ibid., ii. 243.   [52] Ibid., ii. 320.
[51] Ibid., ii. 316-319.   [53] Ibid., ii. 298.

the Apostles and finds that, though the Apostolic Church had no rights and privileges, it had very worthy ministers, who paid taxes to the State and submitted themselves to the powers that be, and did not, as the priests now do, insist on all kinds of rights and immunities. The clergy complain that the laity are their enemies, but it does not occur to them to ask the reason, which consists in the fact that though so highly privileged and beneficed, they are very unworthy of their office. If they claim all manner of rights and privileges, let them at least show themselves good priests.[54] He is of opinion that the State compares favourably with the Church in the matter of efficiency. Whilst the secular power rigorously punishes thieves, murderers, and other criminals, the Church, though quick enough to complain of the invasion of its rights and privileges, not only does not punish, but nurtures pomp, ambition, luxury, and contentions. So bad is the state of things that it would be safe, he thinks, to place the temporalities of the clergy under the supervision of the temporal power, since the Church not only does not debar ignorant, unsuitable, and useless persons from the holy ministry, but even promotes them to the highest offices. It does this, too, with full knowledge of the facts, and yet by promoting these pestiferous men, it provokes the infringement of its rights and is itself the cause of the scandal of which it complains.[55] He has no high opinion of the bishops in general, and in view of the worldly character of the episcopal office and the mercenary conduct of so many of its holders, writes strongly, in a letter to Spalatin, against the Elector's project to appoint Staupitz to a bishopric. " To be a bishop nowadays," he tells him, " is to live as in Greece, as in Sodom, as in Rome of old, which you will understand sufficiently well if you compare the works and pursuits of the ancient bishops with those of the high priests of our age." The Elector, though so farseeing in secular affairs, " is sevenfold blind " in religious matters, and he earnestly dissuades his friend from . countenancing what he regards as, from the spiritual point of view, a most inadvisable project.[56]

[54] " Vorlesung," ii. 299.   [55] Ibid., ii. 300.
[56] Enders, i. 40-41 (June 1516).

At the same time, he does not spare the secular power. " The princes and rulers of the world drain to themselves the goods of their subjects, not indeed by actual violence, but by threatening them if they do not cede them and by abandoning them in their necessities. . . . Thus you will find few princes who are not thieves and robbers, or at least the sons of thieves and robbers, as St Augustine has truly said, ' What are great kingdoms, but great robberies ? ' They seek their own interest and not the public good, and heap up riches, whilst neglecting the care and the welfare of their subjects." [57]   By what right, he asks, do they preserve the game for themselves and punish as a thief every rustic who kills a single bird ? Do they not thus deprive the community of its rights, simply because they are powerful enough to do so, and not by any inherent right ? In this connection he reminds them of the story of Alexander the Great and the pirate. Why, asked Alexander, do you infest the seas ? Why, retorted the pirate, do you infest the whole earth ? If I do this with my small vessel, I am called a robber. If you do the same with a great fleet, you are called an emperor ! Similarly, he denounces the oppressive expedients, such as the arbitrary depreciation of the coinage, by which they exploit their subjects. The spiritual princes are among the worst of these oppressors, since they make use of the spiritual arms of the Church, of excommunication and interdict, for their selfish ends, to the utter devastation and ruin of the Church.[58] The quarrels and animosities of rulers and peoples fill the world with strife and war. Italians, French, Germans think only of their own national interest, and seem to forget that they are Christians.[59] Under this baneful influence the jurists are far too prone to consider justice only from the particular point of view, not from that of the universal justice by which God governs the world. Thus Pope Julius waged war with the Venetians for his particular interest, under the pretext of vindicating justice. Thus, too, Duke George of Saxony pursues his claims against the Frisians, and even his own Bishop of Brandenburg and his own sovereign, the Elector Frederick,

[57] " Vorlesung," i. 22.   [58] *Ibid.*, ii. 30-31.   [59] *Ibid.*, ii. 294.

are not above reproof in this respect. If only such
potentates would remember their own shortcomings
in the sight of God, from the point of view of universal justice, they would learn to be more forbearing,
less exacting in the pursuit of their own ends in the
name of justice.[60]

These outspoken strictures sound rather revolutionary.
Luther stands for a thorough transformation of Church,
and State, and society. But he stops short at a moral
revolution. He is not the apostle of a political
or a social upheaval. It is not a question of political
liberty, he says in reference to Romans xiii. 1, since
subjection to the powers that be is incumbent on all.[61]
The duty of the Christian is to bear the cross even
under wrong and oppression.[62] This doctrine, which
he seems to have derived from the mystics, might
well appear a sufficient safeguard against the freedom
of criticism which he allowed himself against all in
authority, from the Pope and the Emperor to his local
bishop and the territorial princes.

Luther is the champion of spiritual, not of political
liberty. He would emancipate the soul from the externalism
that distorts religion and hinders the apprehension of the
Gospel and the spiritual life, in dependence on God's grace.
At this stage he does not fully realise what this emancipation
implies. He would modify and improve rather than sweep
away the ecclesiastical usages and institutions which have
encrusted personal faith. He believes in these usages and
institutions out of respect to the authority of the Church.
But he also feels, and feels strongly, that there is something
wrong in the state of Denmark, and he boldly attacks the
many abuses which disgrace the Church and paralyse its
spiritual life. On the clamant necessity of the reform of
these glaring abuses he speaks with no uncertain voice.
As to the institutions of the Church in themselves, he is

[60] " Vorlesung," ii. 271-273.

[61] *Ibid.*, ii. 303. De potestate autem seculi nullam facit questionem
libertatis. Neque enim servitus illa est, cum sit omnium hominum in
mundo.

[62] *Ibid.*, ii. 34.

only at the stage of incipient doubt. Whether the doubt
would increase or decrease would depend on the question
whether the Pope and the hierarchy would come some way
towards meeting his demand for a thorough reformation
of the Church in a spiritual direction.

CHAPTER X

THE REFORMER AT WORK (1516-1517)

I. The Attack on the Scholastic Theology

LUTHER did not begin his career as an active reformer with the attack on indulgences towards the end of 1517. He was already from 1513 onwards propagating his views, with growing insistence, in his lectures, sermons, and letters, as well as criticising current dogmas, institutions, and usages. In teaching his students, he was at the same time training disciples who should become the heralds of his distinctive ideas. He only, indeed, gradually became conscious that he was in fundamental antagonism to the teaching of the Church, and so far his polemic was directed against what he deemed the errors of the schoolmen and what were generally recognised as abuses of the religious life. At the same time, this active polemic against the scholastic doctors and the usages, of which these doctors provided the theoretic basis, did not begin with the indictment of indulgences in the autumn of 1517. Fully a year earlier he had formally challenged the adherents of the old theology on the fundamental question of free will and grace.

The challenge took the form of a disputation for the degree of *Sententiarius* on the 25th September 1516, over which he presided, and in the course of which the candidate, Bartholomew Bernhardi, one of his students, maintained the professor's distinctive views on this question. The candidate was obviously but the mouthpiece of his teacher in contending, with the aid of copious quotations from Scripture and St Augustine, that man, though created in the image of God, is totally incapable, because of inherent concupiscence, of keeping the commands of God without grace, or of preparing himself for grace, and that without

274

grace the human will is not free, but enslaved by sin, albeit unwillingly. Man is free only to sin when he does what in him lies to attain the good, since of himself, by reason of original sin, he cannot desire or purpose the good. As a bad tree can only bear bad fruit, so man without grace, however much he may strive to will or do the good, necessarily sins without faith operating in love. Only he is righteous whom a merciful God reputes such. Christ alone is our righteousness, and it is a mere superstition, a human device to think that the saints can help us. To him who believes in Christ all things are possible. He is all sufficient for salvation.[1]

The candidate was only repeating what Luther had dogmatically taught again and again in his lectures and sermons. But the significance of the theses does not lie in the repetition of what had become the commonplaces of his master's teaching, but in the fact that Luther himself was deliberately proclaiming war, in a public academic deliverance, on the old theology in the most uncompromising terms. They were a public manifesto against the teaching of the Nominalist school in which he had been trained— of his old teachers Trutvetter and Usingen, and other followers of Gabriel Biel. He had got to know, he informed Lang in a letter in September 1516, that the Erfurt theologians, as well as some of his colleagues at Wittenberg, were objecting to his teaching, and he had adopted this expedient to stop the mouths of these detractors.[2] He had farther given offence to the Gabrielists, especially to his colleague Carlstadt, by denying that Augustine could have written the work on " True and False Penitence," which the schoolmen, following Gratian and Peter Lombard, incorrectly ascribed to him. They made use of this work to torment, instead of healing the consciences of penitents, although nothing could be farther removed from the mind and teaching of Augustine than this insipid and inept production. In conclusion he asks Lang to tell " these astounded and wonderful Erfurt doctors " that he is not to be gainsaid

---

[1] The theses are entitled, Quæstio de viribus et voluntate hominis sine gratia. The best edition is that of Stange, " Die Aeltesten Ethischen Disputationen Luthers " (1904).　　[2] Enders, i. 53.

whatever Gabriel Biel, or even Raphael and Michael say. "I know Gabriel's views. They are altogether good, except when he speaks of grace, love, hope, faith, virtue. In these matters he is as much a Pelagian as his leader Duns Scotus." [3] The challenging note of these words is unmistakable. Luther is already on the warpath as an aggressive reformer of theology. He is beginning to pit his theological convictions against the world.

For him it is not merely a question of scholastic theology. These doctrines are of the essence of salvation, and he will maintain and propagate them not only against the schoolmen, but against even Erasmus. "You would say," he wrote to Spalatin, "that I am rash in bringing men of such reputation under the rod of Aristarchus; did you not know that I do this on behalf of the true theology and the salvation of the brethren." [4] "What is more wholesome than Christ and the Gospel," he writes to the same correspondent, who consulted him about his plan of translating certain works into German, "though they are held in little esteem by so many to whom they are a saviour of death unto death, and not, as in the case of only a few, of life unto life." Let him discard the current theology and read Tauler's sermons. [5]

He had come to the conclusion that the corruption of theology was due to the domination of Aristotle in the schools. He had, in fact, long been convinced, as his early lecture notes on the Sentences show, that the theologians had erred in basing their systems on his philosophical and ethical principles. Hence the incidental polemic against Aristotle in the lectures on the Psalms and the Epistle to the Romans. It was still, it would seem, part of his duty to lecture to the monks on the Physics. This enforced study he regarded as a waste of time, [6] and he now determined to dethrone the pagan dictator of the schools and to emancipate theology from his baneful influence. To this end, he sent to Lang in February 1517 a number of propositions, in his most drastic style, against the corrupter of Christian truth, with a request to submit them to Trutvetter and find

[3] Enders, i. 55.   [4] Ibid., i. 64.   [5] Ibid., i. 74.   [6] Ibid., i. 86.

out what he and others thought of them. These propositions have not been preserved. But the letter is explicit enough as to his own opinion of the false idol of the theologians. In his early lecture notes on the Sentences he had, as we have seen, given rather violent expression to his sense of his baneful influence on theology, and he renewed his dissent in several passages in the Commentary on Romans,[7] whilst admitting that, if properly understood and applied, his philosophy might to a certain extent be serviceable.[8] In the letter to Lang the condemnation is unqualified. Aristotle is the most sophistic of conjurors who, through his credulous followers, has foisted on theology such absurdities that an ass, nay the very stones, could not keep silent. He has nothing so much at heart as to tear the Greek mask off this stage player, who has imposed his sophistries on the Church, and expose his ignominy to all. If Aristotle had not lived in the flesh, he would not hesitate to assert that he is the very devil.[9] The language cannot certainly be called judicial. But Luther's violent aversion was not so much to Aristotle the philosopher, as to the pseudo-Aristotle of the schools, whom the theologians had established as their infallible mentor in theology and had thereby led themselves and the Church into a labyrinth of false doctrine.

Here, at all events, was a man with the courage of his convictions, a forceful personality which bade fair to go far in the crusade in behalf of personal religious conviction. To Martin Pollich, the Professor of Law, it seemed that " this brother with the deep-set eyes " would yet revolutionise the teaching of the universities. He was already, in fact, a power in the University of Wittenberg, and was winning over his colleagues, including Amsdorf and Carlstadt, who at first opposed him, to his views. In April 1517 Carlstadt published 152 theses on nature and grace in which, to Luther's joy, he set forth the Augustinian view. " Blessed be God," wrote he to Scheurl in May, " who has commanded again the light to shine forth from the darkness." [10] " Our theology (*Theologia nostra*)," he informs Lang a few days

---

[7] " Vorlesung," ii. 108, 178, 183, 192, 221.
[8] *Ibid.*, ii. 266.   [9] Enders, i. 85-86.   [10] *Ibid.*, i. 97.

later, " and St Augustine advance prosperously and reign
in the university through God's agency. By degrees
Aristotle descends from his pinnacle and inclines to fall into
ruin, perhaps permanently. It is wonderful how the
lectures on the Sentences begin to become tedious. No
one can hope for hearers unless he professes the new
theology, *i.e.*, the Bible and St Augustine, or some other
teacher of real ecclesiastical authority." [11]

On the 4th September another of his students, Francis
Gunther, arraigned the scholastic theology in a public
disputation for the degree of Biblical Bachelor. In a series
of ninety-eight theses, the candidate, as Luther's mouthpiece,
categorically asserted the views of Augustine on free will
and grace against the teaching of Scotus, Occam, D'Ailly,
Biel, and others. In his opening thesis he did not hesitate
to claim a monopoly of truth for Augustine against his
opponents, and roundly averred that to object to his views
as " excessive " was to espouse the side of Pelagius and all
heretics. The assumption all through is that the scholastic
theologians, who differ from Augustine, are false teachers,
enemies of sound doctrine. The candidate was certainly
not lacking in audacity. It is true, he insists against the
objections to the former series, that man, like a bad tree,
cannot do otherwise than will and do evil. He has no
choice in the matter, since he is not free, but a captive. It
is therefore false that the will can conform itself naturally
to the prescription of reason. While it is not, as the
Manichæans hold, evil in its very nature, its nature is
inevitably corrupt. It is absurd to say that, because erring
man can love the creature above all things, he can, therefore,
love God above all. This is a figment of Scotus and Biel.
The opposite conclusion is rather the true one that, because
erring man can love the creature, it is, therefore, impossible
for him to love God. Only by predisposing grace can he
attain to the pure love of God. By nature he is capable
not of love, but only of concupiscence ; in other words, of
egotism. The disposition to receive grace is conditioned,
not by the will of man, but by the predestination and

[11] Enders, i. 100-101.

election of God. Whilst it is thus false to say that a man can do what in him lies to remove the obstacles to grace, it is not true that his inveterate ignorance and disability do away with his responsibility for sin. Though both intellect and will are corrupt and he is not the master but the slave of his actions, his actions are none the less sinful. Without justifying grace no one is acceptable to God, since without grace he cannot fulfil the law. It is futile to say, with the scholastics, that he can conform, without grace, to the mere letter of the law, that he may abstain from murder, or adultery, or theft in external obedience to the precept. A mere external conformity is of no avail in the sight of God, who has regard, not to the external act, but to the inward disposition. It is the spirit or disposition in which the act is done, not the mere doing of it, that is the great thing with God. Without His grace operating in the heart, the disposition and, therefore, the acceptable observance of the law in God's sight are impossible.[12] The law and the human will are two implacable opposites without God's grace ; for what the law desires, the will does not desire unless from fear or a mere pretended love. Though good in itself, the law only makes sin to abound, as Paul says, since it only irritates and rebuts the will. Grace, on the contrary, makes the righteousness of Christ to abound, because it makes the fulfilment of the law possible. By the law is meant not merely the ceremonial, but the moral law, the fulfilment of which consists in the love of God diffused in our hearts by the Holy Spirit. The evil, he concludes with the mystics, is in us, in self-love, not in it. To love God is to hate self, to know nothing besides God, and to conform our will to His.

In thus sharply defining the new theology in opposition to the scholastics, the candidate, *alias* Luther, believes that he has asserted nothing that is not in agreement with the teaching of the Church and its doctors. Evidently, however, he does not reckon among these doctors those who have

[12] The reference here is to the scholastic distinction between the observance of the law *quoad substantiam*, *i.e.*, the mere prescription, which is possible without grace, and its observance *quoad intentionem præcipientis*, for which grace is necessary.

been led astray by that false guide, Aristotle. Almost the whole of the Aristotelian ethics, he insists, is the worst enemy of grace, and it is an error to hold that his conception of the highest good is not contrary to Catholic doctrine. Equally erroneous the assumption that without a knowledge of Aristotle one cannot be a theologian. On the contrary, no one can be a true theologian unless he discards Aristotle ; for the application of his teaching to Christian truth has been the bane of theology. In brief the whole Aristotle is to Christian theology as darkness is to light, and it is extremely doubtful whether the early Latin fathers knew anything of his philosophy. It would have been well for the Church if Porphyry, with his doctrine of universal ideas, had never been born.[13]

In thus condemning the use of the dialectic and philosophy of Aristotle for the purpose of demonstrating Christian truth, he was only applying the Nominalist principle of revelation as the sole source of the knowledge of God. Trutvetter, Usingen and their Nominalist predecessors were, in fact, contravening a fundamental of their own school. On the other hand, he himself, in his subservience to Augustine, was in danger, in demolishing one theological idol, of setting up another in its place. There was much to be said for his attempt to free Christianity from the extraneous ideas which, in the course of time, it had absorbed from Greek philosophy. We may not appreciate his violent language, which seems to suit the obscurantist monk rather than the cultured critic. It is none the less certain that the schoolmen had overcharged theology with a dead weight of ideas and terms which were alien to the simpler teaching of Jesus and the Apostles. It was high time to make a clearance of this lumber, and so far Luther was doing a real service to Christian theology. His demand that the Bible, not the schoolmen, as dominated by Aristotle, should be the norm of Christian truth was eminently sound. But in thirling theology to

---

[13] The best edition of the Disputatio Contra Scholasticam Theologiam is that of Stange, " Die Aeltesten Ethischen Disputationen Luthers," 35 f.

Augustine, he was imposing a dialectic and philosophical incubus on Christian thought, from which it would have been better if he had kept himself freer. After all, there was some force in the objection of his opponents that, in his controversy with heretics like Pelagius, Augustine was inclined to make "excessive" statements. Luther was certainly not the man to mitigate the dogmatic spirit of the new oracle, or to woo by persuasion the older theologians from their allegiance to Aristotle. The Erfurt doctors do not seem to have taken any notice of his offer to debate with them the new theology.[14] On the other hand, Scheurl and his Nürnberg friends had avowed themselves as enthusiastic followers and zealously circulated the theses far and near, including one copy to Eck, to whom Luther refers as "Our Eck."[15] To them Luther is "The Restorer of the Theology of Christ."[16] He had, he learned from Spalatin, secured the Elector's goodwill,[17] and the students and his younger colleagues of Wittenberg ranged themselves at his side under the banner of Augustine.

II. ORIGIN AND PRACTICE OF INDULGENCES

The warfare in the schools on behalf of the true theology was the prelude to the warfare against the errors and evils of the religious life. Within two months after the Disputation on the Scholastic Theology, Luther nailed to the door of the castle church at Wittenberg his Ninety-five Theses on Indulgences (31st October 1517). He had already in his sermons and lectures criticised the abuse of this practice, which had largely become a mere expedient for filling the coffers of the papal treasury. The theses in which he now arraigned it, if couched in less uncompromising terms than the polemic against Aristotle and the schoolmen, were far more fateful in their effects. They proved, in fact, to be the decisive step in his career as an aggressive reformer, though he little anticipated the revolution that this comparatively

---

[14] Enders, i. 106-107.
[15] *Ibid.*, i. 110.
[16] *Ibid.*, i. 111-112, 119.
[17] *Ibid.*, i. 73.

moderate academic document was to call forth.   In itself the attack on indulgences was of far less importance than that on the teaching of the schools.   Its importance lies in the fact that the resounding controversy, to which it gave rise, gradually revealed to him the inherent antagonism between his religious convictions and the teaching of the Church, and finally brought him to the inevitable parting of the ways and the disruption of the Western Church

The practice of indulgences had gradually developed in connection with the penitential system of the Church. In the ancient Church grave sin was punished by exclusion from the Christian community until the delinquent had rendered satisfaction by submitting to the prescribed penitential discipline.   In the early Middle Age the practice came into vogue of making satisfaction, in part at least, in the form of a contribution for some good object, such as the support of the poor or the erection and maintenance of a church.[18]   As we learn from the complaints of Abelard, in the twelfth century, and Pope Innocent III. in the early thirteenth, it was liable to become a mere expedient for obtaining money on the part of many of the clergy.[19]   It was, nevertheless, extensively taken advantage of by successive popes, during these centuries, as a means of inciting the faithful to take part in the Holy War against the infidel and the heretics.   It became, in fact, the most effective method for enlisting recruits for the crusades for the deliverance of the Holy Land from Moslem domination.[20] The Cross Indulgence, as it was called, guaranteed to the

[18] Moeller, " History of the Christian Church," ii. 117-118, 219-220 (2nd edition, 1910).   For early examples of this indulgence from penance, see that granted by the Archbishop of Arles to those contributing to the building of a church (1016), and by Pope Urban II. for the support of a monastery (1091).   Köhler, " Documente zum Ablass-streit," 5-7 (1902).

[19] Köhler, " Documente," 8-9.   Sunt nonnulli sacerdotum non tam per errorem quam cupiditatem subjectos decipientes ut pro nummorum oblatione satisfactionis injunctæ pœnas condonent vel relaxent ; non tam attendentes quid velit dominus quam quid valeat nummus (Abelard).

[20] On this subject see Gottlob, " Kreuzablass und Almosenablass," (1906), and Boehmer, " Luther im Lichte der neueren Forschung," 78 f. (5th edition, 1918).

crusaders the relaxation of the penance due for their sins, or even the plenary remission of sins, with the promise of an increased reward in the day of judgment. Erelong the indulgence was extended to those who, whilst not actually taking part in the crusade, contributed money, or men, or vessels to the enterprise.[21] Whilst contrition and confession were presupposed and usually expressed as a condition of these spiritual benefits, the indulgence preachers were not always careful to remind their hearers of this condition, and did not hesitate to assure the worst criminals that, by taking the cross, they were freed from guilt and penalty, and in case of death during the expedition, would secure an immediate entrance into heaven.[22]

With the decline of the crusading spirit in the thirteenth century and the consequent diminution of the contributions to the papal treasury, it became necessary to discover other methods of fanning the devotion and the generosity of the faithful. Hence the indulgence proclaimed by Boniface VIII. in the Jubilee year 1300, which offered the fullest remission of sin to all who should visit the Roman churches once a day during a period of thirty days, in the case of Roman citizens, and half this number in the case of strangers.[23] The Jubilee indulgence brought in a rich harvest of offerings, and in order to ensure a more frequent repetition of it, subsequent popes reduced the interval between the Jubilees from 100 to 50, 33, 25 years, and even shorter periods.[24] Moreover, Pope Boniface IX., following the example of Innocent III. in the case of

---

[21] See, for example, the Cross Indulgence proclaimed by Urban II. in 1095 and Innocent III. in 1215. " Documente," 7, 10, 11. The same privileges were accorded by Innocent III. to those who took the cross in the crusade against the Albigensian heretics. " Documente," 11.

[22] Moeller, ii. 343-344.

[23] " Documente," 18-19. Vere pœnitentibus et confessis . . . non solum plenam et largiorem, immo plenissimam omnium suorum concedemus et concedimus veniam peccatorum. The phrase *Remissio Peccatorum* occurring in such mediæval ecclesiastical documents is held by Roman Catholic theologians to refer only to the remission of the temporal punishment, not the guilt of sin. Grisar, i. 346.

[24] Jubilee Indulgence of Clement VI. for the year 1350 ; Urban VI. for 1390 ; Paul II. for 1470. " Documente," 19-24.

the Cross indulgence, decreed that the benefit of the Jubilee indulgence of 1390 could be secured by those who, though not actually making a pilgrimage to the churches of the Holy City, should pay a contribution to the papal treasury through the agents whom he sent to collect them [25] In the course of the fifteenth century the war against the Turks and the rebuilding of St Peter's gave the popes further opportunities of making use of this expedient for increasing their revenues. By the beginning of the sixteenth century the indulgence system had become one of the most productive devices of papal finance.

In order to increase its efficacy, the benefit of indulgences was extended to souls in purgatory. It had long been a debated point whether an indulgence was of avail for the dead as well as the living. In 1447 Calixtus III. declared in a letter to the King of Castile that the indulgence granted to those taking part in the war against the Moors in Spain was valid for the relief of souls in purgatory.[26] Thirty years later (1477) Sixtus IV. formally decreed that contributions to the fund for repairing the church of St Peter at Saintes, made by the living for their dead relatives or friends, and supported by the intercession of the Church, availed for the relaxation of the pains of purgatory.[27] A papal Bull did not, however, necessarily decide such a matter for the whole Church. Many, in fact, questioned the power of the Pope to issue a dogmatic deliverance on a question of this kind, without the counsel and consent of the Church, to which alone belonged the right to decide what was to be esteemed an article of faith. Sixtus, indeed, in view of " the errors and scandals " to which the Bull gave rise, found it necessary to issue an explanatory brief in the

[25] " Documente," 32 ; Creighton, " History of the Papacy," i. 113.
[26] " Documente," 37.   Eadem venia vita functis concedebatur.
[27] *Ibid.*, 37-39.   Si qui parentes, amici aut ceteri Christi fideles, pictate commoti pro ipsis animabus purgatorio igni pro expiatione pœnarum ejusdem secundum divinam justitiam expositis. . . volumus ipsam plenariam remissionem per modum suffragii ipsis animabus purgatorii, pro quibus dictam quantitatem pecuniæ aut valorem per-solverint, ut præfertur, pro relaxatione pœnarum valere et suffragari.

following year to the effect that the indulgence, whilst valid for this purpose, did not do away with the necessity of prayer and ordinary almsgiving for the benefit of souls in purgatory.[28]   Even so, it still remained a matter of doubt whether, and how far, an indulgence could profit the dead, and Luther, in calling in question its validity, was not necessarily guilty of infringing an indisputable dogma of the Church.

III. THEORY AND SIGNIFICANCE OF THE PRACTICE

Such was the practice, as it had developed by the beginning of the sixteenth century. What now was the theory on which it was based? The theory was found in the doctrine of the superabundant merits of Christ, the virgin, and the saints, enunciated by Alexander Hales and elaborated by Thomas Aquinas in the thirteenth century. According to this doctrine, which was officially sanctioned by Pope Clement VI. in the Jubilee Indulgence Bull of 1343,[29] this superabundance of merit (*Thesaurus Meritorum*, or *Ecclesiæ*) was available for all the faithful, in virtue of the fact that, as the Church constituted the one mystic body of Christ, its members could participate in these benefits.[30] This inexhaustible treasury, which far exceeds all the penalties owing by the living, has been committed to the Pope as the successor of Peter, the keeper of the keys of heaven, and the Pope can draw on it for the benefit of all those whose own merits are insufficient. This benefit is, however, limited in its scope. It does not secure the remission of the guilt of sin, which can only be obtained by contrition and confession to the priest who, in the Sacrament of Penance, absolves the penitent from the

[28] " Documente," 39-40.   [29] *Ibid.*, 20.
[30] " Documente," 17.   Ratio autem quare valere possunt, est unitas corporis mystici, in qua multi operibus pœnitentiæ supererogaverunt ad mensuram debitorum suorum et multas etiam tribulationes injuste sustinuerunt patientes, per quas multitudo pœnarum poterat expiari, si eis deberetur—quorum meritorum tanta est copia, quod omnem pœnam debitam nunc viventibus excedunt—et præcipue propter meritum Christi (Aquinas).

guilt and the eternal punishment of sin in hell and thereby reconciles him with God, whilst imposing certain satisfactions or penalties to be rendered by him for actual sins. It can at most apply only to the remission of the temporal punishment for these sins, to which the sinner, in spite of absolution, is supposed to be still liable in this life or in purgatory. Moreover, in regard to this temporal punishment, it was assumed that the remission held only as far as the jurisdiction or forensic power of the Church (*forum ecclesiæ*) extended, and, as we have seen, there was considerable doubt whether it could apply to those in purgatory, and not rather be limited to the satisfactions imposed by the priest on penitents in accordance with canon law. Thomas Aquinas held that it was applicable to those suffering in purgatory, in virtue of the privilege of remission conferred on Peter.[31] But, as we can see from the objections that he attempts to refute, there were many sceptics in the thirteenth century. In the fifteenth this scepticism found growing expression in the schools. Whilst Paltz maintains the affirmative,[32] in accordance with the opinion of Aquinas, Jacob of Jüterbock is very doubtful.[33] His pupils, John of Wesel and Wessel Gansfort, went much farther in their scepticism and not only denied that the Pope's power extends beyond the penalties imposed on the living by canon law, but called in question the whole theory and practice of indulgences.[34]

[31] " Documente," 17. Sed quidam dicunt quod non valent ad absolvendum a reatu pœnæ, quam quis in purgatorio secundum judicium dei meretur, sed valent ad absolutionem ab obligatione, qua sacerdos obligavit pœnitentem ad pœnam aliquam, vel ad quam etiam ordinatur ex canonum statutis. Sed hæc opinio non videtur vera. Primo, quia est expresse contra privilegium Petro datum, ut quod in terra remitteret et in cœlo remitteretur. *Cf. ibid.*, 34-35.

[32] Cœlifodina, " Documente," 65 f.

[33] *Ibid.*, 47. Whilst admitting in one passage of his " Disputation Against Indulgences " that an indulgence may have an indirect efficacy for those in purgatory, he roundly denies this assumption in another passage on the ground that it can only benefit those who are under the jurisdiction of him who gives it. *Cf.* Ullmann, " Reformers Before the Reformation," i. 252-253.

[34] For Wesel, see Ullmann, i. 260 f. ; for Wessel Gansfort, Miller and Scudder, ii. 194 f.

There was also diversity of opinion on the question whether an indulgence could secure remission from the guilt as well as from the temporal punishment of sin.[35] The language of some of the indulgence Bulls had, to say the least, been rather ambiguous on this point. Some of these certainly assured the remission of guilt as well as penalty.[36] In general, however, it seems to have been understood and taught by the theologians that the remission secured by an indulgence referred only to the temporal punishment of sins, and that remission from guilt could be obtained, not by means of an indulgence, but only in the Sacrament of Penance as the result of contrition, confession, and absolution by the priest.[37] The distinction was, however, by no means strictly observed by the indulgence preachers (*quæstores*) who, in their striving to promote the sale of a particular indulgence, were not too careful to explain to the people the intricacies of the system, and freely preached remission from guilt and penalty.[38]

So much for the theory. As to the religious significance and efficacy of the practice, it may be granted that, from the religious standpoint of the age, it might be a means of quickening the spiritual life. The mission of the indulgence preacher was, theoretically at least, intended to stimulate

[35] Remissio a culpa et a pœna.

[36] For instance, the Bull of Celestine V., 1294, which was revoked by his successor, Boniface VIII., in the following year. " Documente," 30-31. See also that granted to St Mary on the Capitol at Cologne by Boniface IX. in 1393. " Documente," 31-32.

[37] See the teaching of Aquinas in " Documente," 1718, and Paltz, *ibid.*, 53-55. Et ideo sequitur quod indulgentia sit remissio peccatorum quantum ad solam pœnam temporalem . . . sequitur quod virtute indulgentiarum proprie loquendo nullus absolvitur a pœna et culpa, sed solum a pœna ; sed per sacramentum pœnitentiæ fit absolutus solum a culpa, alias sacramentum pœnitentiæ esset frustra. *Ibid.*, 54. The modern Roman Catholic view is stated in the article " Indulgence " in the " Catholic Encyclopedia." " An indulgence is the extra sacramental remission of the temporal punishment due, in God's justice, to sin which has been forgiven, which remission is granted by the Church in the exercise of the power of the keys through application of the superabundant merits of Christ and the saints and from some just and reasonable motive."

[38] See, for instance, the decree of Clement V. against the abuse of indulgences (1312), " Documente," 33-34.

the sense of sin. Its benefits were, on paper at any rate, limited to those who had made confession and professed repentance for their sins, though the lower form of repentance, known as attrition, was esteemed valid.[39] The indulgence preacher was supposed to instruct the people in the real significance of the practice, to emphasise true repentance, to make his mission the means of a religious revival. It was accompanied by special religious exercises to this end. It was in this spirit that earnest preachers like Geiler of Kaisersberg in the fifteenth century championed indulgence preaching. An attempt has, in fact, been made to represent the sale of indulgences as a mission for the benefit of souls comparable to the popular mission preaching of to-day.[40] At the same time, it is indisputable that the practice had too often been, and in the opening decades of the sixteenth century largely was, a mercenary traffic, which really had precious little to do with religion and the salvation of souls. The association of spiritual benefits with a money payment was in itself very questionable. It might easily give rise to the crude notion that one might buy the grace of God in accordance with an ecclesiastical tariff. It might be and was, in fact, popularly regarded as a form of insurance against the pains of purgatory and might thus foster the idea that, in virtue of this insurance, one might commit sin with impunity. No wonder that, to serious minds, the whole thing appeared as an artificial ecclesiastical device without real religious validity or efficacy. Throughout the Middle Ages there had been, in truth, a tendency, as the objections, which the schoolmen attempted to refute, show, to regard it as at best a pious fraud by which the Church sought to entice to the performance of some good work. To such critics it seemed that it would be much more fitting to submit oneself to the discipline of the Church by making satisfaction for one's sins, than to seek thus to compound for sin, and that it is morally and religiously advisable to face the consequences of sin rather than seek to evade them in this mercenary fashion.

[39] Paltz, Cœlifodina, " Documente," 62-63.
[40] Pastor, " History of the Popes," vii. 336-338 ; Grisar, " Luther," i. 35, 55.

Moreover, there was recurring opposition to the system on material as well as moral and religious grounds. To the nations and their rulers it was a mere financial expedient for draining the national wealth to Rome for the benefit of a swarm of parasites and grasping curial officials. " When Rome comes to your door, draw your purse-strings tight," was a saying of the preacher Berchtold of Ratisbon. And yet, adds the chronicler, the credulous people were only too ready to throw away their money on this worthless object.[41] Nor can there be any doubt that, on the eve of the Reformation, and for long before it, the traffic was fostered by a corrupt curia largely from financial motives. At the beginning of the sixteenth century the management of it in Germany was in the hands of the banking firm of the Fugger of Augsburg, who shared in the profits and whose interest it was to push it with all the vigour of the modern lottery agent. The same motive held good in the case of too many of the preachers, the subordinate agents who undertook the actual selling of the indulgence, and whose chief aim was to extract as much as possible out of the pockets of the faithful.[42] The traffic had, in fact, become a gross scandal which reflects only too realistically the crass corruption prevalent in the curia, and may without exaggeration be described as a travesty of religion and a grave danger to morality. There can be no question at all that, in challenging it and demanding the suppression of its abuse, Luther was rendering a clamant service to both. He was, in truth, by no means alone in this demand. Among its severest critics were reforming churchmen like Cardinal Ximenes and theologians like Eck and Emser, who were among the most zealous of his later antagonists. Their criticisms have been repeated by modern Roman Catholic historians like Pastor. " All the popes of the latter days of the Middle Ages," says Pastor, " driven by crusade difficulties and other embarrassments, or else moved by the constant requests for assistance from clergy and laity, granted indulgences to quite an extraordinary extent, both as to number and area. Though in the wording of the Bulls

[41] " Documente," 32.   [42] Boehmer, " Luther," 85-86.

19

the doctrine of the Church was never departed from, and confession, contrition, and definitely prescribed good works were made the conditions for gaining the indulgence, still the financial side of the matter was always apparent, and the necessity of making offerings of money was placed most scandalously in the foreground. Indulgences took more and more the form of a monetary arrangement. . . . No wonder that loud and violent complaints were heard on every side." [43]

IV. THE INDULGENCE OF 1515-1517

The particular indulgence which called Luther into the arena was more than ordinarily scandalous. Albrecht, Prince of Brandenburg, and brother of the reigning Elector, Joachim, who was already Archbishop of Magdeburg and acting Bishop of Halberstadt, coveted, in addition, the vacant electoral archbishopric of Maintz, and managed in March 1514 to secure his election by the cathedral chapter to this high office. The ambitious prince was only in his twenty-third year and, therefore, on this ground alone, ineligible, according to canon law. Moreover, the holding of three such offices was also barred by the canon law. The election was, therefore, illegal and required a special papal dispensation. Such trafficking in episcopal benefices was, however, common enough in the case of high papal officials, and the Elector of Brandenburg, from family and political reasons, plied Pope Leo X. with arguments in favour of granting the necessary dispensation. Leo was at first disposed to refuse such an enormous demand. But the prospect of securing a large sum for the dispensation was tempting, and at the suggestion of an official of the papal treasury, and as the result of a good deal of bargaining with the Elector and the archbishop elect, the Pope at last agreed to grant the necessary dispensation in return for a payment of 10,000 ducats, in addition to the customary fees for confirmation of the election and the pallium. This sum was paid in Albrecht's behalf by the Fugger, from whom he also borrowed 21,000 ducats to enable him to pay the additional fees. The obligation

[43] " History of the Popes," vii. 340-341.

was a heavy one, and in order to enable him to meet his debt to the Fugger, the curial officials suggested the sale of a Jubilee indulgence for the building of St Peter's, to run for eight years throughout the wide region subject to the archbishop's enlarged jurisdiction.[44] By this secret arrangement, which was completed in March 1515 by the issue of an indulgence Bull, only half of the proceeds were to go to the Pope. The other half Albrecht was to retain. In the Bull itself the indulgence was issued solely for the purpose of raising funds for the building of St Peter's, and nothing was said about the private arrangement for the division of the spoil between the curia and the archbishop.

The Bull offered the largest possible inducement to take advantage of its benefits. On reading the document one feels that the scribe who wrote it (Sadoletus, who later became a cardinal) was especially concerned, under cover of the lavish use of pious phrases, to get the largest possible amount out of the pockets of the faithful. The contributors are assured of the fullest remission, after confession, of all their sins, "however grave and enormous," with a few specified exceptions. They are empowered to choose their own confessors. Contributions to the money chest of the indulgence commissary are equivalent to the benefits to be gained by a pilgrimage to Rome, or Compostella in Spain. These benefits are open to those guilty of simoniacal practices, to those who have contracted uncanonical marriages, to those admitted to clerical orders under the canonical age. They are available in the case of those who have obtained possession of property by usury and other means of extortion, or have been guilty of perjury. They can secure remission and participation in the full benefits of the prayers, masses, intercessions, pilgrimages, etc., of the Church universal for the dead as well as the living.[45]

The task of applying the indulgence was committed by the Pope to the Archbishop of Maintz as chief commissary

[44] The statement that Albrecht petitioned the Pope to grant the indulgence Bull for this purpose is erroneous. The suggestion came from the curia. Kalkoff, " Luther und die Entscheidungsjahre der Reformation," 16-18 ; Boehmer, " Luther," 86-87 ; Grisar, i. 347-350.

[45] " Documente," 83 f.

and the subcommissaries to be appointed by him. In his
" Instruction " to the subcommissaries and confessors the
archbishop prescribed the procedure to be followed by these
officials. In whatever place they erected the indulgence
cross, all other religious services were to cease during the
days on which they prosecuted their mission. They were
to explain the Bull and to extol in their sermons the immense
benefits to be gained by their hearers and their dead relatives.
They were to dilate, in particular, on the four principal
" graces " or benefits which the Pope, in the plenitude of
his power, had conceded. The first of these assured to
the living the plenary remission of sin, including the punishment due for sin in purgatory. This grace could be secured
by all confessed penitents who should contribute in accordance with a tariff, fixed in keeping with the social status and
the means of the contributor, ranging from twenty-five gold
florins for a prince and a bishop to half a florin at the bottom
of the scale. Remission evidently depended upon the rank
and wealth of the beneficiary. The second grace, they
were to point out, conferred the right to choose a confessor,
with the most complete powers to absolve even the gravest
sins. The third assured to the contributors and their
dead relatives, now and for ever, participation in the benefit
of all the prayers, intercessions, alms, fasts, pilgrimages,
masses of the Church militant and all its members, and this
immeasurable boon was obtainable even without confession
by simply buying an indulgence ticket. The fourth grace
secured for souls in purgatory the plenary remission of all sins
in return for a contribution made by the living to the chest of
the commissary, and in this case also confession and contrition
were not necessary on the part of the contributor. Only in the
case of notorious sinners was a public profession of penitence
necessary, and in this case the commissary was only to accord
absolution after scourging the delinquent with three strokes
of the rod, with befitting religious ceremonial.[46]

In this document, as in the Bull itself, the main concern
of the scribe was evidently to incite the generosity of the
faithful on behalf of the object for which the Bull was
ostensibly issued. All its specious pious phraseology does

[46] " Documente," 104 f.

not succeed in hiding this patent fact from the critical eye.
The "Instruction" does, indeed, officially impose caution
and care on the subcommissaries in pushing the sale, and
professes anxiety for the good of souls. But the mercenary
spirit of the whole business is not conjured away by such
professions, and one is none the less shocked by the cool
assumption that the mere purchase of an indulgence ticket
can secure the remission of sin for those in purgatory.
Moreover, the reiterated assertion that the proceeds of the
sale were to be devoted entirely to the building of St Peter's
was nothing less than an unblushing fraud. The archbishop
knew well enough that one half was to be devoted to the
payment of his debt to the Fugger, though he took good care
not to say so in his "Instruction," and the subcommissaries
gave no hint of the fact in their sermons. From this point
of view, the document is simply a piece of pious "humbug."
And what applies to the "Instruction" applies to the Bull,
since the expedient of a Jubilee indulgence originally
emanated, not from the archbishop, but from the curia.

The mercenary spirit appears still more prominently in
the huckstering tone of the sermons of the indulgence
preachers. Of these the most skilful and pushful was John
Tetzel, the prior of the Dominican monastery at Leipzig,
to whom, as subcommissary, the archbishop assigned the
dioceses of Magdeburg and Halberstadt, and whose gift
of rough and ready eloquence had already earned him no
little reputation as a popular indulgence preacher.[47] He
had some learning and, to judge from his extant sermons,
seems to have assumed the conventional doctrine, which
required contrition and confession as a condition of the
efficacy of an indulgence, and distinguished between the
remission of guilt and that of the temporal punishment due
for sin. But whilst adopting the conventional phraseology,[48]

[47] See N. Paulus, "Johann Tetzel der Ablassprediger," 88 f. (1899).
[48] "Documente," 125. Scito quod quicunque confessus et contritus
eleemosynam ad capsam posuerit, juxta consilium confessoris, plenariam
omnium peccatorum suorum remissionem habebit. Ser. ii. ; cf.
ibid., 126. Potestis jam habere confessionalia, quorum virtute in vita
et in articulo mortis, et in non reservatis totiens quotiens habere plenariam
remissionem pœnarum pro peccatis debitarum. Ser. ii.

it does not appear that he made the distinction clear to his uninitiated hearers. His object was rather to magnify the salutary effects of a mere contribution to his money chest than to set forth the spiritual and moral aspect of the transaction. Johann Lindner, a fellow Dominican and a contemporary, severely criticises his methods.[49] Certain it is that, as far as the deliverance from purgatory was concerned, he did proclaim that a mere money payment in behalf of the departed, without contrition on the part of those who made this payment, sufficed to work this miracle. " As soon as the money in the coffer rings, the soul from the fire of purgatory springs." [50] This notorious saying cannot be actually traced to him. But it appears from his antitheses [51] and other writings against Luther, and from the testimony of reliable witnesses, that he did preach in this sense.[52] In order to drive it home, he luridly described the pains of purgatory and pathetically pictured to his hearers the souls of their dead relatives crying to them for help. Would they callously abandon them to the torments of the flames, when for a mere trifle they might deliver them? Such appeals could not fail to filch the money of the crowds that flocked to hear the melodramatic popular preacher, and the preacher was doing a brisk trade in pardons for the living and the dead when, on the 31st October 1517, All Saints' Eve, Luther intervened by nailing his ninety-five theses on the subject on the door of the castle church at Wittenberg.

V. LUTHER'S ATTACK ON INDULGENCES

As the sermons on indulgences delivered during the years 1516-17 show, Luther had been no indifferent observer of this mercenary traffic. The critical note of these sermons was sharpened by the reports of the gross utterances of

[49] Grisar, i. 343.

[50] Luther's Theses against Indulgences, " Werke," i. 234.

[51] " Documente," 132.

[52] Grisar, i. 343-345. For that of Myconius, who heard him preach, see Gieseler, " Church History," v. 362.

Tetzel and his fellow-pardonmongers.[53]   The Elector had
prohibited the traffic within his territories.   But he could
not prevent his subjects from crossing the border to hear
the popular preacher at Jüterbock and Zerbst and acquire an
indulgence ticket.   What this benefit practically meant in
too many cases, Luther discovered in the confessional.
When he refused to absolve those guilty of gross sin unless
they abandoned their vicious life, they produced an
indulgence ticket and threatened to report him to Tetzel,
who was empowered to excommunicate anyone attempting
to gainsay his holy enterprise.   His indignation at the
discovery of the evil practical effects of the traffic was
intensified by the perusal of the " Instruction " of the archbishop, which came into his hands.   This document appeared
to him nothing less than a travesty of religion, and he felt
bound publicly to protest against it, at all hazards, as a
perversion of the truth, which his own experience of the
fact of sin and salvation had burned into his soul.   " On
this account I could no longer keep silent about these
enormities." [54]   The theses against indulgences were the
outcome both of his indignation at the crass practical abuses
of the system and his conviction of the false conception
of religion on which the system was based.   Moreover,
he had been led, as he wrote to Staupitz, by his study of the
New Testament in the original (evidently with the help of
Erasmus) to the true apprehension of the word Repentance.
Repentance, he found, meant a change of mind and heart
(*transmutatio mentis et affectus*) inspired by the grace of
God.   This conception is totally at variance with the
scholastic and ecclesiastical notion of penance as a
satisfaction rendered for sin by penitential works.   Repentance and penance are by no means the same thing, though
the Latin term may be the same.   Repentance has to do
with the inward condition, not with the outward works of

[53] See his letter to the archbishop, Enders, i. 115 : " Documente,"
144.   Circumferuntur indulgentiæ papales sub tuo præclarissimo titulo
ad fabricam S. Petri, in quibus non ideo accuso prædicatorum exclama-
tiones, quas non audivi, sed doleo falsissimas intelligentias populi ex
illis conceptas, quas vulgo undique jactant.

[54] " Documente," 144.   Idcirco tacere hæc amplius non potui.

the penitent. " When my heart was burning within me as
the result of this discovery, behold there arose around us all
this hubbub about this new kind of indulgences, all this
trumpeting of remission, by which we are not, nevertheless,
incited to the strenuous pursuit of the war against sin.
Briefly, neglecting the doctrine of true penitence, these
noisy shouters are concerned with magnifying, not sin, but
the lowest form of penitence, which is called satisfaction,
and extol the remission of this lowest form of it with unheard
of exaggerations and with the denunciation of those who
call it in question as heretics, worthy of eternal damnation." [55] It was against this false and heretical teaching,
he adds, that, in the interest of the truth, he determined to
testify.

The attack took the form of a series of theses, which he
drew up with a view to an academic disputation. According
to the preface, the object of the disputation was simply
" to elucidate the truth," and the theses are certainly not
to be regarded as a popular manifesto, though it is evident
that they grew out of his conviction of the evil practical
effect of the traffic, as carried on by the indulgence preachers,
and the urgent necessity of putting a stop to it. They were
an appeal to the theologians of Wittenberg and other
universities, and there was nothing unusual in such an
appeal. Discussions of this kind were, in fact, regularly
held in the university, and the subject of them was publicly
notified beforehand on the door of the castle church.
There were, besides, not a few difficulties and obscurities
in the whole doctrine, in regard to which opinion was in
a very nebulous state, as some of the theses point out.
Luther himself long afterwards asserted [56] that, when he
penned them, he was by no means clear on the subject.
They prove, indeed, that he knew the conventional doctrine.
But they also show that he had his doubts about many
debatable points and was eager to obtain more light on
the subject. At the same time, it is evident that he had
formed certain definite convictions in the light of his own

[55] Enders, i. 197-198.
[56] In the philippic, " Wider Hans Wurst," 1541.

experience of sin and grace, and that his purpose was to enunciate and defend a more spiritual conception of the practice, in opposition to the mercenary and pernicious application of it by the popular indulgence preachers.

Hence the emphatic distinction at the outset between true repentance and mere penance. Christ, he contends, following St Bernard, in calling sinners to repent, demands that the whole life of the believer should be one of repentance. In this summons he was not referring to sacramental or ecclesiastical penance, consisting in confession and satisfaction, which is ministered by the priest, but to the inner experience of repentance, which manifests itself outwardly in the mortification of the flesh, in self-discipline and conflict with sin (*odium sui*). As long as this true inward repentance remains, *i.e.*, throughout the whole life, the sense of the penalty or punishment of sin (*pœna*) also remains.[57] In other words, as he explains more amply in the " Resolutions "[58] on the theses, the true Christian life is the life of the Cross, suffering, and conflict with sin, not an attempt to evade these by such an artificial expedient as an indulgence.

This spiritual conception of religion is for Luther the touchstone of the whole problem. It is from this point of view that he considers both the theory and the practice of indulgences. He does not, on principle, reject the practice as an ecclesiastical institution. His polemic is directed only against its abuse, and he assumes throughout that his contentions are in accord with the mind of the Pope and all good Christians. Practically, however, these contentions materially circumscribe the papal power and involve a radical reform of the ecclesiastical institution as well as its practical abuses. His main contentions are as follows :—

1. Indulgence is only a remission of ecclesiastical penalties (*pœnæ*). The Pope can only remit penalties imposed by his own authority, or that of the canon law, and so the phrase " remission of all penalties " in the papal Bulls must

---

[57] Theses 1-4.
[58] The amplification of the theses later sent to the Pope.

be understood. These penalties ought to be imposed, as was formerly the case, before and not after absolution as tests of true contrition.[59]

2. God alone can remit the guilt of sin (*culpa*), and the Pope and the priest have only a declaratory power. They can at most only declare or warrant in the Sacrament of Penance that guilt is remitted by God, and this declaration by priestly authority is essential, since God only forgives those who humbly subject themselves to the priest as His vicar. Luther still recognises the validity and even the necessity of the authoritative declaration of the priest, given in absolution, for the forgiveness of sins. Without this authoritative declaration, he insists in the " Resolutions," the sinner cannot have the assurance of salvation. His personal conviction is not sufficient to bring peace and comfort of conscience. Only through the priest does God give this assurance. At the same time, without personal faith in Christ's promise, the absolution of the priest does not of itself avail to secure forgiveness, which is due to the grace of God appropriated by faith. It only assures the penitent of the efficacy of his faith.[60] As for papal pardons in the form of indulgences, they are absolutely impotent to take away even the least of venial sins, as far as guilt is concerned.[61]

3. The remission of canonical penalties applies only to the living and does not extend to those in purgatory. Death, that implacable " necessity," is the grand exception, with which even papal decrees must reckon. The cardinal error that carries the remission of penalties over to purgatory must have been sown, like tares, whilst the bishops were nodding. The dead have done for ever with canon law and are by right relieved from its penalties. The Pope rightly recognises that he can help souls in purgatory, not by the power of the keys (absolution), but only by way of intercession (*per modum suffragii*). He has no more power over purgatory than any bishop in his diocese or any priest in his parish.[62]

---

[59] Theses 5, 20, 21, 34 ; " Werke," i. 233 f. ; " Documente," 127 f.
[60] " Werke," i. 540 f.
[61] Theses 6, 7, 38, 76.   [62] *Ibid.*, 8, 9, 10, 11, 13, 22, 25, 26.

4. Many of the assertions of the indulgence preachers are false and pernicious. To say that papal indulgences absolve and save from all penalties is necessarily to deceive the people by hollow promises. To proclaim that as soon as the money clinks in the chest, the soul flies straight to heaven is to preach only after the manner of man, *i.e.*, in the worldly, advertising spirit. Whilst the preachers certainly increase gain and avarice, their preaching does not change the fact that the intercession of the Church for souls depends solely on the will of God. No one can, in fact, be sure of the reality of his contrition, much less of the obtaining of plenary remission, since the truly penitent are rare, and still rarer one who rightly buys an indulgence. Those who trust to letters of pardon for salvation will be damned along with their teachers. We should, therefore, beware of these false teachers who proclaim that these papal pardons are that inestimable gift of God by which man is reconciled to Him, or that contrition is not necessary in those who would buy souls out of purgatory or purchase confessional licences (*confessionalia*).[63]

5. Religion, being spiritual, is entirely independent of such an artificial, mercenary expedient. Every truly penitent Christian has by right plenary remission from punishment and guilt (*a pœna et culpa*) and participation in all the benefits of Christ and the Church, without these letters of pardon. It is extremely difficult for even the most learned theologian to extol and lavish these pardons to the people and at the same time enlarge on true contrition. True contrition seeks and loves punishment (the way of the Cross), whereas this lavishing of pardons leads the people merely to hate it and seek relief from it. It is false and misleading, inasmuch as it begets the notion that these pardons are to be placed before other good works of charity. The buying of them is not to be compared in any way to works of mercy. He that gives to the poor or lends to the needy does better, because by a work of charity love is increased and a man becomes better, whereas by merely buying pardons a man is not made better, but is only supposed to be freer from

[63] Theses 21, 23, 24, 27, 28, 30, 31, 32, 33, 35.

punishment. To neglect the poor for the sake of buying these pardons is to purchase, not the indulgence of the Pope, but the wrath of God. Unless a man has superfluous wealth, he ought to keep his money to provide what is necessary for his household, and not throw it away for such a worthless object. Contributions for this object ought to be voluntary and not to be pressed as an obligation. Moreover, it should be made clear that the Pope, in sanctioning this traffic, desires that devout prayer should be made for him, that he would prefer that the Church of St Peter should be burned to ashes rather than that it should be built out of the skin, flesh, and bones of his flock, and that he would rather sell it in order to supply the needs of the poor people, from whom the indulgence preachers extort as much as they can. These pardons are, in fact, only useful if people do not confide in them, even if the commissaries, yea the Pope himself, should pledge their own souls for them. They are most harmful if, on account of them, they lose the fear of God. As preached by these noisy hucksterers, these so-called "graces" are only such in the sense of promoting money-making. They are, in reality, in no way to be compared to the grace of God and the piety of the Cross. As an ecclesiastical institution, the papal indulgence is to be reverently regarded and the bishops and priests are bound to receive the papal commissaries with due respect. He that speaks against this usage, rightly understood, let him be accursed. But the actual practice is a sham and a fraud, and the bishops are bound to see to it, with the utmost care, that those preachers do not proclaim their own imaginings in place of the Pope's commission. To say, for instance, that they are empowered to absolve, even if a man had been guilty of violating the mother of God, is madness, and he who denounces such enormities, let him be blessed. [64]

6. The mission of the indulgence preachers is most detrimental to the Word and worship of God. To silence the preaching of God's Word in the other churches for the purpose of pushing the sale of these pardons is to be an enemy of Christ. To devote an equal, or even a longer

[64] Theses 36-52, 67-75.

time to the extolling of them in the same sermon is to do injury to the Word. An indulgence is not in the least to be compared in importance to the Gospel, and if the sale is prosecuted with such pomp and ceremonial, surely the Gospel, which is the supreme thing, should be preached with a hundredfold more devotion. To say that the indulgence cross, set up with all the insignia of the papal arms, is of equal power with the Cross of Christ, or that the Pope has greater graces to grant than the Gospel is blasphemy.[65]

7. The indulgence traffic has no real basis or justification in the doctrine of the Treasures of the Church. There is great dubiety and uncertainty in regard to this belief, and it is not sufficiently explained or made known to the people. It is evident, at anyrate, that the Treasures, in virtue of which the Pope claims to grant indulgences, are not temporal treasures, for many of the indulgence preachers do not so readily lavish these, but only strive to collect them. They are not the poor, as St Lawrence held, for these preachers do not concern themselves with this needy class. Nor do they consist of the merits of Christ and the saints, for these are always working grace to the inward man, and the Cross, death, and hell to the outward man. Moreover, as he points out in the " Resolutions," there is no such thing as superabundant merits of the saints, since not one of them has sufficiently fulfilled the commandments of God. The martyrs and saints are rather to be regarded by us as examples of suffering and self-discipline, and this suffering, not the evasion of it, on such an imaginary pretext as this so-called superabundance of merit, is the divinely appointed lot of the Christian. As to the merit of Christ, who fulfilled the law for us, and by whose merit we are justified and forgiven, this is, indeed, the unique Treasure of the Church. But it is a very different thing from the so-called Treasure in virtue of which the Pope professes to give indulgence.[66] Whilst the phrase has been variously interpreted, the Treasures of the Church are, he holds, the power of the keys of the kingdom of heaven, the power of loosing and binding, conferred by the merit of Christ, whilst in the matter of

[65] Theses 53, 54, 55, 77, 78, 79.   [66] " Werke," i. 605 f.

indulgences, the Pope does not exercise the power of the keys (*i.e.*, the remission of guilt), but only that of remitting canonical penalties. The true Treasures of the Church are thus the holy Gospel of the glory and grace of God, from which the remission of sin is derived, not this supposed extra source, from which the Pope draws for the purpose of an indulgence. These true Treasures, being purely spiritual, are, however, most hateful to the indulgence mongers, because this conception makes the things on which they lay the most stress—the material contributions to the money chest—the least important. Of old the Treasures of the Gospel were nets by which the preachers fished for men of wealth, whereas the indulgence treasures are nets by which the preachers of them, with shameless effrontery, fish for the wealth of men.[67]

8. This traffic does harm not only to religion, but to the papal authority and the Church. Apart from its questionable moral effects, it breeds scepticism and irreverence. People are talking and asking questions, of which Luther gives a number of samples by way of conclusion. Why does not the Pope, if he has the power, empty purgatory out of compassion for souls ? Is not this a far juster reason than doing it for the sake of money for building a church ? Why do funeral masses and anniversary masses for the dead continue, and why does the Pope not return or permit to be returned the funds for this purpose, since it is wrong to pray for those already redeemed ? What is this new goodness of the Pope that, for the sake of filthy lucre, he allows a wicked man to redeem a pious soul, instead of doing it out of free charity on account of its need ? Why does not the Pope, who is wealthier than all the greatest millionaires, not redeem souls out of his own funds, instead of extracting money from the poor for the building of St Peter's ? What does he remit or impart to those who, in virtue of true contrition, have a right to full remission and participation, etc. ? [68]

In posting up these theses, Luther's object was neither to excite a popular disturbance nor to attack the legitimate

[67] Theses 56-66.   [68] *Ibid.*, 82-95.

use of indulgences. In the " Resolutions " or amplification of them, which he subsequently sent to the Pope, he vehemently disclaimed the charge of heresy. The charge should rather be brought against the indulgence preachers, who distort the truth and expose the Church to mockery and ridicule. The theses contained nothing contrary to Scripture, the fathers, the canon law, and the papal decrees, and it was not his intention to maintain anything that could be so construed. At the same time, he claimed the liberty to accept or refute the mere opinions of Aquinas, Bonaventura, and other schoolmen or canonists on the subject, on the ground of Paul's counsel to prove all things. He might err, but he was no heretic, however loudly others, who differed from him, might rage against him.[69]

The proposed disputation did not take place, and he refrained from printing the theses in order, if possible, to avoid scandal. He contented himself with sending them, along with a letter, to the Archbishop of Maintz in the hope of persuading him to put a stop to the reprehensible doings of his agents, and to some of his friends. He was, however, unable to prevent their circulation in both Latin and German through the printing press, and before the end of the year they were being discussed by friends and foes far and near.[70] The tale that he had been instigated by the Elector of Saxony for the purpose of discrediting the archbishop and the Elector of Brandenburg, his rivals in power, Luther described as a monstrous invention.[71] Whilst ready to defend his opinions, he was not eager to court popularity or start a popular movement against the Pope and the Church.[72] Nor had he any idea of the storm that these academic propositions were about to conjure. At this stage his attitude is that of a reformer within the Church. He still reverences the Pope and the priesthood, still believes in the Sacrament of Penance, the use of indulgences, and

[69] " Werke," i. 524-530.   See also his letter to the Bishop of Brandenburg. Enders, i. 148 f.
[70] Enders, i. 165-167.   [71] Ibid., i. 156; cf. 121.
[72] Ibid., i. 161.   Primum quod miraris, he wrote to Scheurl, cur non ad vos eas (the theses) miserim, respondeo non fuit consilium neque votum eas evulgari, etc.

other usages, whilst emphasising their spiritual significance and striving to impart to them a deeper religious significance. The forgiveness of sin is, indeed, due solely to the grace of God, appropriated by faith ; whilst the priestly declaration is essential to the assurance of salvation on the part of the believing soul. The doctrine of justification by faith is assumed in the theses and finds explicit expression in the " Resolutions." It is at the bottom of his antagonism to the crass conception of such an ecclesiastical expedient as the papal indulgence. It is, in reality, alien to the traditional ecclesiasticism, with its rampant formalism and its manifold abuses. But he is not as yet fully conscious of any serious divergence from the doctrine and institutions of the Church, and he certainly is not deliberately making an insidious attack on either, with a view to undermining the legitimate power of the Pope or revolutionising the traditional faith. He did not in these theses set out to cast down the walls of Jericho by a trumpet blast of defiance to Rome, as he was ultimately to do in the great Reformation treatises three years later. His aim was " to elucidate the truth," as he conceived it, within the limits of ecclesiastical obedience, by means of free discussion, untrammelled by scholastic dogmatism, in the light of the teaching of Scripture and the fathers.

At the same time, he was not the kind of man to be browbeaten by opponents of the type of Tetzel, Wimpina, Eck, and Prierias, who were already on the warpath against him.[73] Nor, humbly as he writes to the archbishop and later to the Pope, will he be scared by threats or demands for recantation against his religious convictions. When his enemies threatened to burn him, and his friends tried to persuade him not to risk the journey to the Chapter of his Order at Heidelberg in the spring of 1518, he calmly replied that he would do his duty at whatever cost.[74] It was here that the momentous significance of this incipient controversy lay. Luther is not the mere propounder of certain scholastic theses. The theses were the revelation of a great religious personality, an original, dynamic man. In calling this

[73] Enders, i. 164, 170, 172-173.   [74] Ibid., i. 169.

original, dynamic man into the arena, with the powerful Elector of Saxony as patron and protector,[75] his opponents were the unwitting authors of the evangelical Reformation. In controversy, as in teaching, one is, or ought to be, always learning, and it was through the antagonism of his opponents that Luther ultimately became conscious of the fundamental opposition between his religious convictions and the teaching and usages of the Church, and was ultimately brought face to face with the alternative of recantation or resistance.

Meanwhile the rapid decline of Tetzel's reputation and his sales among the people is convincing evidence that he was already a force to be reckoned with. When Tetzel's counter-theses were hawked in Wittenberg, the students laid hands on them, and, without Luther's approval, made a bonfire of them.[76] " I have not begun this enterprise for fame, nor will I abandon it because of ignominy," wrote he to Staupitz. " If God is at work in it, no one can stop it. If He is still, no one will set the thing in motion." [77] It was in this spirit that he met alike the onslaughts of his opponents and the misgivings of his friends. He was learning the secret of all great leaders—how, if need be, to stand alone with God against the world. Significantly enough, he now, in letters to Spalatin and Lang, signs himself *Martinus Eleutherius*, Martin the Emancipator.[78]

[75] Enders, i. 170.
[76] *Ibid.*, i. 170.
[77] *Ibid.*, i. 176.
[78] *Ibid.*, i. 122, *passim*.

INDEX

A

Abelard, 63, 68, 69, 83, 87, 88, 282

Abgar, King, 241

" Address to the German Nobility," 21, 22, 142

Ægidius, General of the Augustinian Order, 140, 143

" Æsop's Fables," 13

Agricola, German humanist, 243, 244, 246

Albrecht, Prince of Brandenburg, 290

Alexander VI., Pope, 259

Alexander the Great and the pirate, 271

Alsace, 244

Amsdorf, Luther's colleague, 277

Anhalt, Prince William of, 15

— Adolf of, 140

Anselm, 63, 68, 69, 157, 159, 160, 221

Antheus, 182

Aquinas, Thomas, 20, 21, 54, 55, 70-72, 75, 76, 78, 80, 82, 83, 86, 87, 88, 172, 221, 234, 246, 285, 286

Aristotle, dominant authority of, in mediæval universities, 21-23 ; opposition to, 23-24 ; influence on scholastic theology, 66 ; Luther denounces his philosophy, 135-136 ; Luther rejects his conception of righteousness, 187-189 ; Luther attacks his philosophy, 276, 277, 280

Athanasius, 42

Augsburg, 243

Augustine, Luther's early study of, 54 ; theology of, 55 f. ; sources of, 56 ; doctrine of original sin, 56-57 ; redemption through Christ, grace, faith. justifica-

tion, 58-59 ; divergence from Paul, 59-60 ; elimination of merit, predestination, 60 ; sacerdotal, ecclesiastical element, 60 ; the Church as the medium of grace, 61 ; divergence of the Church from Pauline teaching, 61-62 ; Augustine accommodates his doctrine of salvation to teaching and practice of the Church, 62 ; Luther and Augustine, 63 ; idea of merit, 66 ; Luther's early study of the works of, 132 ; early influence of, on Luther, 137, 139 ; Luther proves one of his works to be spurious, 134 ; influence of the " De Litera et Spiritu " on Luther, 154 ; Luther's use of his works in the lectures on the Psalms, 157 ; Neoplatonism of, and its influence on Luther, 159-160 ; influence of, on Luther's view of human nature, 162 ; Luther's use of his works in the lectures on Romans, 172 ; confessions of, 174 ; misinterpretation of Paul, 185 ; Luther values him above Jerome, 254

Augustinian Eremites, 18, 20, 29, 37 f., 260

B

Bacon, Roger, 240

Basle, 132, 213, 246

— Council of, 81

Bebel, Heinrich, 244

Beccadelli, 242

Beghards, the, 262

Bembo, Cardinal, 143, 237

Berchtold of Ratisbon, 289